The Coltrane
Church

The Coltrane Church

Apostles of Sound, Agents of Social Justice

NICHOLAS LOUIS BAHAM III

McFarland & Company, Inc., Publishers
Jefferson, North Carolina

All photographs are courtesy the St. John Will-I-Am Coltrane African Orthodox Church unless otherwise noted.

Frontispiece and back cover: "Dancing Coltrane icon": The Dancing St. John Coltrane icon, by the Rev. Mark Dukes, is from the "100 Dancing Saints" mural project in the rotunda of St. Gregory of Nyassa Episcopal Church in San Francisco (photograph by David Sanger).

LIBRARY OF CONGRESS CATALOGUING-IN-PUBLICATION DATA

Baham, Nicholas Louis, III, 1965–
    The Coltrane Church : apostles of sound, agents of social justice / Nicholas Louis Baham III.
        p.   cm.
    Includes bibliographical references and index.

    ISBN 978-0-7864-9496-5 (softcover : acid free paper) ∞
    ISBN 978-1-4766-1922-4 (ebook)

    1. Saint John Coltrane African Orthodox Church.   2. Jazz—Religious aspects.   3. Jazz—California—San Francisco—History and criticism.   4. Coltrane, John, 1926–1967.   5. African Orthodox Church.   6. African American political activists.   7. African Americans—California—San Francisco—Religion.   I. Title.

ML3921.8.J39B34 2015
289.9—dc23   2015013154

BRITISH LIBRARY CATALOGUING DATA ARE AVAILABLE

Printed in the United States of America

McFarland & Company, Inc., Publishers
  Box 611, Jefferson, North Carolina 28640
  www.mcfarlandpub.com

Table of Contents

In this modern jazz, they heard something rebel and nameless that spoke for them, and their lives knew a gospel for the first time. It was more than a music; it became an attitude toward life, a way of walking, a language and a costume; and these introverted kids ... now felt somewhere at last.

—John Clellon Holmes, *Beat* novelist

Acknowledgments

"I will do all I can to be worthy of thee, O Lord"—St. John Will-I-Am Coltrane

The Coltrane Church is a humble offering to my father, Nicholas Louis Baham, Jr. (January 28, 1935—September 22, 1992), who introduced and nurtured in me a love for jazz music and the redemptive songs of my people, who taught me how to listen and what to listen for and who first introduced me to John Coltrane.

This book is a humble offering to my mother, Betty Joyce Baham, who introduced and nurtured in me a love of the Holy Scriptures and Jesus Christ the Teacher, the Son of God, the Son of Man. I love you and hope to honor you with this work.

This book is a humble offering to my dear wife and best friend, Angela Faith Dean-Baham, who trusted and assisted me in the realization of my vision. Thank you for lending the gift of your voice to St. John's African Orthodox Church. Thank you for urging me forward through the days when my inner fire was waning. You taught me what it means to love and that this work could only proceed from love.

For Nicholas IV, my dear son, watching your initial forays into jazz improvisation committed me to the vision of explicating the communal imperative of the Coltrane Church and gave me that last spark that took me over the finish line.

For Elizabeth, my dear sister. Through you the circle is unbroken and the life and spirit of our dear grandmother, Mildred "Honey" Bacon, continues. Your journey was a vital metaphor to everything I have written here about black womanist power. From the very beginning Honey could see how brightly the fire burned within you.

The Coltrane Church: Apostles of Sound, Agents of Social Justice was written with a love supreme for the community of the St. John Will-I-Am Coltrane African Orthodox Church. This book is dedicated to the vision of John Coltrane and the Holy Ghost shared by Archbishop King and Mother Marina on September 18, 1965.

All of my love and gratitude to Archbishop King, Mother Marina King, and Pastor Wanika King-Stephens in particular for welcoming me as a member of their community and family. Your vision and its fulfillment have brought untold joy into my life. This document is an expression of that joy and a testimony to the victory that the music and sainthood of John Will-I-Am Coltrane has earned in my life. I hope that I have done justice to your extraordinary journey. I remain committed to your vision and I look forward to the future of Coltrane Consciousness optimistically.

For Pastor Wanika King-Stephens, I know that under your leadership we look forward to the future optimistically!

A very special thanks to the Rev. Mark Dukes for allowing me to reprint your inspired Coltrane icons. Your work continues to expand my consciousness and my capacity to embrace the contradictions and heterogeneity of our experience as African Americans. I look forward to our future endeavors together.

Thanks to David Sanger for allowing me to reproduce your amazing photo of the dancing St. John Will-I-Am Coltrane icon from the Rev. Mark Dukes' Dancing Saints iconography that adorns St. Gregory's Episcopal Church in San Francisco.

Thanks to Shahada Hull for allowing me to write about the miracle of the music that saved your life. Keep the faith!

Thanks to Deacon and soon to be Father Max Hoff for assisting me with the selection of photographs contained in this book, for your parallel efforts in a Coltrane scholarship and your efforts in preserving the history of the St. John Will-I-Am Coltrane African Orthodox Church.

Thanks to you Rev. Deacon Franzo Wayne King, Jr. Your powerful sound, the barrelhouse honks and growls of the spirit-driven John Coltrane, so moved my soul every Sunday. It was in the sound of your horn that I first heard the voice of God speaking to me in the services.

Thanks to the St. John Will-I-Am Coltrane African Orthodox Church Master of Music, Frederick Harris, for your brilliance on the keys as you took me through the entire history of the music in every inspired solo and musical testimonies. I so loved your preludes to "Lonnie's Lament," how your solos would traverse an entire history of jazz music; I think you've been there before, Bro. Fred, playing stride piano in a tremendous cutting session with Fats Waller or Art Tatum.

Thanks to the late Father Roberto De Haven (Blue Water) for the ministry of your powerful sound praise, for piercing the altissimo limits of my aural consciousness, for all the great conversations we had, and for being an example for me of a mystic and a seeker of the truth. The road trips to Stanford University and the Santa Cruz for the Zion Trane experience as well as your consultation and encouragement in Paris were invaluable. I remember you encouraging me to solo and asking only that I "end it just right so that you can set me up."

Thanks to the entire community of worshippers and friends at the St. John Will-I-Am Coltrane African Orthodox Church. Ohnedaruth. The Sisters of Compassion. Your work has been a tremendous blessing on my life.

One Mind.

Preface

Welcome is that feeling that you have when you finally do reach an awareness, an understanding which you have earned through struggle. It is a feeling of peace. A welcome feeling of peace.[1]

— St. John Will-I-Am Coltrane

In the heart of San Francisco's upscale Jazz District on Fillmore Street in the redeveloped Western Addition neighborhood, there's a storefront church known popularly as the "Coltrane Church,"[2] where souls are baptized in the free jazz improvisations of local musicians playing the compositions of the great American classical music[3] innovator John Will-I-Am Coltrane.

Every Sunday at noon the Archbishop blows a conch shell and leads the procession of priests and musicians. He wears a purple chasuble signifying repentance over a white alb signifying baptism. The Apostles of Sound process from the upper room,[4] dressed in black cassocks and white surplices and blowing glimmering saxophones. They are followed by a small choir of five called the Sisters of Compassion, two bassists, a drummer, and the pianist and Master of Music. The drummer marks the eternal return with a crashing cymbal. The congregation rises, expectant.

Inside, the walls of the sanctuary are covered with beautiful Byzantine—style[5] portraits of Saint John Coltrane, Christ the Teacher, the Virgin Mary and the Christ child, and Moses.

One of the wall portraits portrays Coltrane seated in a white robe, a golden halo around his head, holding his soprano saxophone in his left hand. He holds an unfurled scroll in his right hand, which reads: "Let us sing all songs to God to whom all praise is due ... praise God." Off to the

1

side and above the pulpit is another and smaller portrait of John Coltrane wearing an emerald green suit, a golden shimmering halo around his head, holding forth his tenor saxophone tied with a red ribbon, with the red flames of the Holy Ghost raging in the bell, and again in his right hand another unfurled scroll, this time reading: "Let us sing all songs to God. Let Us Pursue Him in the righteous path. Yes it is true; 'Seek and ye shall find.'" A third icon depicts John Coltrane standing in a white robe and holding his tenor saxophone in his left hand and a scroll in his right with a phrase from his poem for "A Love Supreme: Psalm." "God breathes through us so completely ... so gently we hardly feel it ... yet it is our everything. Thank you God."

The Saint John Will-I-Am[6] Coltrane African Orthodox Church is a place for jazz pilgrims, devotees of the late jazz legend John Coltrane, and people from diverse corners of the earth who have either heard about a place where John Coltrane is lauded as a saint or who have felt some sense of the divinity of this music and in the person of John Coltrane. Whatever their social station, the pilgrims and devotees arrive and wait patiently for the "Coltrane Liturgy," the integration of orthodox Christian liturgical practice and improvised jazz music.[7] Many come with the expectation of

The St. John Will-I-Am Coltrane Church at 351 Divisadero Street near Oak Street. The church conducted services at this location from 1972 to 2006.

finding a great free Sunday concert in this sanctuary. Still others, bringing their instruments, hope to find a suitable place to jam. By the time the Coltrane Liturgy has ended, most will encounter more than they had bargained for as Jesus Christ and the Holy Spirit are invoked in a message of social justice and the late jazz giant John Coltrane is revered as a messenger of a modern gospel and a new testament of sound.

The St. John Will-I-Am Coltrane African Orthodox Church has an extraordinary beginning. On September 18, 1965, Franzo and Marina King attended a performance of the John Coltrane Quartet at the Jazz Workshop in San Francisco, California, to celebrate their first wedding anniversary.[8] Seeking little more than a romantic evening and the pleasure of good music and drinks, a would-be preacher with roots in the Pentecostal movement in St. Louis and Los Angeles and his young bride, the daughter of a respectable middle-class black Episcopalian family from Cleveland with a lineage in the history of jazz, found themselves "arrested" by the spiritual presence of John Coltrane. They saw a vision of the Holy Ghost as Coltrane took the bandstand. Their shared vision, referred to by church members as the "Sound Baptism," initiated a new religious and aesthetic movement called "Coltrane Consciousness"—defined as a set of social, cultural and political practices inspired by the life and music of John Coltrane—that has been at the vanguard of subaltern struggles against corporatism; religious intolerance; sexism within the African American church; police brutality; urban redevelopment; race, gender, and class inequality; and African American removal in the San Francisco Bay Area since the late 1960s.

The Sound Baptism of 1965 initiated an extraordinary history of ideological transitions and alliances. What began in 1965 as a spiritual vision yielded cultural gatherings and an after-hours jazz club and then the incorporation of a nascent spiritual practice structured around the devotion of John Coltrane that was accompanied by alliances with the Black Panther Party and John Coltrane's widow, Alice Coltrane, and the creation of a Hindu ashram and finally, in the wake of a $7.5 million lawsuit filed by Alice Coltrane, integration within the African Orthodox Church whose institutional roots reach back to the 1920s and alliances with Marcus Mosiah Garvey's Universal Negro Improvement Association. The St. John Will-I-Am Coltrane African Orthodox Church has attempted to put into practice what cultural studies theorist Chela Sandoval has termed "differential ideological positioning" critical to the effective formation of counterhegemonic ideologies and practices, and a fluid, improvisatory strategy of social moves that have enabled it to transverse domains of culture, religion, and politics (Sandoval).

The sanctuary at 351 Divisadero Street was transformed into a dining hall to feed the homeless during Thanksgiving in the mid–1990s, and music was performed by Ohnedaruth. This photograph also shows the iconography of the Rev. Mark Dukes.

The Coltrane Church: Apostles of Sound, Agents of Social Justice offers a critical history of 50 years (1965–2015) of the ideological evolution and transition of the Coltrane Church from the 1965 Sound Baptism to the present. I present a history of the church situated within the specific historical and cultural landscape of the San Francisco Bay Area from the mid–1960s to the present. The Apostles of Sound thrived in San Francisco in an era of new church movements marked by the rise and fall of personality cults and Eastern spiritual experimentation. The early manifestations of the church as the Yardbird Club and the Coltrane-worshipping Yardbird Temple and the One Mind Evolutionary Church of the Hour survived beyond the inevitable disillusionment with counter-cultural spirituality caused by the Peoples Temple and the mass-suicide at Jonestown in Guyana (1978) because each manifestation of the Coltrane Church was capable of strategic ideological and material transition and of emerging in 1986 as the St. John Will-I-Am Coltrane African Orthodox Church. That kind of ideological adjustment, the willingness to move from the deification of John Coltrane to his accommodation as a saint, alone speaks to the ideological fluidity of the Coltrane Church, to say nothing of its alliances with the Black Panther Party, Alice Coltrane, the Nation of Islam, and the Occupy SF movement. Embedded in their history are a host of other strategic cultural and religious transformations that have sustained them through a 50-year history marked by the peaks and valleys of jazz patronage in the Bay Area, the rise and fall of community civil rights organizations, the vicissitudes of urban development and social protest, and the far-ranging social, cultural, and political implications of California's economic cycles.

In many senses, this book is also a critical history of San Francisco since the mid–1960s. Members of the Coltrane Church have witnessed and resisted transformations of the city's economic, political, and cultural life from the provincial blue collar and bohemian "Baghdad by the Bay" to the contemporary mini–Manhattan landscape of massive capital and master builders (DeLeon). Their involvement in social protest against urban redevelopment marks them as participants in a more radical coalition of critics of the ineffectual slow growth progressivism. Their experimentations with Eastern mysticism speak to the era of new religious movements and the flower power innocence of the 1960s. Their shift from Alice Coltrane and the Vedanic Center to the African Orthodox Church is played out against the horrific nightmare of the Peoples Temple. Their engagement with the Black Panther Party in the 1960s, the 2009–10 Oscar Grant Movement against police brutality, and the 2011–12 Occupy SF movement inextricably links them to 50 years of a broader history of struggles of the underclass in the San Francisco Bay Area.

From the perspective of this historically situated narrative, I argue that the transitional, fluid, integrative theology and practice of "differential ideological positioning" of the Coltrane Church is the central factor that has enabled the Coltrane Church as a religious, cultural, and political organization to effectuate successful counter-hegemonic strategies in response to the exigencies of local histories of urban redevelopment, the corporatization of jazz, civil rights militancy, post–civil rights urban black politics, and the rise and fall of new church movements (Sandoval). The ability of the Coltrane Church to create a theology from whole cloth and consistently participate on its own terms in highly contested fields of culture, religion, and politics testifies to the efficacy of strategic ideological positioning for subaltern movements, generally speaking, working within broader contexts of corporate and state power. It is in this regard that the story of the Coltrane Church is instructive to any subaltern congregation and/or new church movement in America that is interested in either long-term sustainability or social, cultural and political relevance.

I have selected the most significant, strategic ideological moves of the Coltrane Church and evaluated these within the perspectives of critical musicology and cultural studies. Theoretically, I have built upon Fischlin, Heble, and Lipsitz's understanding of the link between improvisation and rights discourses. As Fischlin, Heble, and Lipsitz have suggested in *The Fierce Urgency of Now*, the St. John Will-I-Am Coltrane African Orthodox Church must be understood as first and foremost a cultural happening, rooted in the ethics of free improvisation, and with a history that suggests an evolving and "wider reference as a form of cultural practice that resonates with and disturbs other forms of being social, being in culture" (19). Beginning with the birth of the church and Coltrane Consciousness at the Jazz Workshop September 18, 1965, the free improvisation of John Coltrane similarly resonated and disturbed a broader range of religious, cultural, and political practices. Referencing Albert Ayler's notion of the "freedom" inherent in the music, Fischlin, Heble, and Lipsitz comment, "What if, in fact, improvisation as a musical practice filters into other cultural practices, virally spreading its aesthetic and ethical challenges in as yet misunderstood or unstudied ways?" (19).

What if?

Most importantly, I have integrated the work of Chela Sandoval on "differential ideological positioning" to make sense of the wide-ranging 50-year evolutionary trajectory of the church as a cultural, religious, and political organization. Sandoval's work is broadly suggestive of strategies of long-term survival and sustainability of subaltern and counter-hegemonic communities.

I have also utilized jazz studies paradigms of *intermusicality*, and notions of community formation through musical performance provided by noted jazz scholars Ingrid Monson, Paul Berliner, Ajay Heble, and Mark Anthony Neal to explain the Coltrane Church as a rational outcome of cultural interactions between artists and audiences. Furthermore, the divinity of John Coltrane is evaluated within the context of my concept of a "Religious Phenomenology of Sound," and illustrates a sophisticated and ecstatic blend of different forms of communication and expression, a fusion of Western and non–Western spirituality, and multi-sensory engagement to explain the experience of miracles.

Finally, the path-breaking work of African American religious scholar Arthur Huff Fauset has been particularly inspirational in helping to bind the many disparate elements of the history of the St. John Will-I-Am Coltrane African Orthodox Church. In the 1971 edition of *Black Gods of the Metropolis: Negro Religious Cults of the Urban North*, Fauset noted,

"Negroes are attracted to the cults for the obvious reason that with few normal outlets of expression for Negroes in America due to the prevailing custom of racial dichotomy the cults offer on the one hand the boon of religion with all its attendant promise of heaven either here or above or both; and on the other hand they provide for certain Negroes with imagination and other dynamic qualities, in an atmosphere free from embarrassment or apology, a place where they may experiment in activities such as business, politics, social reform, and social expression; thereby these American Negroes satisfy the normal urge of any member of our culture who wishes to contribute positively to the advancement of the group" (Fauset 107–108).

Edward E. Curtis IV and Danielle Brune Sigler's contemporary collection of essays inspired by the work of Fauset, *The New Black Gods: Arthur Huff Fauset and the Study of African American Religions*, has been equally inspiring in its overall mission of explicating and updating Fauset's vision of assimilating so-called "marginal" African American religious expression within broader and more mainstream African American cultural and political prerogatives. Curtis and Sigler write, "He [Fauset] was able to conceptualize an African American universe of religious activity in which black bodies did more than perform emotional worship –black religion for Fauset was much more than a 'jig and a song.' In Fauset's view, Americans of African descent were modern and rational persons possessing as much human agency as anyone else. Democratic to the core, Fauset's vision also resisted the idea that black religion, especially 'cult' religion, was a tragic, ultimately misguided, and ineffective political protest against social alienation and oppression. To the contrary, Fauset saw the seeds of effective social and political protest in the activism of cult members" (Curtis and Sigler 7). In this spirit I have similarly focused on the rationality, strategic ideological constructions, and actions of the founders and members of the Coltrane Church, rather than to glorify their difference and ecumenical "exoticism" and dismiss any possibility of cultural and political relevance as so many magazines, short films, and brief asides about the Coltrane Church have done.[9]

Any analytic engagement with the history of the Coltrane Church has to employ a similarly eclectic fusion of theoretical perspectives that range from the cultural politics of representation to jazz studies and theories of intermusicality to phenomenological and often esoteric analyses.

The Coltrane Church: Apostles of Sound, Agents of Social Justice is also a chronologically structured critical history that undertakes analyses of "multiple coexisting social processes," examining the differential ideological positioning of the Coltrane Church in cultural, religious, and political domains (Rosaldo). Chapters that emphasize the cultural impact of the Coltrane Church as an African American community-based jazz institution, what Herman Gray refers to as the "Jazz Left," contextualize the church against a history of the corporatization of jazz music and its exodus from traditional African American communities in San Francisco (Gray). Chapters that emphasize the impact of the theology and religious practices of the Coltrane Church contextualize the church's theological embrace of Coltrane's spirituality, spiritual universalism, and Eastern mysticism against a Bay Area marketplace of alternative spiritual practices and new religious movements from the 1960s forward. Chapters that emphasize the Coltrane Church as a politically active interest group contextualize the church's anti-police brutality, environmental, and anti-redevelopment activism and its steady embrace of black woman-centered leadership against the broader histories of racialism, urban gentrification, redevelopment, and sexism in the black church in the San Francisco Bay Area.

I chose as my primary evidence the reflective oral narratives—often referred by my informants in religious terms as "testimonies"—of church founders and leaders Archbishop Franzo Wayne King, Mother Marina King, and Pastor Wanika Kristi King-Stephens. I have clearly been led in this regard by the work of Monson and Berliner in privileging interviews of the musicians, priests, and founders of the Coltrane Church. Monson claims "the only ethical point of departure for work in jazz studies ... remains the documentation and interpretation of vernacular perspectives, contemporary or historical, no matter how much we must rethink the claims we make for them in light of post-structural discussions of representation and the politics of knowing and being" (Monson 6–7).

The story of the St. John Will-I-Am Coltrane African Orthodox Church answers the question of whether music, culture and religion matter. Specifically, does either jazz music or African American religion materially enhance the lives of its participants? Can either expression effectuate meaningful political or economic change?

The answer to these questions, I believe, is affirmative in specific contexts, particularly where there has been a willful desire and pragmatic strategy to effectuate counter-hegemonic practices through the explicit rejection of orthodoxy and embrace a fluid, transitional, indeed improvisatory posture of "differential positioning." My extensive ethnographic experience with the Coltrane Church and my ongoing relationship with the church as Ph.D. in residence and guitarist have restored my faith that subaltern groups can in fact create effective and empowering ideological positions and productive political realities in spite of the limitations imposed by dominant society. Sandoval further reflects, "All social orders hierarchically organized into relations of domination and subordination create particular subject positions within which the subordinated can legitimately function. These subject positions, once self-consciously recognized by their inhabitants, can become transfigured into effective sites of resistance to an oppressive ordering of power relations" (55). The Coltrane Church is one among many possible spaces for transfiguration and resistance.

The question of community relevance has been central to many contemporary critical histories of jazz. Since Herman S. Gray prioritized the distinction between a community-centered "Jazz Left" and the institutional and corporate grounding of the "Jazz Right," in *Cultural Moves: African Americans and the Politics of Representation* (2005), contemporary jazz scholarship has taken a decided turn towards the investigation of jazz practice within specific local, community settings. George E. Lewis' *A Power Stronger Than Itself: The AACM and American Experimental Music* (2009); Daniel Fischlin, Ajay Heble and George Lipsitz's *The Fierce Urgency of Now: Improvisation, Rights, and the Ethics of Co-Creation* (2013); and Steve Isoardi's *The Dark Tree: Jazz and the Community Arts in Los Angeles* (2006), to name a few, all explore the efficacy of jazz practice within the context of community arts movements from Chicago to New Orleans to St. Louis to Los Angeles from the 1940s to the present. In similar fashion, *The Coltrane Church* connects the cultural performance, theology, and religious practice of the church to a sustainable narrative history, locally as well nationally. Here, in the historical and cultural landscape of functionality, lies the relevance and purpose of the Coltrane Church in the San Francisco Bay Area from 1965 to 2015.

In the Coltrane Church jazz music and religious expression matter because of their fundamental ability to bring people to spiritual, cultural, political, and other forms of social engagement. For 50 years, Coltrane Consciousness has brought unbelievers to Christianity and, for a time, Hinduism. It has brought addicts to sobriety, the unhealthy to vegetarianism, the apathetic to political action, and spurred the silent and the meek to creative articulation. The Coltrane Church has served in the battle for liberation in the Black Panther era of the 1970s. In 2009 it was at the forefront of social protest against police brutality in the wake of the tragic shooting of an unarmed and handcuffed Oscar Grant by Bay Area Rapid Transit police at Fruitvale Station in Oakland. In that same year it presented an impressive proposal to the San Francisco Redevelopment Agency for the restoration of a historic Fillmore Street property and the initiation of a St. John Coltrane University of Arts and Social Justice. From 2009 to 2012 it was allied with the broader Occupy movement in efforts to seek justice for the exploitation of big bank mortgage lenders, and continues fighting bank foreclosures of African American home and business owners in the Western Addition and Bayview-Hunter's Point neighborhoods. In 2010 the St. John Will-I-Am African Orthodox Church was the first African Orthodox Church to consecrate a woman as pastor. But all of these material challenges have been implemented on the grounds of ever-shifting ideologies and practices and the willingness to evolve and recognize ideological evolution as a spiritually heightened and politically pragmatic principle.

At stake are African American cultural politics and the project of constructing affirmative counter-hegemonic ideologies for subaltern African American communities. The Coltrane Church, Coltrane Liturgy, and Coltrane Consciousness are contested discursive practices resulting from the deliberate symbolic activity of a counter-public seeking to contest power and project its own image and identity. For reasons perhaps most directly explicated by the social, cultural, and political context of San Francisco on September 18, 1965, Franzo and Marina King *needed* to interact with John Coltrane. They *needed* the Holy Ghost to walk out on the stage and speak with them through John Coltrane. They *needed* an agenda from John Coltrane that they could further and through which they could locate themselves. Indeed, as Stuart Hall once commented, "You can only get something out of the image if you position yourself in relation to what it's telling you. What we've only gradually come to see is the way in which the viewer himself or herself is implicated" (Hall 16).

In *The Coltrane Church: Apostles of Sound, Agents of Social Justice* I seek to affirm the agency and sovereign politics of representation of the Coltrane Church and subaltern cultural communities and congregations generally speaking. My interest is in how the ideologies and practices of the Coltrane Church have met the social, cultural, political, economic and spiritual needs of a particular counter-public for the past 50 years. I have absolutely no interest in validating the theology of the Coltrane Church according to the standards of established religious institutions or in validating the specific "religious training" of these Apostles of Sound. These are self-proclaimed apostles who have expressly and definitively rejected established religion and claimed an extraordinary vision and baptism in sound by and through the person of the late jazz visionary John William Coltrane. The ideas that were communicated through the interaction between Coltrane and his young listeners, Franzo and Marina King, were predicated upon discrete cultural understandings and resulted in the creation of a community that expressed the yearnings of its members, the community of the St. John Will-I-Am Coltrane African Orthodox Church. The Coltrane Church is undoubtedly only one of many possible ideological representations and interpretations of John Coltrane and his music but it is singularly important because it fundamentally represents community-based anti-establishment cultural and political expressions of religious faith.

I do not purport to present exhaustive histories of jazz music, urban redevelopment, police brutality, new religious movements, or political resistance in the San Francisco Bay Area. It is merely my goal to properly contextualize the 50-year history of differential ideological movement of the Coltrane Church against the relevant historical backdrop of social, cultural, and political movements in the region between 1965 and 2015 to properly illuminate the significance and assess the efficacy of each stage of the church's evolution. Further, I have no intention of presenting a thorough biography of John Coltrane, but merely to present the relevant aspects of his life, music, thought, and practices that have influenced the development of the Coltrane Church.

After 21 years (1994–2015) and counting of involvement with the Coltrane Church, as an ethnographer, member, Ph.D. in residence, and guitarist, I've experienced a measure of the revolution I'd anticipated and something with even broader implications than I had ever imagined. I've been with the Coltrane Church as it has sojourned from its long-time location on 351 Divisadero Street to the St. Paulus Lutheran Church on 930 Gough Street to its current location on 1286 Fillmore Street in the heart of San Francisco's new Jazz District. I've watched members come and go, alterations in the liturgy, changes in community outreach programs, productive forays into social advocacy, and the rise and fall of plans for expansion. I've attended hundreds of worship services on Sundays and Wednesdays, untold numbers of outreach performances, community gatherings, and even one wonderful trip to Paris in February 2008. It took 20 years to experience and fully understand the Coltrane Church for what it is, what it has always called itself: an evolutionary, transitional body of believers.

1

Apostles of Sound

*To perceive again and this time it must be said, for all who
read to know that no matter what, it is all with God. He
is gracious and merciful. His way is in love, through which
we all are. Wherever and whoever you are, always strive
to follow and walk in the right path and ask for aid and
assistance ... herein lies the ultimate and eternal happi-
ness which is our through His grace.*
—St. John Will-I-Am Coltrane

The Coltrane Church is the product of Franzo and Marina King's
vision of the Holy Ghost at John Coltrane's September 18, 1965, performance at the Jazz Workshop in San Francisco. This event is referred to by
the community as the initial Sound Baptism that gave rise to Coltrane
Consciousness and a church in John Coltrane's honor. It is a foundational
moment for the Coltrane Church that is widely accepted as a matter of
faith by church members, and an important cultural happening that speaks
to the endless possibilities of performative communication and the critical
role of subjectivity in the interpretation of performance. But the Sound
Baptism was also the singular experience of two migrant seekers who
experienced the spirituality of John Coltrane and his music in a cultural
and religious vacuum outside of the context of established black cultural,
religious and political organizations in San Francisco. This was, in every
sense of the word, something new.

In order to understand the Sound Baptism and critically assess whether
the kind of communication that created a new religious movement was
even possible as a cultural phenomenon, it's necessary to first understand
who Franzo and Marina King were, how they were situated as persons
when they arrived at the Jazz Workshop and what set of expectations they

Archbishop and Mother Marina King singing during the Coltrane liturgy at the present church location, 1286 Fillmore Street.

brought. It is necessary to understand their position as marginalized out-siders to the African American religious, cultural, and political establish-ment of the 1960s and '70s in the San Francisco Bay Area and their belief that they were both destined to be agents of change.

In the first year of our interviews, Archbishop King—then Bishop King—and I would meet at regular intervals in a small back office space near the kitchen of the 351 Divisadero Street facility. There were pictures and posters of Coltrane, Marcus Garvey, Hazrat Inayat Khan and Bob Marley on the walls. Plaques of recognition from the greater African Orthodox Church. Memorabilia from the church's former manifestations as the Yardbird Temple, and the One Mind Evolutionary Transitional Body of Christ Church and scattered papers addressed to the Archbishop's title during this transitional period, Bishop Ha'qq.[1] Photographs of many of the children of the church, and snapshots of former members from pre-vious eras. A framed picture of Archbishop Hinkson. A beautiful pencil sketch of a pensive John Coltrane. Pictures of the Archbishop with his magnificent dreadlocks in the pre–African Orthodox era.

What was noticeably missing in this space was any documentation of Archbishop King's relationship with the significant African American cultural, religious, and political power brokers of San Francisco since the 1970s. There were no plaques of recognition from the NAACP and Urban League. There was no proclamation honoring their community service and food programs in the 1970s from Terry Francois, the first African American member of the Board of Supervisors, nor from Mayor George Moscone, nor Wilbur Hamilton of the city's Redevelopment Agency that had substantively re-made the landscape of the Western Addition, nor "Da Mayor" Willie Brown. There was nothing to suggest affiliations with any of the major black churches and church organizations in the city from the greater Church of God in Christ to the Baptist Ministerial Alliance, nor evidence of substantive relationships from any of the more notable activist churches in the city's history including Jim Jones' People's Temple and Cecil Williams' Glide Memorial.

In the late 1960s and '70s Franzo and Marina King resided in a space of active resistance at the edge of significant cultural and political schisms within the black community. They steadfastly maintained an uncompromising position of resistance to not only the city's largely white corporatist power structures but also to that system's black accomplices and most celebrated discontents.

Writing in the early 1990s, San Francisco historian Richard Edward DeLeon notes that since the 1970s, African Americans, although consistently the smallest of the three major ethnic groups in the city (including Latinos and Asian Americans), had developed an influential ethnic political power bloc: "African Americans are now the smallest of the three major ethnic minority groups in terms of population size, but they have mustered the highest rates of voter mobilization, consensus on issues, and representation in government. Supported by political organization and leadership at the state and national levels, the city's African American leaders have converted limited numbers and economic resources into a power bloc to be reckoned with in local politics" (DeLeon 28). DeLeon further addressed the significant political schisms within San Francisco's black communities that perhaps limited the full realization of African American political power in the city: "Despite the current ascendancy of African Americans among San Francisco's ethnic minority groups, there are signs that the African American power base is eroding, mainly because of demographic attrition and developing schisms within African American leadership groups over issues such as growth controls" (28).

That schism, centrally focused around urban redevelopment in the mid- to late 1960s and 1970s as one the most significant racial events in San Francisco politics, included on one side local community activists and their allies, national civil rights organizations, and local black political insiders. Community activists included the Afro-American Association, Council of Civic Unity, the NAACP, the Baptist Ministerial Alliance and the Inter-Denominational Ministerial Alliance and the Bay Area Urban League, all of whom had been officially consulted on the redevelopment of Western Addition Area 2 in 1964[2] and had failed to demonstrate any critical consciousness regarding the project. The Afro-American Association, for example, notably fell short in 1964 and only voiced concerns that there should be provisions made to assist with social problems that might be incurred as a result of relocation.[3]

Allied with local community black activists were progressive European-American and Japanese-American Christian organizations in the Western Addition that did manage to sound the alarm but found only limited success in slowing the rate of redevelopment. Among the more prominent of these organizations were WACO, or Western Addition Community Organization, funded in part by the Christ Church United Presbyterian Church, originally organized in 1885 as the First Japanese Presbyterian Church, the oldest Japanese Christian Church in America.[4] WACO, an umbrella for approximately 40 Western Addition organizations, was an alliance of diverse churches, civic organizations and trade unions organized in January 1967. WACO called attention to the inequities of redevelopment, created a newspaper (*The WACO Organizer*) for raising awareness, halted the construction of the Martin Luther King, Jr., Square, and convinced the San Francisco Board of Supervisors to provide guarantees for relocated residents.

The established national opposition included black civil rights organizations that unsuccessfully attempted to block redevelopment in lieu of a Citizens Review Committee. Henry Marshall, chairman of the Western Addition Target Area Board of the Economic Opportunity Council; Bill Bradley, chairman of the San Francisco office of the Congress of Racial Equality (CORE); and Arthur Latham, chairman of the local NAACP, were all significant players in these efforts.

Local political insiders unsuccessfully attempted to ameliorate the effects of relocation, including civil rights activist, attorney and former city NAACP chapter president Terry Francois, who was serving as the first African American member of the Board of Supervisors (1967–1978). Francois at one point accused white Presbyterian ministers of WACO of manipulating Negroes, and proposed a dead-end 2 percent hotel tax to provide for housing for relocated persons.[5] Wilbur Hamilton, whose family has significant leadership connections in the African American Church of

God in Christ, served as project manager of the Western Addition Area–2 Project in 1968 and was appointed assistant executive director of the San Francisco Redevelopment Agency by Mayor George Moscone in 1971, deputy executive director in 1974, and in 1977 as agency head, a position he held for 10 years.[6] There is little that can be said of how his "insider" status helped stem the ravages of redevelopment.

Between the political insiders, established civil rights organizations, community activists, and their allies, however well-intentioned, none of their efforts managed to stop the ultimate success of redevelopment and relocation, a phenomenon that continues to displace African American residents in San Francisco at nationally unprecedented rates.

For Archbishop King and Mother Marina, black activists, allies, and insiders alike were merely playing out a self-serving drama that, in their opinion, was never intended to materially benefit the largely African American and poor residents of neighborhoods like the Western Addition or Bayview-Hunter's Point. In the midst of this drama, the Coltrane Church worked from the margins, showing up at protest meetings when asked, helping to fill the room, even as it continued to bag groceries for the growing indigent populations of the Western Addition from its Divisadero location, feeding students engaged in protest at San Francisco State University, and creating a community emergency response and policing system. Archbishop King:

> What would happen, Reverend Townsend would tell me, "Hey Franzo, we need people to come up to this meeting." I would take 20 or 30 people out of the food program line and go to the meeting but I don't know what they're meeting on or about. I'm just going because they're people from the street, people that I know.

With the notable exception of their relationship with the Black Panther Party, the early manifestations of the Coltrane Church engaged in community work and political activism from the margins. They were often "accidental" figures in larger dramas of urban redevelopment and police brutality, performing small acts without significant alliances to mainstream black political figures, activist organizations, or political insiders. Archbishop King:

> What protected me is that I was apolitical up until Dr. Huey P. Newton. And even then we were the vanguard revolutionary. In other words, we didn't incorporate, we didn't want anything from the state, no and nothing. Even going back to being a youngster and getting married, I didn't want to go and ask any white man for a license to marry a black woman. So I had that kind of consciousness about the whole wicked system.

You know how they say "keep yourself unspotted from the world, separate yourself and come from amongst them"? That was my attitude before
I knew anything about politics, I didn't want to be a part of the world, I
didn't need to have some kind of acceptance from established churches or
anything. No, this is an underground movement. Matter of fact, we didn't
let everybody in. That kept me from getting involved.

Because of their fierce independence and skepticism, the Coltrane
Church cannot retrospectively be counted among the various "slow
growth" activist community coalitions who ultimately failed to halt redevelopment and the relocation of many of the Western Addition's African
American residents. The cultural history of the Fillmore/Western Addition
includes the failure of many of these activist organizations, and a legacy
of seemingly "righteous" leadership that would ultimately abandon the
cause only to take up other more fashionable causes at a later date. But
the Coltrane Church is not remembered among these.

Furthermore, the Coltrane Church, as Western Addition residents,
never materially benefited from the presence of African American insiders
like Hamilton or Francois, nor it could it be properly located within the
broader coalitions of insiders and so-called progressive black political
power within the city. There were always prominent figures in San Francisco's African American churches seeking the limelight amidst the city's
redevelopment insiders. The most notorious of these was Jim Jones, leader
of the People's Temple and one-time liberal elite darling, who was
appointed to the San Francisco Housing Authority in 1976 by then Mayor
George Moscone whom he assisted in a tough mayoral campaign against
the conservative John Barbagelata. "Moscone, a charming and handsome
state legislator, had electrified San Francisco progressives with his campaign for city hall. A champion of gays, women, minorities, tenants and
organized labor, Moscone was locked in a tight race with a pack of oppo-
nents led by conservative realtor John Barbagelata, whose campaign
evoked a nostalgia for an older San Francisco, when it was ruled by traditional Catholic values. A meeting was set up between Jones and Moscone
in the office of Don Bradley, the candidate's veteran campaign manager.
Bradley was initially cautious. 'I was a little leery we were getting into
something like the Moonies,' he later recalled. But after he looked into the
temple's campaign history and saw how effective it was in delivering victories, Bradley enthusiastically embraced Jones's volunteer army. Nearly
200 temple members showed up at Moscone headquarters, fanning out
to campaign in some of the city's toughest neighborhoods, and helping
the candidate finish first in the November 1975 election."[7]

Contrastively, the founders of the Coltrane Church have a marginal and subaltern history as cultural outsiders and seekers who were ready to see John Coltrane take the bandstand on September 18, 1965, and embrace him as the uncompromising iconoclastic saint of constant evolution and hear him communicate a message that would serve as the ultimate catalyst for social action and, to paraphrase John Coltrane himself, "a force for real good."

Cultural Outsiders

As a cultural and political outsider, the Archbishop was the kind of man I would have expected John Coltrane to embrace. Tall, lean, angular with the wiry strong build of a middleweight prizefighter, and enough charisma to fill up all of San Francisco. Archbishop King immediately impressed me with the kind of spirit and energy that had, according to legend, endeared Elvin Jones to Coltrane. He was charismatic and open, a visionary and yet a man without pretensions. He could speak esoterically and punctuate his thinking with common sense wisdom. He understood the ways of the mystic and the machinations of Machiavellian politics.

Archbishop King, Mother Marina and Ohnedaruth bassist and warden Clarence Stephens at services at 930 Gough Street.

During the course of the next 21 years and counting I would watch him negotiate with government officials and local merchants alike with a unique fluidity and familiarity. Wherever you were coming from, he seemed to have been there. And he was always the same man, refusing to sign on to anyone else's agenda, defending his ideological position in the bowels of west African slave castles with Dr. Cornel West and politician and civil rights activist Al Sharpton[8] or affirming the sainthood of John Coltrane at the African Orthodox Synod in Miami or highlighting the paradox of social liberalism and pro-growth policies in a closed session with then San Francisco Mayor Willie Brown or publicly decrying police brutality before the police commission.

The everyman/outsider aura of Archbishop King is certainly well earned. A St. Louis native who migrated with his family to California, this was a man who lost his father when he was only 2 years of age and was raised by a single mother. Like so many young African American men, Franzo King was repeatedly targeted and arrested by a notoriously racist and predatory Los Angeles Police Department in the 1960s. But Franzo King's narrative would take a different turn than so many others in his ability to avoid a long-term prison sentence and his ever-present awareness of a possible future as a preacher, a belief he carried like a birthright, an inheritance from parents who were ministers.

His self-conscious awareness of a birthright to the ministry is the product of belonging to a family of founding and pioneering members of the Church of God in Christ (Pentecostal) in St. Louis and southern California, when the black Pentecostal movement was itself an outsider movement in the broader history of black migrations. This was the second wave of a black Pentecostal movement in Los Angeles, following on the heels of the 1930s demise of William J. Seymour's Azusa Street Revival (1906–1909),[9] and based on the inspiration of Bishop Charles Mason after his attendance at Seymour's revival.[10] It was a new religious movement of African Americans who were, by virtue of social class, excluded from the established African Methodist Episcopalian and Baptist social circles and whose membership generally constituted the latest and most impoverished black migrants from the American South.

His great-grandmother, Benny Roberts Benbow, built the first podium from which Bishop Charles H. Mason, the founding Apostle of the Church of God in Christ, preached. His grandfather, Elder E.C. Benbow, was a member of the inner circle of elders who labored with Bishop Mason to lay the foundation of the black Pentecostal movement in St. Louis in the early 1900s. Bishop B. R. Benbow established the New Life Church of God in Christ and pioneered the church in Venice, California. Elder E.C. Benbow's wife, Mother Elizabeth Benbow, was a missionary and founder of Y.P.W.W. (Young People's Willing Workers), a central and enduring organization for the religious training of young people in the black Pentecostal church. Their seventh child, Mildred Phyllis Benbow, known familiarly within the Coltrane Church community as "Supreme Mother," became an evangelist and carried the word in Pentecostal revivals across the country. Her husband, Landres Charles King, Sr., was also a young preacher with an ambition for the bishopric, but his death at an early age left Mildred Phyllis a widow with three young children. Her second-born was Franzo Wayne King, whom she was to groom as a little preacher.

This was the man who claimed to be the first son born of Sound, the man who, together with his wife and spiritual partner Marina King, had heard through the horn of John Coltrane the voice of God. This was the man who was bringing to the world a universal gospel of brotherhood through the language of sound. And there were no airs about him, no hierarchy demanding obsequiousness to penetrate. His Pentecostal, working class, and recent migratory status gave him, in spite of his fierce antiestablishment defiance, great warmth and humility. If Sister Deborah, or Sister S. Elizabeth were there to join us for tea and conversation, he would defer to their corrections in the chronology or on matters of specific detail. There was often doubt in his voice and sometimes our meetings would begin with him questioning my return and continued affiliation with the church. "I thought I might have scared you away the last time," he would say. And later he would tell me, "I still feel that I'm holding back." Inevitably he would defer everything to the opinion of Mother Marina to provide the final clarification, claiming, "I've got to ask Mother Marina, she would know."

Mother Marina King, the first daughter born of Sound, was his equal in every sense of the word. Commanding attention with a quiet grace, Mother Marina could be a woman of few words, certainly fewer words than the Archbishop, but her every utterance demanded respect and contained a significant "reading" or commentary delivered with a gentle smile. She was the consummate manager of the menagerie of personalities and egos that made up the Coltrane Church and its official touring band, Ohnedaruth.[11] She had a way of bringing clarity and direction to every contentious situation and there was hardly a member of the Coltrane Church who would have ever dared question her authority.

Contrastively, Mother Marina King, formerly Marina Lynn Robinson, has deep credentials in the more established African Methodist Episcopal

Church, black activism, and jazz that undergird her authority and leadership. She was anything but an outsider. Her mother was an administrator at the University of California, Los Angeles, her father was a jazz trumpet player, and her uncle, Freddy Robinson, was a trombone player in Louis Armstrong's Hot Five band, notably appearing on Armstrong's paradigm shifting "West End Blues" recording.[12] Her grandfather was an A.M.E. Zion minister and active member of the Honorable Marcus Mosiah Garvey's Universal Negro Improvement Association (U.N.I.A).

Born and raised in Cleveland until her teenage years, Mother Marina's family moved to Los Angeles and subsequent decisions, particularly regarding her education, in effect rendered Marina King an immediate cultural outsider. Mother Marina:

> In junior high school when I moved from Cleveland, where my school experience had been African American teachers, principals, students, going to Los Angeles I experienced a lot of culture shock. My parents didn't want me to go to a black school, they wanted me to go to this Jewish school so we were like the flies in the buttermilk and I think my way of acting out was that I was anti-social and didn't try to get along with anybody but just stayed with myself. One of the girls came up to me and said, "Well, we sing, let me hear you sing. Oh, well you can sing." So we would sing together mainly for fun.

Dislocated from a predominantly black middle class school environment and from her family's church in Cleveland, Marina King found a great measure of cultural and personal identification in the milieu of the civil rights struggle in Los Angeles:

> As a teenager and when all of the civil rights disturbances were going on and with experiencing racism here, it wasn't hard for me to be ready for change, it sounded good to my ears and I felt that I needed to be a part of that change. It was like a high to me. It was the thing to be doing. And I still feel that way.

A West Side Story Love Supreme

The Coltrane Church is at its core the product of the love of these two extraordinary people, one an outsider from more established African American social circles and the other a classic black middle-class insider. There is an incredible love story that undergirds the founding and ongoing evolution of the Coltrane Church and speaks to the common spiritual, cultural, and political yearnings of these two unlikely lovers. There are at least five key components of the love story between Franzo and Marina

King that created a church: the incredible "Romeo & Juliet/West Side Story" insider/outsider narrative of the early years of their courtship; a shared sense of being destined to create the Coltrane Church together; a shared and uniquely profound love and admiration for John Coltrane; a shared sense of being outsiders and revolutionary agents for change; and their shared self-identification as mystics and visionaries. Franzo and Marina came together as two of John Coltrane's greatest fans, outsiders given greater purpose and identity through their love of John Coltrane, who both believed that Coltrane's music had a power that extended well beyond mere entertainment and could reform African American culture, religion, and politics. Through their mutual admiration of John Coltrane, Franzo and Marina found a sense of belonging and an enduring commonality from which they could build a life's work.

Archbishop King speaks of meeting Mother Marina, who had only recently arrived from Cleveland, for the first time. His narrative is rich with the self-consciousness of his lower class status in relationship to Mother Marina, the very real possibility of rejection, and the very real excitement of crossing class borders within the black community:

Archbishop and Mother Marina King in the late 1980s at their home in the Bayview-Hunter's Point neighborhood.

The first time I met her was on the last day in high school. I was introduced to her by a mutual acquaintance. She had just gotten to Los Angeles from Cleveland. Everybody was in a celebratory spirit. I had a car and me and two of my partners were rolling. Three of us, one in the back seat. One of them, Bobby Dunlap, he was younger than me, about a year younger, and he was Mother Marina's age. He was telling me about these beautiful girls from Cleveland that he met. He actually knew where she lived and her and her girlfriends were there and I went over and met her and stood on the porch and talked with her for a little while. She didn't go out and ride with us that day, but I did meet her and I was quite impressed. And then I got a chance to see her again at a party.

The group that I was hanging out with we called ourselves the Clique Brothers and her girlfriends called themselves The Group. And so the Group and the Clique Brothers were together, having a party. A house party. I show up and Mother Marina was literally running from me. When I saw her I didn't realize that it was the same girl. Bobby brought her to the party. I told him, she was a higher class, she was outta his league. I came in and said, nice to see you and she went over to this room and that room … she was literally running from me. But I was insistent and I think she kinda liked my humor and personality. And then a wild romance begins.

I never even thought that I was good enough for her, to be honest. I was always fearful that somebody better was going to come along and crash my scene. I guess I was insecure. I was only about eighteen or so. And I used to quit her every other week or so, you know, before she quit me. I got my teeth busted out, I got my nose broken, my face was all swelled up, and I looked in the mirror and said, Oh, this is it, it's over. So I called her up and said, "You know, I think we ought to end this, I mean, who are we kidding? We should leave this alone." And she told me, "You know, I'm really tired of you breaking up with me every other week, and if you're going to pull this stunt again, don't call me no more."

Archbishop King recognized that the one thing that might miraculously hold them together in spite of the very real barriers of class and privilege was his desire to become a preacher, a long-respected occupation within all class levels of the African American community. Archbishop King recalls his understanding in that moment of his future life in the ministry and the centrality of prayer and spirituality in their burgeoning romance. His willingness to engage Marina in prayer would be emblematic of his respectability within her circles and of his true calling, however far he had strayed up to that point. He recalled:

> And I knew that I was going to preach, even though at that point in my life it didn't look like I was on the road to the ministry. But I knew I was and my thing to her was, "Do you think you could be a preacher's wife?" And she said, "Yeah, my grandfather's a preacher."

When I would bring her home after the movies or something like that we would always have prayer. So I mean, that was in the very beginning of our relationship I would tell her that you need to know that I'm going to be a preacher. And I need a preacher's wife. I knew that that's what my calling was. And Mother Marina was aware of it very early on in our relationship and it was just a very intense courtship.

We used to talk on the phone and fall asleep and wake up and find we were still there on the phone. And my brother would be telling me, "Man, would you get off that phone, talking to that woman all night!" And I was out. I was in love. I think her parents had to take her phone out of the room. She had a phone in her room. They had to take it out of her room. I mean we were ridiculous with it.

Mother Marina's subsequent pregnancy combined with their pronounced class differences prompted her family to send her back to Cleveland. This is a classic strategy of the African American middle class in this era, as her family attempted to hide the "shame" of Marina's out-of-wedlock pregnancy and discourage any further contact with Franzo King. Here their love story meets its first challenge. Archbishop King followed Mother Marina to the Midwest, traveling by bus to Chicago to attend cosmetology school and later back to Los Angeles and the Bay Area. Archbishop King:

And then there was the separation. She was sent to Cleveland. I was not the ideal person that her parents had seen for her. I came over to ask for her hand and her mother looked at me and she said, "You know what, I think you need to get out of her before her father gets here because he's not going to be very pleased to see you." And he was the guy I had come to see. But I took her advice and left.

And something we don't talk about too much, Mother Marina was pregnant. So they sent her to Cleveland. That was 1963. They sent her to Cleveland to cut off our communication. That's why I went to Chicago, because it was close to Cleveland. I went out there and studied to be a hairdresser. I never thought about being a hairdresser. Cosmetology school never entered my head. My aunt came out and asked me what I was doing and then said that she was going to make an artist out of me. That was being a hairdresser. She said that she was going to send me a bus ticket so that I could come. And that's how I ended up in Chicago. That's why I ended up in Chicago. I was trying to get close to Cleveland where Mother Marina was.

And when I get to Chicago my letter gets to her, because my letters were not getting to her, they were being intercepted. And Anne's [Mother Marina's sister] husband came in and told her one day, "Marina, I got a letter for you … and it's from Franzo!" So he opened the door and gave her the letter and made that contact. Now she's on her way back to Los Angeles. So there was no way I was finishing cosmetology school because I'm on my way back.

It was way out. It was thundering back there and the thunder is calling her name. It was intense for me. So I came back to LA and I looked at LA and the crowd that I was hanging out with when I was in Cleveland and Chicago, and I said if I stay here I'm going to the penitentiary or the graveyard. So I got up out of there and went to San Francisco, which is where my mother was. Later Mother Marina and Wanika [their first child] came up. And you know, it was a story of perseverance, and neither one of us would let go. We were committed. And when I think back on it, it wasn't a long courtship. It was probably only less than a year that we were courting. And the rest is history.

Spiritual Destiny

The testimonies that they shared with me reflected attempts to retrospectively understand how they had been destined to meet and arrive at this position of leadership. Certainly the circumstances surrounding Marina's pregnancy and sojourn to Cleveland support the notion that Franzo and Marina were destined to be together and that their passion for one another endured the trials of class and an out-of-wedlock pregnancy. But there is also a profoundly spiritual dimension to the sense of destiny that characterized their relationship.

There was always a sense in their telling and re-telling of the stories of their lives that it had all been like that moment at the Jazz Workshop in 1965, that they had always been "set up" by God, even by John Coltrane himself, to create a church and bring Coltrane Consciousness to the world. There had been no wasted moments. It had all been a part of God's plan. There was a sense of destiny that would propel Franzo King toward preaching and Marina King toward a greater relationship with jazz music.

Archbishop King, for his part, would consistently claim that from the beginning he was blessed with an understanding communicated through his mother that he was to accomplish something special in the world. There can be no overestimation of the impact of his mother, Dr. Phyllis Proudhomme, on his emotional, intellectual, and spiritual development and the constant source of inspiration that she provided. In the absence of a father, Phyllis Proudhomme provided a young Franzo Wayne King with a sense of importance by attaching significance to his birth, his name, and by instructing him as a preacher. Indeed, as Archbishop King reflects through his testimonies on his life, it is clear that his mother provided a road map and a religious training for him with which to make significance of all the disparate influences and events in his life:

You see I always tease her saying that she knows that I'm hers, and because of the fact that there wasn't any room for any switching to take place. I was born at home. And the fact that I came out head up first, facing the world. That's what the doctor said. He said, "He's really gonna be somebody, he came facing the world." And I've always had that in my mind because it was something that from time to time if I would accomplish something she would make that reference that "you know you're gonna be more than that because you came facing the world." I don't know what else to say about it other than that it helped to kind of shape my psyche, it was a source of inspiration for me, thinking that just from the very instance of my being born that it was dignified and distinguished from other births.

Archbishop King's sense of belonging to the music is derived from his name. He was named by his mother after a famous musician of the period, Wayne King, the Waltz King, and for him the name foreshadowed the importance of music in his life. This was a power given to him by his mother, and Archbishop King has long recognized his mother's central role in shaping his spiritual life and, consequently, the possibility for his creation and leadership of something like the Coltrane Church:

My name is Wayne, and there was a great orchestra player called Wayne King, and Archbishop Hinkson told me, he said, "Wayne King, the sweetest music this side of heaven," and that's the way he used to advertise himself. I was thinking it has to be some kind of hook up there, me being Wayne King. My mother used to say, "Wayne King, the Waltz King," and that was another name that he had because he played a lot of waltzes and stuff.

And so it was Wayne King the Waltz King and when I think about the stuff that John does that I can identify the most with, are the 6/8 things, which is an elongated 3/4. On the drums I have the tendency to play 3/4 or 6/8, I am so free in that time. And the idea of being the Waltz King and then hooked up with John Coltrane is this music which is the sweetest music this side of heaven. I don't know, I think they were on to something. She dropped that name on me.

Archbishop King's specific understanding of himself as a preacher of the Word of God is part of an understanding passed on to him through his mother who encouraged and tutored him as a child, instilling in him a sense that he would one day become a preacher:

And that's a very early age, probably like five and six years old, a son is born, and it wasn't the kind of thing she did that distinguished me. You grew up in the church, you know that around Easter time and Christmas they have the kids' program and people they get up and say "For God so loved the world that he gave His only begotten Son" and everybody says, "Oh, they cute," ... but my thing was "For unto us a child is born, for unto

Mother Marina King singing the 23rd Psalm.

us a Son is ... and the government shall be upon His shoulders ... and His name shall be called wonderful." She would say, "Let your voice drop there, son." And she was grooming me for the preaching.

The sense of spiritual destiny shared by Archbishop and Mother Marina King is also fundamentally linked to black womanist theology and a shared understanding of the role of women in communicating and making covenants with God and leading a ministry. Part of this is demonstrated through narratives of the importance of Dr. Phyllis Proudhomme, Supreme Mother, in guiding the spiritual path of Archbishop King. Another part of this is demonstrated in Mother Marina's testimony of the Sound Baptism, which resonates the origin narrative of Hagar, the Egyptian handmaid of Sarah, wife of Abram, and archetypal figure of black womanist theologians, many of whom derive their spiritual authority from the experience of Hagar.

In her book *Sisters in the Wilderness: The Challenge of Womanist God-Talk*, Delores Williams develops the Old Testament story of Hagar as archetypal black womanist theologian. Taken from Genesis 16:1–16 to Genesis 21:9–21, the story of Hagar involves themes of forced motherhood, slavery, homelessness, motherhood, domestic violence, rape, single-parenting, ethnicity, survival, flight, and ultimate redemption. In Williams' work, Hagar becomes an important focal point for black womanist theology because her concerns resonate those of black women—particularly in the midst of slavery—and because she is the first woman in the Bible to liberate herself from slavery and oppression, and to do so with the ultimate blessing of God (Williams 19). Hagar's story reveals "the faith, hope and struggle with which an African slave woman worked through issues of survival, surrogacy, motherhood, rape, homelessness, and economic and sexual oppression" (33). The most critical element of Hagar's narrative is the covenant that God makes with Hagar that she will give rise to a great tribe and a nation. Thus, when God speaks directly to Hagar in the desert He does so without an intermediary and makes His promise directly to Hagar. Without an intermediary between herself and God, Hagar experiences the power of God autonomously, and immediately earns a relationship with God that is separate from that of her former masters.

Similarly, when Mother Marina witnessed the manifestation of the Holy Ghost through John Coltrane, in spite of the fact that Archbishop King also witnessed it, she secured for herself the possibility of an independent relationship with God, and one that continues through visions and miracles wrought by her faith. The true locus of womanist power in Coltrane Consciousness, that which would later enable the leadership of Alice Coltrane and the ordination and leadership of Pastor Wanika Kristi King-Stephens, was formed in that moment in which the Holy Ghost simultaneously appeared to both Mother Marina and Archbishop King.

Another compelling black womanist archetype for Mother Marina King is Jarena Lee, a free black woman and leader in the African Methodist Episcopalian Church. Frances Smith Foster discusses the transformation of the trope of spiritual autobiography by Jarena Lee in *The Life and Religious Experiences of Jarena Lee, A Coloured Lady* (1836). "Jarena Lee writes from the tradition of spiritual autobiography. In the manner of the Puritan and Quaker conversion narratives, hers has three major parts: confession, testimony of conversion, and demonstrations of subsequent commitment to God's work. While the bulk of her narrative concerns her conversion, the work transcends the conventions of spiritual autobiography" (Foster 27). Specifically, Lee's work does not focus on details of her daily life, and she does not reveal the number of children that she bore. "Her interest is clearly in recording 'for the satisfaction of such as may follow after me, when I am no more ... how the Lord called me to his work, and how he has kept me from falling from grace, as I feared I should'" (28).

The testimonies of Mother Marina from the Sound Baptism of 1965 forward similarly transcend the traditional women's spiritual biography. Like Jarena Lee, Mother Marina eschews traditional motherhood tales, victimization, patriarchal femininity, and focuses instead on her own spiritual development and relationship to God and community. Thus, Mother Marina's co-ownership of the origin narrative of Coltrane Consciousness not only locates her as a co-founder with her own mystical path, but also within the broader histories of black womanist theology.

Mother Marina's claim to an independent relationship with God necessarily also means an independent relationship to John Coltrane, an independent sense of predestination, and an independent sense of always knowing that her life would involve a relationship with jazz music:

> I think that I knew that the Lord was with me when I was a child, but to say that I had vocal lessons or that my parents really steered me in this way, it really wasn't like that. I grew up in a family that did love the arts. My father played the trumpet and my mother sang. She won't say that she did, but she did. It was a musical family, aunts and uncles. My father played with Louis Armstrong and so did my uncle. When my father was young he made his pilgrimage to New York and he had an older sister there and he played with the cats and he had a horn that Louis Armstrong gave him but when we moved from Cleveland my mother didn't move it with us so it's gone. He always talked about playing with those guys and he held them in high esteem. My uncle, Fred Robinson, played trumpet also and actually recorded with Louis Armstrong. He's in the *Encyclopedia of Jazz*. My sister, she really sang, she was a jazz singer, she danced, she performed ballet, and she paints. We were encouraged in art in that way. I took dancing lessons, piano, and I think it was almost more of a way of preparing you just in case you do want to go in these directions; it was an introduction to the arts.
>
> But I just always felt a closeness with the Lord. My grandfather being a

minister, and I felt very close with him. My husband was just a great inspiration to me and he really ushered me and actually literally pushed me into singing. I would sing quietly when he wasn't there, I think it was the shyness that I had. I always loved to sing and I remember in elementary school, actually I was in the third grade, and I was gung-ho about singing in the glee club and they said that you had to audition and I said, "Sure, I'm there." There were all of these people sitting there and singing in front of people I just got all choked up and of course I didn't make the glee club. I was crushed.

Mother Marina further comments, establishing her role in the early musical development of Archbishop King and the young church:

As a child I was raised up hearing Billie Holiday. My mother loved her. Once she left Cleveland and caught a bus to New York to hear Billie Holiday sing and her name is Elnora so it's Billie Holiday's name. I listened to that music and I really liked that music. I always had the language of the music but was a little shy in expressing it and when we started to put together this church Bishop was learning to play the music so that's one area that you might say that I taught him in. We learned together.

The culmination of Mother Marina's role in the musical development of the church is the Coltrane Liturgy, perhaps one of the more vital spiritual practices of the church. This practice is inseparable from the voice of Mother Marina. Supported by a chorus of the Sisters of Compassion, it is Mother Marina King's lead vocals that breathe life into the Coltrane Liturgy, that unique marriage of John Coltrane's music with the words of an orthodox Christian liturgy. Her vocal rendition of Psalm 23 ("The Lord is my shepherd; I shall not want") to the theme of "A Love Supreme: Acknowledgement," the first suite of Coltrane's four-part masterpiece written as a devotion to God for the Coltrane's deliverance from heroin addiction, encapsulates both the essential creativity of the Coltrane Church and the depth of its passion with smooth melismas.

Agents for Change and Critics of the African American Religious Establishment

Franzo and Marina King were also self-consciously aware of the historical moment and the spirit of change, revolution, and evolution that characterized America in the 1960s. Evolution is a fundamental discursive practice of Coltrane Consciousness. But it is fundamental precisely because it was central to the self-understanding of Franzo and Marina King who already considered themselves future agents of revolutionary change even before witnessing John Coltrane's 1965 performance.

Prior to the Sound Baptism it is clear that this shared understanding was primarily focused on possibilities for effectuating spiritual change. Arthur Huff Fauset eloquently encapsulates the yearning for change of Franzo King and Mother Marina, children of a post–World War II African American migration to the urban north and west. "The church, once a *sine qua non* of institutional life among American Negroes, does not escape the critical inquiry of the newer generations, who implicitly and sometimes very explicitly are requiring definite pragmatic sanctions if that are to be included among churchgoers, or if indeed they are to give any consideration at all to religious practices and beliefs" (Fauset 7).

In the spirit of understanding themselves as agents of change, Archbishop King reveals his particular disenchantment with organized religion within a broader cultural conversation about religion in the 1960s:

> Coming from a Pentecostal background it was quite obvious to me that when the music began that there was something beyond just an entertainment but that something powerful was taking place. I could feel the anointing in the music. I could feel what I would say was the Holy Ghost just falling. I've since then called it a Sound Baptism and I think it was at that time that I felt the effective transference of the Holy Spirit as it was coming through John and the music and it touched me and my life in a way that I was reminded of my youthful desire to be a servant of God. And I think from that point I began a quest on the journey to seek out how I would fulfill that holy ambition and so it began at that point with the very first hearing and then John Coltrane came to town again the next year and I received another dip, another anointing.
>
> I guess I could say that at the time I was disenchanted with organizational churches. This was in the '60s when there were a lot of questions being raised about the position of the church in the community. I say this because I think I was running from God when I went to see John Coltrane. I wanted to break from all of that religious stuff. I was looking for something new but when I went to see John Coltrane I didn't know that I was going to be baptized by the Holy Ghost himself.
>
> What I experienced with John Coltrane reminded me of what we call some of the high services that we had in church, where the emotional content and the presence of the Holy Spirit was so obvious. It was an opportunity to really escape from this dense kind of existence. You felt like you were in the third heaven or something. It helped me to say this is like church to me. It felt like a revival.
>
> It was really a transcendent kind of experience that you're desiring to take place in the music so that you can reach that point where you get that glimpse of freedom or free thoughts so to speak and you want to enter that realm where the music becomes a vehicle for space travel on a spiritual voyage. And John Coltrane said that he would make music that would

make people happy and uplift them. So the idea is to have your spirit uplifted from listening to the music and being a part of the music.

In light of their shared spiritual disillusionment, the Sound Baptism would mark something of a "revival" of the spirit, a re-purposing of their spiritual energies. This positioning of a Coltrane performance as a "revival" affirms the mandate for forming a church or a context for spiritual experiences as much as the perception of the Holy Ghost. What Archbishop King and Mother Marina are referring to is the need for a revival of the entire black religious establishment. The language of a "revival" specifically underscores their disenchantment with organized religion and yearning for something new.

Archbishop King's critique of the black Pentecostal establishment was matched only by Mother Marina's critique of the black Episcopalian Church. Mother Marina speaks to their self-understanding as agents for change engaged in revolutionary spiritual practice against the black religious establishment and how she envisioned John Coltrane's music as a means of rebuilding African American spirituality by returning to a greater engagement with the Holy Ghost:

> I think we pretty much felt that we were letting the Holy Spirit shape and form the service per se. Archbishop King knew that we were in an embryonic stage so we expected to be changing. Change was a great thing that we learned. We didn't want to be the same; we didn't want to be stagnant. There was an element of not wanting to be like other churches. It was definitely there. We had gone through some rebuilding, from being teenagers to not going to church every Sunday as we had once had to do, and seeing things that we felt needed to make better. We'd say, this needs to be better, or that. For example, we said, we're not going to look down on you if you don't have a new suit to come to church in. Anybody can come into the house of the Lord.
>
> I think my rebellion against my background in the Episcopalian church was mostly social. That's one reason that I feel that the Lord put me aside for this work, because I remember being a child and we always had a piano in our house and there were some teenage girls that would come over and they played and they started singing church music and I can remember my heart leaping; I loved the music. I was used to singing the hymns but I loved that music and I never thought ... a lot of times they [people in the Episcopalian church] feel that they're better than others but I never had that feeling. In the Sunday school we were taught not to feel emotion and all of that stuff. I didn't have any problem with showing emotion. I loved going to church; I loved my Sunday school teacher, the services and clergy.... I loved going to church.
>
> The church is still very much in that mode of growth and change. When

you ask about the future, it's interesting because that is a point that we're meditating on and it is really time for us to make a pivotal change now. There are some very serious decisions that have to be made about this church and the way that we are going to go, as far as Archbishop and myself getting older and considering what we have to work with. How are we going to expand it? How are we going to continue to hold it up? We're dealing almost with basic survival right now.

Their shared mandate for reform also carried with it a distinctly secular, cultural dimension and Archbishop King and Mother Marina's oral testimonies frequently conflate church and specifically jazz experiences. This intersection of jazz/cultural and spiritual/religious critiques marks an early moment of the sophisticated multi-dimensionality of the Coltrane Church experience, and how Franzo and Marina King understood the many necessary fronts of the revolution.

Archbishop King speaks of their prior experiences as listeners and jazz aficionados and how these experiences impacted their understanding of Coltrane as a vehicle for cultural as well as spiritual/religious "revival":

> These two times that I saw John Coltrane were not the first times that I heard him. The first hearing of it, my ear was arrested and I was really pulled into and very much interested in what kind of music it was. My brother had come home, my older brother Landres, and he brought a John Coltrane record into the house. It was *My Favorite Things* and at that time the soprano saxophone was not as popular as it is now. It was a strange instrument for me and I remember asking what kind of music is that? What kind of instrument is that? Who's playing? And he said it was jazz, soprano saxophone, and it was John Coltrane. And I remember even finding the name of John Coltrane interesting so that that it didn't even seem like a name to me. Coltrane, is that like a nickname or something? That's what they call him? And that name was arresting, just Coltrane and the music. I can only compare it to other jazz music or so-called jazz music. It was like the first time I heard Billie Holiday. I wanted to know, Who is that? What kind of music is that? When I heard the name I wanted to know if it was a man or a woman.

The Unsuspecting Converts

This shared awareness of leadership and destiny on cultural and spiritual/religious fronts is central to the foundational narrative of the Sound Baptism in which Franzo and Marina are unexpectedly confronted with the spiritual and cultural revelation of John Coltrane in a secular jazz club. This narrative bears great resemblance to the trope of the unsuspecting convert (e.g., Saul/Paul on the road to Damascus) found in so many religious origin narratives. Their narrative also bears resemblance to the classic religious trope of enlightenment (e.g., Siddhartha Gautama under the bodhi tree) in which they realize the presence of the Christian Holy Ghost in the African American musical idiom of jazz through the person of John Coltrane.

Franzo and Marina King claim that they merely intended to celebrate their anniversary in a secular jazz club. They both entered the Jazz Workshop that night as unsuspecting converts. Mother Marina's comments allude to their youth and desire to "party all night" and their lack of preparedness for the message they would receive from John Coltrane that evening:

> It was our anniversary, we were both young and gonna party all night and didn't leave and we didn't talk, you know we were just spellbound, caught up.

Archbishop King also speaks of being "set up by God," who managed to reach him in a secular jazz club, the last place he thought he would have to deal with God. Indeed this reference to God's ability to traverse sacred and secular domains is a common trope of Archbishop King's sermons and reflects many of the sermons he heard growing up as a child in the Pentecostal Church of God in Christ in Los Angeles under the tutelage of his mother. This particular theme reflects not only his belief that God is everywhere, but that God may be found in the least obvious of places and that God may use extra-spiritual and potentially contrary motivations to guide "His people to His Word." The "set-up" therefore describes the manner in which God led the young, loving couple Franzo and Marina King to His Word through an anniversary at a secular jazz club where, despite their intentions, Franzo and Marina King would be led to a life of the Spirit. Archbishop King:

> It felt like a set-up man because we really didn't go there to get saved or anything. We were going to paint the town that night, celebrate her birthday. And then here comes the spiritual father John and he baptized us in that sound and there wasn't any talking.

The trope of the unsuspecting convert is affirmatively linked with the trope of enlightenment as Mother Marina expresses her reaction to the astonishing vision that she and Archbishop King shared when John Coltrane came onto the bandstand and appeared to walk beside the presence of the Holy Ghost:

> When we saw him come out the Holy Ghost came out when he walked out. It didn't just start when he played, he had the power with him when

he walked out onto the stage. He had the peace that the demons are afraid of and tremble at. That's the kind of presence he had.

Archbishop King substantiates their shared vision as unsuspecting converts of the Holy Ghost:

> He came out from the back, and from the moment.... I mean, you could just see an anointing on him. He didn't have to make a sound, it was just the way he looked at you. I knew the Holy Ghost was there, growing up in that culture as I had, I knew what was happening. I said, O God, this is a set-up!

The Visionary Trope

The love between Franzo and Marina King has always been strengthened by their mutual love and admiration for the music and person of John Coltrane. Both Franzo and Marina King shared testimonies with me of ongoing visions and visitations from John Coltrane and the ways in which Coltrane affected and continues to affect their lives. This visionary trope is critical to the formation of their religious community. Church members must fundamentally accept the 1965 vision of Coltrane and the Holy Ghost, the ongoing visionary status of Archbishop King and Mother Marina, and the possibility that they too can function as mystics and visionaries through the power of Coltrane's music.

The ongoing visions of John Coltrane experienced by Archbishop King and Mother Marina since the 1965 Sound Baptism not only provide evidence of their unique bond based on discrete shared principles and values, but also their separate and deeply personal claims to the ministry of Coltrane Consciousness. There are remarkable similarities in each of their independently experienced visions, although fundamental differences are structured in accordance with the very different roles that each play within the church. Mother Marina's visions clearly reflect her connection to Coltrane's music as a singer, mystic and spiritual leader. Conversely, Archbishop King's visions reflect his role as a preacher/teacher and his specific understanding of John Coltrane within the context of a history of spiritual teachers in his life since his mother.

Mother Marina's visions of John Coltrane are always associated with the presence of the Holy Ghost and a profound sense of peace and joy. Mother Marina's testimony suggests that the Holy Ghost was central to both her personal visions of John Coltrane and her vision of a possible reformation of the African American church:

The one thing that I want to talk about is the inspiration that John Coltrane has been to me through is music, and the profound effect that he has had on me. I guess, just to talk about my personal relationship to the music and wisdom of John Coltrane. That is the thing that holds this whole thing together.

I've had visions of John Coltrane and he has literally saved my life. I was going through a period of doubt and I was very disappointed because I didn't think the Lord was answering my prayers. I said aloud that I was tired of this and I just wished the life outside of my body. I felt the energy from my head just draining out and when it got around to my knees, I said, Lord, and no sooner did I say then the spirit of life just reversed and the energy just started going back up. I was in a tent and it was a tabernacle and the Holy Spirit just filled me with energy. I am using this terminology now but at the time I couldn't have expressed it like that. It just started coming around in a circle and that's when I was saying I didn't think I could tell anybody, they would think I was crazy. That's when the Holy Spirit first really filled me like that. John Coltrane was playing and it was just such a peace and a humbling experience that came over me. It was the love of Jesus.

I must have been about 24 years old. This was after I had seen John Coltrane perform. We were living on Galvez, where we had the tabernacle set up, and this was where we first started the first jazz club, the Yardbird Temple. From there we went to Visitacion Valley on Sawyer Street where we first formed a church and set the downstairs aside where we would pray "A Love Supreme." And we would just be slain in the Spirit; we could never get through it. The Lord was just using us. It was just a really high time. I felt like we were a special cadre. We were on Coltrane's meditation schedule and daily worship. We prayed "A Love Supreme" twice a day and it wasn't even to the tune then, to Psalm.

One time in particular Archbishop King and I were having different opinions about something and it was "Naima" that was playing and we were sitting in the car talking and I felt my heart just start moving and turning and melting and we just knew the Spirit was moving. It is amazing.

We have leaned on the music in so many ways, from the birthing room and pregnancies and we'd put on Coltrane for particular tunes, for nurturing a baby. Sometimes we wouldn't know how we were going to make ends meet and we would just say, John's going to get us out of this. Miracles would always happen.

I experienced a dream in which John Coltrane came to me and his hair was flowing and he was just so alive. One time three of us sisters were walking down Geary Boulevard and the sky just opened up and John Coltrane's face appeared. You could see his face, it was always an encouragement. He was always ever-present. And we were in a high level of spiritual awareness, always meditating, praying.

Archbishop King's relationship with John Coltrane can be seen as an outgrowth of his relationship with his mother, and his subsequent relationship with the Holy Ghost and with Christ that were planted in him by his mother. Indeed Supreme Mother planted the seeds that gave birth to Coltrane Consciousness, and made it possible for him to be able to recognize John Coltrane as a messenger of God and a manifestation of Holy Ghost power. But just as Supreme Mother, the Holy Ghost, and Christ led Archbishop King to a full understanding of the power of John Coltrane, his faith in Coltrane led him to greater and greater levels of devotion to Supreme Mother, the Holy Ghost, and Christ. Archbishop King's devotion to Coltrane is one and the same as his devotion to Supreme Mother, the Holy Ghost and Christ, for while those are the foundations of his devotion to Coltrane, it was John Coltrane who ultimately enabled him to grow as a Christian. Archbishop King:

> Well, I've had three, at least three dreams about John Coltrane that I can recall vividly. I remember when I was studying Hazrat and the Egyptian Book of the Dead and all these other things and I can't remember who it was but somebody told me the book is a dead teacher, and you need a living teacher. I used to frustrate people with my Coltrane Consciousness. I was on a soapbox about it all the time, and this is before the church. I'm always preaching that Coltrane was the anointed savior, just short of calling him Jesus Christ. Jesus means savior. Christ means anointed. So I would call him the anointed savior when I was saying Jesus Christ.
>
> I would get on a lot of people's nerves and then I was trying to read something in these books and somebody said, "Man, Coltrane's dead, these books you're reading are dead, you need to get a living teacher." And at that time I couldn't understand what they were talking about. I thought they meant a guru or something. And it kinda disturbed me because I'm looking to find everything that John Coltrane said. Did they write it down? I want to read it, I want to know what John is saying and I'm learning from him in such a way that to be challenged with that was devastating because I did see people that had living teachers and the other and not just music teachers because I had living music teachers but I needed a spiritual teacher.
>
> And John Coltrane came to me in a dream and he was a giant in the sky. But the thing that stood out was that he had this great big afro like they were wearing in the '70s and for me John lives and he's got a new hairdo. You dig what I'm saying? John is alive. That's all I needed was that vision.
>
> And then I had another visit where John Coltrane was on the bandstand and it was like he was at the piano instead of playing his horn and he wasn't playing and it was like when I came up to him he put his hand out like that and I was able to kiss his hand in the dream.
>
> And when I woke up like that I was, Oh, praise God! I'm on the right track!
>
> And so I've had that kind of fellowship with John visiting me like, and those things, I don't play them down, they were very important in terms of me being encouraged to continue with this work. And all of these things

happened before we moved into here. My four a.m. meditation hour. To me this is a visit. If I'm asleep and I go to sleep with the radio on and I wake up because John Coltrane just came on and he's playing and it's four am and it's time for me to meditate, then John came and got me for meditation. You know what I mean? Now you can argue with that if you want to but he shook me with the music. He walked in and I woke up. He came on and I just woke up.

Archbishop King's visions of John Coltrane are a confirmation of his faith in John Coltrane as he who would truly deliver him unto Christ. These visions also confirm his responsibility to take the music higher as had been urged by John Coltrane, and to respect Coltrane's stated wish to become a saint. In an often quoted passage, Coltrane once remarked, "I have a basic desire to go to the basic elements of music and come out with value to go right into the heart, strip myself of the old, and be truly creative. I would like to be a saint" (Analahati 61). Understand that unlike many contemporary jazz critics, the Coltrane Church interprets Coltrane's desire for sainthood quite literally. Archbishop King remarks:

> The intent and the attitude of the music is what John Coltrane left us to work on. The intention of our playing. Of playing all praise to God. John Coltrane said, "In my estimation the music is rising, and therefore it will need somewhere else to be played." And out of that we're going to hear the angels of God breathing fire, the Holy Ghost, that's where it's coming, from right out there.

Conclusions

The love story of spiritual, cultural, and political outsiders Franzo and Marina King provides a foundation for the core discursive practices of Coltrane Consciousness. The narrative tropes of an impossible love, a predestination for the ministry, gender equality and black womanist theology, a central ethic of change and evolution, and a profound belief in the mysticism of sound are all elements of the sophisticated counter-hegemonic discourse of Coltrane Consciousness. The ethic of evolution and the principle of impossible, indeed unconditional love, play out across a 50-year span as the most critical of these discursive practices. As the story of the Coltrane Church unfolds across cultural, religious and political domains, the narrative tropes of the love story of Franzo and Marina King continue to echo through the ongoing evolution of ideas and practices in Coltrane Consciousness.

Evidence of the situated perspective of Franzo and Marina King does not diminish the metaphysical possibilities of the Sound Baptism of 1965. Rather, it emphasizes the role that faith and religion played in answering fundamental existential questions shared by Franzo and Marina King on that night. Such an analysis also begs the question of John Coltrane's subjective awareness of himself as an artist and as a man and the set of expectations that he may have brought to that 1965 performance at the Jazz Workshop.

2

The Self-Representation
and Spiritual Teachings of
John Coltrane the Saint

*I have a basic desire to go to the basic elements of music
and come out with value to go right into the heart, strip
myself of the old, and be truly creative. I would like to be
a saint.*

—St. John Will-I-Am Coltrane

The meaning of that performance on September 18, 1965, at the Jazz
Workshop as something more than a mere jazz event could not have happened before John Coltrane himself began to represent the spiritual possibilities of his music in his landmark *A Love Supreme* album released in
February 1965 nor before the new free jazz movement of the 1960s began
to represent itself as a nationalist expression of a return to African roots and
spirituality and John Coltrane as its high priest. The Sound Baptism was a
manifestation of mutual representations of the spirituality of John Coltrane
on the part of Franzo and Marina King and John Coltrane and was therefore a community event predicated upon a history of communication and
representation between artists and audiences in the African American community.

The enduring belief in the spirituality of jazz music pioneer John
William Coltrane and the investment in him as a cultural phenomenon
and a focal point for a counter hegemonic ideology against the backdrop
of urban black politics, religion, and culture illuminates a complex historical relationship of African American people to their aesthetics and the
use of music in particular as a vehicle for building meaningful communi-

ties and politics of cultural representation. Ingrid Monson is correct in emphasizing, "In music, it is particularly important to talk about the relationship of African American aesthetics to the 'dominant cultural body,' because music is the arena in which the taken-for-granted hegemonic presumptions about race have been turned upside down by the leadership of African American music and musicians in defining and influencing the shape of American popular music" (Monson 103).

If jazz *is* community and John Coltrane *is* its high priest, it is because Coltrane devotees and John Coltrane himself have consistently represented jazz music and John Coltrane as such. The notion of jazz as community and Coltrane as cultural phenomenon or ideological focal point or the divine saint of the Gospel of Jazz, are meanings that cannot be taken for granted. These representations have to be interrogated and evaluated in terms of broader cultural and political projects and agendas. In what ways does Coltrane Consciousness advance critically important dialogues and religious, cultural, and political agendas in the city of San Francisco? How is Coltrane Consciousness even possible given the constraints imposed by dominant society and big capital?

The central challenge of any ethnography or critical history of the Coltrane Church lies with the explanation of how any jazz performance could yield a 50-year cultural, religious, and political odyssey. Monson's *Saying Something* (1996), Paul Berliner's *Thinking in Jazz* (1994), Mark Anthony Neal's *What the Music Said: Black Popular Music and Black Public Culture* (1999), and Ajay Heble's *Landing on the Wrong Note* (2000) have all contributed nuanced and multi-layered understandings of how meaning is communicated in jazz performance. Each theorist deliberately negotiates the minefield of linguocentrism and literal readings of music as language. Each ultimately produces cultural theories of metaphoric and metonymic associations respectively between and within the domains of linguistic conversation and musical improvisation in the manner of Terence Turner (1991), James Fernandez (1986), Steven Feld (1984) and Charles Seeger (1977).

Monson specifically explores metaphors and figurative tropes in her analysis of music as conversation, perhaps the most critical cornerstone for advancing the notion of jazz music as community. Monson writes, "Metaphors point to similarities between contrasting cultural domains or activities, while metonyms suggest part-to-whole (contiguous) relationships within cultural domains. Ironic tropes, on the other hand, assert incongruity, especially between apparent meaning and deeper ironic reversal of that meaning. While cultural theorists have devoted their attention

Archbishop King preaching at the 1286 Fillmore Street location.

mainly to the metaphor, recent work on the theory of tropes has emphasized the relationships among these figurative ways of speaking in cultural
practice" (Monson 76). Further, "To return to the metaphor we're examining, if improvisation is like conversation (subsets of music and language),
then sociable, face-to-face communication (subset of communication)
may be the larger category at stake" (76).

Monson's ethnographic study of jazz drummers introduces the concept of *intermusicality* to deal with jazz performance as discursive practice
in a fashion similar to Berliner's use of the metaphor of conversation in his

exhaustive study of the acquisition of improvisational techniques. Monson identifies three levels along which an improvising musician may interact and say something of value to an audience member: (1) the creation of music through the improvisational interaction of sounds; (2) the interactive shaping of social networks and communities that accompany musical participation; and (3) the development of culturally variable meanings and ideologies that inform the interpretation of jazz in American society" (76).

Monson doesn't take us to that spiritual place of the music that Franzo and Marina King experienced in 1965. However, the second segment of Monson's three-part formulation for intermusicality involving the "shaping of social networks and communities" through music does help us to understand the sense of community that predicated their awakening and which would follow it for 50 years after that extraordinary evening (76.).

Archbishop King references these processes through which music may shape social networks and communities as he comments on his introduction to jazz music through his older brother's record album collection:

> My brother told me, "Music's a pacesetter, the music you listen to is the kind of person you are." And when I was in high school, jazz was called "progressive jazz." So we were listening to progressive jazz and that meant that we were progressively ahead of our peers intellectually just because we were listening to this high intellectual music with this high intellectual content.

He further differentiates church members and others influenced by Coltrane Consciousness from a broader and more mainstream "jazz listening community" in terms of the willingness of Coltrane Consciousness devotees to expect more from the music than others in mainstream American culture:

> I don't think that many of the critics and much of the public in fact have tested the music. They haven't really tried it in that I don't think that within the jazz listening community there's that much expectation from the music. I don't think that they expect as much from music period as say I do and others that I know. I just expect so much from music. I mean music is as Hazrat [Hazrat Inayat Khan] says, music is the source from which the world was created.

Archbishop King's understanding, via Hazrat Inayat Khan, that "music is the source from which the world was created" is a radical extension of "expectations" arising from the communal interaction between African American musicians and audiences. Archbishop King interprets John Coltrane's stated desire to pursue spiritual enlightenment through music as Coltrane's understanding of the relationship between God and

Sound. Archbishop King reads Coltrane's musical and extra-musical cues (liner notes, interviews, composition and album titles, etc.) as evidence of a transcendent ideology that facilitates greater "expectations" from the music, including communication across boundaries of race, class, gender, sexual identity and religious orthodoxy and denominationalism. Coltrane Consciousness pushes the communicative possibilities between performer and audience to its furthest margins, giving music a transcendent power over all other forms of human interaction. All of this is possible because of "expectations" created by the communal interaction between artists and audiences, and the specific *conversation* that Franzo and Marina King believed they were having with John Coltrane September 18, 1965.

If improvisatory *conversation* can, on a larger level, be a subset of community interaction, what happened at the Jazz Workshop in 1965 was part of a broader series of conversations between audiences and performers within African American communities. For Monson and indeed also for Berliner, community is fundamental in jazz performance. Monson writes, "Paul Berliner's monumental *Thinking in Jazz* (1994) has demonstrated beyond any doubt the centrality of the musical perspectives of professional jazz musicians in rethinking our understanding of improvisation. Berliner describes how jazz musicians acquire and develop improvisational expertise through interaction with an ever-changing community of musicians functioning as a learning environment, a musical process that defies explanation by traditional musical analyses of self-contained works" (73). Thus, for both Monson and Berliner, community is fundamental to jazz pedagogy and the continued growth of the music and its forms. Indeed community provides the very opportunities for discursive practices upon which the music is based.

To a large extent the tacit relationship formed between John Coltrane and the founding members of the African Orthodox Church that evening in 1965 can also be explained by the relationship between black popular culture and black popular music in the mid-twentieth century. Archbishop King and Mother Marina were part of a culture and a community that had expectations regarding the communicative abilities of black musicians and black musicians. This foundational moment in 1965 was a communicative, discursive moment between an artist and members of his community set against the countercultural confluence of the new black music of free jazz, Black Power politics, and notions of spiritual universalism.

Coltrane Consciousness is clearly a 1960s phenomenon and a product of populist revolutions against racism and imperialism. To understand the origins of Coltrane Consciousness in that moment in 1965 is to understand the black nationalist following of the free jazz movement and the likes of the Sun Ra Arkestra or the AACM (Association for the Advancement of Creative Musicians) or Horace Tapscott's UGMAA (Union of God's Musicians and Artists Ascension) or *Bitches Brew*-era[1] Miles Davis or, more popularly, the following generated by Jimi Hendrix, Carlos Santana or the phenomenon of Woodstock. The St. John Will-I-Am Coltrane African Orthodox Church "happened" amid the relationship between American popular music and social and political struggles for freedom and self-determination and John Coltrane was a central figure in this precious moment for jazz and non-jazz listeners.

Every Sunday service at the Coltrane Church, where worship services are introduced with almost two hours of music preceding the reading of spiritual texts or preaching, constitutes the kind of community that Monson and Berliner speak of as fundamental to jazz conversation. Archbishop King attests to this in his narrative of a performance in Paris where a listener experiences the visitation of the Virgin Mary in the same fashion that he and Mother Marina King experienced their visitation of the Holy Ghost in 1965.

> When we played in France there was a man that stopped Mother Marina, he was in a wheelchair and he was ecstatic with tears and joy. He said that he had seen the Virgin Mother over the bandstand the whole time that we were playing. So that was some powerful stuff. So, people in this community, a lot of them have those kinds of experiences that they can share. And that might be a part of what needs to be recorded. We have a gentleman that comes here from time to time, big tall fellow that credited John Coltrane with saving his life. He had some horrible fall or something. And there's another man that said that John Coltrane saved him in a foxhole. So I think that would be a good project for somebody, to record the miracles of this saint. And outside of this community too, because they're all over the place where people are giving that kind of testimony.

Coltrane's public presentation of himself as an artist motivated by a spiritual quest helped to create this unique, visionary moment of communication and set of expectations between performer and audience. This understanding of Coltrane the mystic was reinforced for Franzo and Marina King in 1966 when they attended a second Coltrane performance at the Jazz Workshop.[2] Their attendance at the 1966 performance was abbreviated but nonetheless equally powerful. It is not to be conflated with the initial Sound Baptism of 1965, nor is it as important in the establishment of Coltrane Consciousness, but it nonetheless reinforced Coltrane's self-representation as a mystic, ever evolving his music and spiritual power. Archbishop King:

Archbishop King trades lines with Deacon Max Hoff, foreground, at the February 8, 2008, show at Cité de la Musique in Paris.

The second time I didn't get in. Me and Mother Marina were there after being given really inside, up-front action for the first time, the guy that was on the door wasn't there and Mother Marina didn't have her identification, which she was of age, the year before she wasn't. And we got in anyway. And I remember trying to get her in and we couldn't so I asked her to wait for me outside and I stepped inside and I just stood there for maybe about ten minutes or so at the most, and that's when Coltrane was bent all the way over like this here and he had Pharaoh [Sanders] with him and it was like hand drummers and it was a whole new ensemble of people, and he must have had Rasheid [Ali] with him then.

I wasn't current as to the fact that the band had disbanded and that there was a new group with Coltrane or that Alice was in the band and when I think back on that night I just remember looking at the bandstand and just feeling a whole lot of energy. I mean it was like a powerhouse, you know, that had gotten the metal tore off of it and you could see everything running or something man and it was ... it just was a lot of energy.

John was bent all the way over, and had the horn down between his legs like, and I don't know who else was there, like the first time Elvin Jones stood out, Jimmy Garrison.... I didn't know his name but the bass player.... I didn't know if it was one bass or two basses, how many drummers or nothing. What he was doing from that year before to then just blew my mind.

Franzo and Marina King now witnessed Coltrane in a wholly different musical manifestation than his performance in 1965 with the classic Coltrane quartet (McCoy Tyner on piano, Elvin Jones on drums, Jimmy Garrison on bass). Here Coltrane expanded his ensemble and initiated his forays beyond modal improvisation into the world of free jazz. What seems to have most impressed Franzo and Marina King in this second encounter was John Coltrane's energy and hence the power unleashed by his most recent transformation. It is in this sense that John Coltrane appeared to Franzo and Marina King in 1966 to have taken the spirituality and spiritual expectations of his music even higher as he ventured into the realm of free jazz improvisation.

Teaching through Sound

Although numerous quotations, audio recordings, and an elegant letter to *Down Beat* magazine[3] are available, Coltrane did not produce an oral or written document of spiritual teachings or philosophy. There are few written words that accompany any of his compositions, with the exception of "A Love Supreme," "Kulu Se Mama," and "Om." Indeed, even Coltrane himself once admitted "I would like to put out an album ... with absolutely no notes. Just the titles of the songs and the personnel. By this point I don't know what else can be said in words about what I'm doing. Let the music speak for itself," thus emphasizing sound in opposition to the written word as a mode of expression and teaching (Analahati 11).

In the Eastern metaphysics studied by Coltrane[4] and his devotees, music is considered a precursor to language. The Sufi mystic Hazrat Inayat Khan refers to language as an inferior music. Traditional Western-European paradigms reverse that hierarchy and tend to regard music as a language of a distinctly "lower" intellectual order than speech and the written word. Donald Jay Grout, in his *A History of Western Music*, significantly discusses how the Greeks originally conceived of music as inseparable from the spoken word (Grout 7). Further, the Greek origin of music was with both Dionysius and Apollo (3). The notion of music as ancillary to language perhaps has its origins with Aristotle's notion of the doctrine of imitation wherein music affected passions and states of the soul, causing the listener to imitate certain passions (8). Grout discusses how Aristotle's doctrine of imitation ultimately led to the Apollonian/Dionysian dichotomy of two different types of musics: "In the distinctions made among the many different kinds of music we can discern a general division into two classes: music whose effect was toward calmness and uplift, and music which tended to produce excitement and enthusiasm. The first class was associated with the worship of Apollo; its instrument was the lyre [stringed instrument] and its related poetic forms the ode and the epic. The second class was associated with the worship of Dionysius; its instrument was the *aulos* [wind/reed instrument] and its related poetic forms the dithyramb and the drama" (8).

The western European devaluation of Coltrane's sound as an instrument of concrete teaching is therefore originally accomplished through the valuation of the uplifting music of strings against the more emotional music of wind and reed instruments. From the Greek division of Apollonian and Dionysian music, Coltrane's music can also be viewed as well beyond the pale of pedagogy in its more emotional content. Undoubtedly remnants of this division lingered well into the jazz era. As Lawrence Levine notes, "Jazz became associated with what Esman has called the 'vital libidinal impulses ... precisely the id drives that the superego of the bourgeois culture sought to repress.' By threatening to expose and return what was repressed, jazz quickly won the enmity of the respectable arbiters of the society's culture and of segments of the Negro middle and professional classes who desired to become part of the mainstream America and found jazz an anachronistic embarrassment. Jazz was denounced as bar-

baric, sensuous, jungle music which assaulted the senses and the sensibilities, diluted reason, led to the abandonment of decency and decorum, undermined dignity, and destroyed order and self-control" (Levine 293–294).

Levine's assessment of the initial European-American reception to jazz music suggests that the pedagogical impact of Coltrane's sound might be undermined by the heritage of the Greek Apollonian/Dionysian division. Within the parameters of Western art criticism; Coltrane's art can never be anything more than purely Dionysian, emotional, body-centered and beyond the pale of rational inquiries. Indeed this Dionysian-bias has long haunted jazz and perhaps all African-derived music forms in the west.

In order to uncover and appreciate Coltrane's concrete teachings through sound, we have to deconstruct some of the more obstinate and oppressive paradigms of Western thinking: the Apollonian/Dionysian musical dichotomy, the Cartesian duality of mind and body, and the primacy of language in "legitimate" spiritual experience. By emphasizing sound over language, members of the Coltrane Church actually explode the parameters of the traditional Western European mind/body, Apollonian/Dionysian understandings that value and legitimate language, so-called "high art," and published written material as rational, concrete and intellectual over and against sound. Within the parameters of a John Coltrane religion, Coltrane's chosen method of teaching was through sound, and specifically the sound of jazz, and for the Apostles of Sound, Coltrane's music went beyond producing abstract feelings and waves of emotions. The Coltrane Church explicitly foregrounds practical, concrete ideas and practices communicated through sound that must be paired with the abstract emotionalism of sound. Coltrane's music is therefore a complete teaching of body, mind, and soul. As such, Coltrane's teachings unite traditional Western dualities of mind/body, Apollonian/Dionysian, etc., and further complement these with the dimension of soul.

What are the sound teachings of Saint John Coltrane and how are these to be comprehended? I will argue that through sound Coltrane teaches selflessness and oneness with God, love, grace, the purpose and practice of meditation, the imperative for spiritual renewal, an appreciation of man within the context of a vast universe, and the spiritual value of African and Eastern aesthetics and philosophies. Coltrane's suggested mode for comprehending these teachings through sound is simple: repeated listening and meditation.

In response to a question regarding how he hoped his music to be understood, Coltrane once remarked,

I think that it's a thing that they, the person that doesn't understand will understand in time or upon repeated listening, or it is something he will never understand and you know that's the way it is. There are many things in life that we don't understand and we go on anyway [Analahati 10].

Here Coltrane not only suggests a method for understanding the teachings of his music but also accepts that there will be those who will not understand and perhaps will not want to understand. Indeed Coltrane seems to implicitly recognize the difficulty of interpreting concrete teachings through his music, and the documents of his many interviews reveal his awareness of the critical misperceptions of his music as "angry," "tortured," and "overpowering" (11). But John Coltrane steadfastly emphasized a great faith in the power of sound, and continued despite popular misconceptions to pursue a path that he felt truly ordained of God to pursue. Coltrane further remarked:

Some people say "your music sounds angry" or "tortured," or "spiritual," or "overpowering" or something; you get all kinds of things you know. Some say they feel elated, and so you never know where it's going to go. All a musician can do is get closer to the sources of nature, and so feel that he is in communion with the natural laws. Then he can feel that he is interpreting them to the best of his ability, and can try to convey that to others [11].

The difficulty in apprehending the concrete teachings of St. John through music rests with his lack of clarification on the nature of "repeated listening." What does it mean to listen? Do we have to be musicians to truly appreciate these teachings? Are there any textual or visual aids that Coltrane provides that can assist the process of listening? What is the role of the Coltrane Church in assisting in this process of repeated listening?

Coltrane's process of repeated listening urges the devotee to deduce metaphorical images from the initial sensory perception of music, and from this metaphorical understanding to meditate toward the realization of more concrete ideas. Repeated listening is a meditation, it is a process of directed concentration on the music that requires us to do much more than treat the music as the background of existence but to put music to the forefront of our lives precisely because it can serve as a powerful pedagogical vehicle. Through repeated listening we can indeed do much more than allow the music to obliquely and abstractly influence us. In this sense, repeated listening can be compared with the process of understanding that Jesus Christ the teacher, Siddhartha Gautama, and other great spiritual teachers have urged through parables and seemingly elliptical questions and fragments given as responses to be meditated upon by the student and devotee.

Paul Berliner has also emphasized the importance of parables and metaphors in the pedagogy of jazz improvisation. Similar puzzle structures and images are frequently provided to students of jazz to assist their development. Berliner argues that the jazz musician constantly inhabits a world between sound and more concrete ideas, and he gives the jazz musician an important role as a storyteller (Berliner 201). Berliner quotes Paul Wertico remarking, "The real great cats can write novels" (202). Here, Berliner underscores this movement between Dionysian and Apollonian art forms through which concrete ideas may be rendered comprehensible through sound. Further, Berliner's work serves to highlight the fact that music is a language, and as such it is a vehicle for communication and the transmission of ideas.

The titles that John Coltrane gave his compositions also help to point the listener to a particular direction, providing an initial path for the listener through meditation and repeated listening. There are a number of significant points of entry with which to contextualize metaphorical images produced from repeated listenings of Coltrane's music. The foregoing analyses of the core spiritual teachings of Coltrane's music highlight the usefulness of everything from Sunday sermons to album liner notes. Certainly composition and album titles can also be useful in planting the initial metaphorical reference for understanding Coltrane's spiritual teachings.

In 1966 LeRoi Jones (Amiri Baraka) identified the spirituality of Coltrane's music through Coltrane's composition titles. Jones wrote, "The titles of Trane's tunes, 'A Love Supreme,' 'Meditations,' 'Ascension,' imply a strong religious will, conscious of the religious evolution the pure mind seeks. The music is a way into God. The absolute open expression of everything" (Jones *Blues People*, 193). Archbishop King frequently uses composition titles as an initial reference point for meditation and repeated listening. "If you just examine some of the compositions and some of the titles of the compositions that Coltrane either wrote or selected to play on they were compositions that would invoke just by the titles." Indeed he suggests that the composition titles represent a move to influence that "initial thought pattern" which might lead the listener down further paths of meditation and prayer.

Most importantly, the composition titles that Coltrane used are clearly a sign of his belief in the power of music and, in particular, the power of music to present certain concrete teachings and ideas. The fact that he uses titles such as "Meditation," "Transition," "The Father, the Son, and the Holy Ghost," "Ascension," "Love," "Selflessness," etc., is suggestive of his belief that these compositions in some way embody and present to the listener his own teachings and understandings of these concepts and ideas.

In order to further appreciate what repeated listening—as meditation or a process of deductive reasoning from metaphor—can yield in terms of concrete teachings, it is necessary to simply begin dealing concretely with each of Coltrane's spiritual teachings according to the Coltrane Church.

The Spiritual Teachings of St. John Will-I-Am Coltrane

Among the most important of Coltrane's teachings emphasized by the Coltrane Church is the notion of selfless devotion to God. The Eastern-influenced notion of the obliteration of ego is taught as absolutely a prerequisite for spiritual development. This lesson is transmitted emphatically through the musical form of Coltrane's composition for free group improvisation "Ascension." Metaphorical understandings can proceed from listening, and a more thorough understanding of the context of Coltrane's

Mother Marina and Archbishop King conducting a service at 1286 Fillmore Street.

spirituality, for example through a reading of his testimony in *A Love Supreme,* assists the listener in arriving at even deeper meanings.

In a brilliant and comprehensive analysis of the musical form of "Ascension," Ekkhard Jost argues that what the seven soloists play is less important than the whole of the composition. In terms of the structure of the composition and improvisation, Jost points out that "a large number of rhythmically independent lines are set against one another by the seven wind instruments, with the resultant overlappings. This superimposition produces rapidly moving sound-fields whose rhythmic differentiation is provided as a rule by the rhythmic section, rather than coming from within. When seven independent melodic-rhythmic lines coincide, the relationships between them lose clarity, fusing into a field of sound enlivened by irregular accentuation" (Jost 89).

Jost's observation of the overlapping of seven wind instruments fusing into a sound field can be gleaned from reading the liner notes to "Ascension" as well. David Wild's liner notes, including quotations from the participants of the "Ascension" session, includes descriptions of the "powerful joining of voices." Archie Shepp emphasizes the union of many voices into a whole in terms of the union of gender dualities: "It achieves a certain kind of unity; it starts at a high level of intensity with the horns playing high and the other pieces playing low. This gets a quality of like male and female voices. It builds in intensity through all the solo passages, brass and reeds, until it gets to the final section where the rhythm section takes over and brings it back down to the level it started at. The idea is similar to the action painters do in that it creates various surfaces of color which push into each other, creates tensions and counter-tensions, and various fields of energy" (*Impulse!* GRD-2–113, 1992).

Shepp's process of rendering his experience with the music to metaphorical understandings of "surfaces of color" and gender is the first step in concentrated listening. The more concrete assessments regarding the unity of voices into a sound field of energy proceed from the metaphorical renderings. Jost's assessment of the manner in which the compositional structure of "Ascension" sublimates the individual against the whole can be interpreted in the context of the composition title and the context of Coltrane's spiritual testimonies. The lesson involves the manner in which the self must be joined with the whole in devotion to God in order to complete the spiritual journey.

Shepp's comments also suggest that Dionysian sound can be compared to Apollonian art forms like painting, and how music can suggest metaphors and concrete colors and shapes, which, contextually, can be interpreted as concrete teachings. Shepp's comments suggest a process of interpreting a spiritual teaching through music in which the listener or participant works metaphorically to build a mental picture of the experience in sound. This is how Coltrane's sound serves to teach. The fusing of seven wind instruments into one sound field on "Ascension" is heard and experienced and translated into words like "sound-field" and "unity." Through "repeated listenings" the listener may come to an awareness of how seven distinct voices are rendered indistinguishable and yet so much more powerful through a compositional structure that emphasizes the unity of sound.

On a deeper level, these meditations on sound and musical structure can be viewed in the context of Coltrane's testimony accompanying *A Love Supreme.* Here Coltrane reveals his concerns with Christian spirituality, employing terms such as "grace," which is suggestive of the dispensation of the Christian Gospels. In this light, "Ascension" refers to reunification of the Son, Jesus Christ, with the Father following Christ's sacrifice for the sins of mankind on the cross. Coltrane can be interpreted therefore as insisting that Christ is the paramount example of selfless love and devotion; Christ's selfless sacrifice before God necessarily precedes his ascension to sit at the right hand of the Father, just as our passage must be marked by selfless love and sacrifice.

A basic awareness of the structure and organization of music is of paramount importance for the transmission and understanding of the content of Coltrane's teaching at the Coltrane Church. Listening implies attention to the structure of sound, a conscious meditative practice rather than a subconscious or purely bodily reaction. Listening demands a higher level of concentration, however, the initiate need not be completely versed in the intricacies of musical theory in order to meditate on the structure of Coltrane's sound. Indeed even the most superficial observation of form can yield the principal lessons. I have been greatly aided in uncovering many of these lessons no doubt by my experiences with the musical ministry of St. John's African Orthodox Church but also by studying the wealth of liner notes, reviews and commentaries on Coltrane's music.

Every Sunday sermon delivered by Archbishop King involves a complex interweaving of reflections on Coltrane's life, music, and words with interpretations of Old and New Testament Scriptures. Every sermon is, in effect, an explanation of the teachings of Saint John Coltrane, and these teachings of a latter-day saint are placed alongside the teachings of Old Testament prophets, the words of the apostles, and the wisdom of Jesus Christ. Archbishop King provides a large measure of guidance for repeated listenings that will reveal the substance of Coltrane's sound teachings. In the context of Sunday worship service I have often heard Archbishop King contrast listening with merely hearing. There is a constant process of listening that members of the community of St. John's African Orthodox Church are involved in and many are the testimonies of lessons learned and spiritual wisdom gained through repeated listening.

The greatest of St. John Coltrane's teachings involves his instruction on love. *A Love Supreme*, for example, urges the listener to conceive of a higher love and of love in purely unselfish terms. In spite of the decidedly Eastern mystical appreciation of music, meditation, and the emphasis on selflessness, the teachings of St. John Coltrane are entirely consistent with the Gospels and particularly with Christ's imperative on grace and love. Coltrane illustrates a path of spiritual growth in four phases as the *A Love Supreme* suite unfolds with "Acknowledgment," "Resolution," "Pursuance," and "Psalm." Archbishop King elaborates:

> "Acknowledgement" symbolizes awareness of one's sins and a prayer act of contrition. You have to acknowledge that you have sinned and are a sinner. "Resolution" symbolizes the willingness to pursue the right path revealed through prayer. You have made that step of fully committing yourself to the right path. "Pursuance" symbolizes the action of proceeding down that right path, living cleanly and with a right heart. Now you have to go and pursue that life because the devil surely puts obstacles in our path, even as soon as we leave the church building. "Psalm" symbolizes a mode of praise and thanks to God for providing a means for deliverance. And that's why we use "Psalm" as a prayer and when we say that we pray on *A Love Supreme* that's what we are talking about, saying the words for the final movement in that suite.

Archbishop King has come to understand Coltrane's *A Love Supreme* album as spiritual formula, and emphasizes that this teaching and this album was indeed the cornerstone of Coltrane Consciousness and, in particular, the first organized church founded around Coltrane Consciousness, the One Mind Temple:

> It is what we call the Love Supreme Thesis. Acknowledgment, Resolution, Pursuance, and Psalm refer to a process of analysis, interpretation, application, and manifestation. It's like Father, Son, and Holy Ghost. It's like a Trinity within that and it is a formula in the sense that in life you have to acknowledge what the problem is, then you have to resolve that you are going to do something about it, then pursue that, and then you have the manifestation of a Love Supreme. So for me, I just saw that a Love Supreme in the four parts was more than just titles of songs. It was some formula. So then in that sense we see that.
>
> *A Love Supreme*, that album, is very important to us because it also con-

tains John Coltrane's testimony and witness to his own spiritual awakening and it also has the written psalms in there. So in the early forming of the One Mind Temple Evolutionary Transitional Body of Christ we held onto this because we all believed in the possibility of transcending into Christ-like beings. This remains at the center of our belief. With Coltrane's *A Love Supreme* we used to call it the cornerstone of the church in the sense, in the Christian sense that we know that Christ is the cornerstone but in terms of motivating us and pushing us into establishing a spiritual community.

A Love Supreme had a lot to do with the spirituality that we found in the music, the formula that we found in the composition of that album and the weight and value of John Coltrane's testimony when he says "Dear Listener..." There's something really wonderful in the way John endears the listener in that statement, the way he says "Dear Listener, All Praise be to God for whom all Praise is Due. Yes, it is true, seek and ye shall find. Only through Him can we know the most wondrous bestowals." And I thought, when I look back on it, that that was a very courageous thing for John Coltrane to do because there were people who really wanted to praise him for his musical accomplishments but John was saying if you really want to know what wondrous bestowals that God has for you then you need to seek him out.

Certain of Coltrane's other composition titles specifically refer the listener to Coltrane's prerogative of unconditional love. For example, the title of a composition on the album *Coltrane's Sound* is "Fifth House." The "Fifth House" refers to an astrological term signifying "love." Jazz historian Lewis Porter explains, "The title has several meanings: it has astrological significance, and it tells us that the piece is based on Tadd Dameron's 'Hot House,' one of the tunes Coltrane played at his first, informal recording session in 1946, 'Hot House,' you'll recall, is itself based on 'What is This Thing Called Love?' and the fifth house is said to represent love" (Porter 166).

Coltrane's interest in astrology was shared by many African Americans at that time and would come to be of increasing importance in the '60s and '70s; the meaning of the title of the composition therefore hardly eluded many listeners. The piece is also a demonstration of what Coltrane does with pentatonic scale forms in forming melodies, and in an interesting way refers us by its structural use of African musical forms to a path to love through African aesthetics. Five is not only the referent to love within astrological terminology, but it is also the number of notes in the pentatonic scale form of "Fifth House" which is used to shape the melody. Coltrane is making an impassioned call to love through "Fifth House" and is accomplishing that call on a number of levels.

There are also elements of Coltrane's biography that demonstrate his understanding of an unconditional love. Archbishop King frequently refers to Coltrane's relationships with other members of the classic quartet.[5] Archbishop King reminds his congregation that Coltrane loved Elvin Jones, in spite of Elvin's problems with drugs and alcohol and his sometimes violent nature. Archbishop King recalls that Coltrane waited for Elvin to be released from jail before forming the quartet that would take his music to greater heights. In *Ascension: John Coltrane and his Quest*, Eric Nisenson also speaks of this relationship to Elvin Jones. Nisenson writes, "He needed Elvin—there simply was no other drummer who could play with the polyrhythmic density he required. He also loved Elvin, not always an easy thing to do. When sober, Elvin could be warm, brilliantly articulate, sensitive, and lovable person. But when he was high, particularly when he was drunk, it often was a different matter. He could be irresponsible, nasty, mean, and even violent. Coltrane's patience apparently knew no bounds. One night Elvin totaled Coltrane's car, which he had borrowed. When Coltrane heard that Elvin was all right he breathed a sigh of relief, without a trace of rancor, and said, 'I can always get a new car, but I'll never find another Elvin.' After Coltrane's death, Elvin would tell an interviewer that he felt he had been touched by something supernatural when he was with the quartet, so angelic was Trane's treatment of other people as well as his ability to produce music on an otherworldly plane" (Nisenson 140).

Perhaps one of the more easily discernible of St. John Coltrane's teachings is expressed through the "Prayer and Meditation Suite" on the *Transition* recording. The composition is divided in five parts titled "Day," "Peace and After," "Evening," and "Affirmation," and "4 a.m." Each composition is a musical rumination around a single scale, in many cases either diminished, pentatonic, or Dorian as is characteristic of much of the music from Coltrane's avant-garde period, and the sheet music indicates a single chord (although other chords are suggested for accompaniment).[6] "Day," for example, is written with F diminished accompaniment and the melody primarily centers on tones within an F diminished half-whole scale.[7] "After" is written with E minor 11 accompaniment and the melody revolves around E Dorian and E minor pentatonic sounds. "Evening" is also to be accompanied by an F diminished chord and its melody is similarly derived from an F diminished half-whole scale. "Affirmation" is accompanied by an A flat minor 11 chord and most of the melody revolves around A flat minor pentatonic and A Dorian sounds. "4 a.m." also explores F diminished tonalities.

The organization of the suite provides a schedule for meditation and prayer. Interestingly, the suite is organized in five parts, unfolding in a manner similar to the Islamic prayer schedule.[8] Since the days of the One

Mind Temple, Archbishop King and the core members of the congregation have maintained a prayer schedule that includes the 4 a.m. prayer and meditation time. Coltrane's suite has taught them the need to have a disciplined prayer schedule and to keep their minds on God throughout the day. Archbishop King:

> We started waking up at 4 a.m. and listening to the music and meditating on the music and John was giving us a schedule for the day so that throughout the day we could keep our minds on God. I really think that with that album what John Coltrane was giving us was a discipline and a way to organize our days around prayer and devotion.

He further reflects,

> If people go and get his album *Meditations*, this will help them to consider their need for maintaining a disciplined and spiritual life. Coltrane has "Meditation 4 a.m.," "Meditation afternoon," "Meditation Evening." Coltrane is telling us that there's a need for us to be constantly involved throughout the whole of the day with the knowledge of God and with the process of seeking to find oneself and one's purpose in life.

Archbishop King speaks of encouraging younger members to appropriate a practice of meditation. In the following narrative he addresses Sis. Erin, the daughter of Sis. Analahati, and her attempts at meditation:

> There is something that has happened recently with one of our young sisters, Sis. Erin. She's at a point where she approached me and she wants to study with me and just be up close and be a personal assistant just for the sake of learning something. She had an experience likened to mine in meditating on the music. This is really something. I should have had her to talk about this.
>
> She was having some problems you know and trying to get past something and she said she just went down by the Golden Gate Bridge where you can go down there and park, put some Coltrane on and started writing.
>
> And she shared with me what she was writing and I looked at it and said, this is really beautiful. It was real stuff, very intimate kinda stuff. And she was crediting it to the music. She said the music just opened me up and God was talking to me.
>
> And I'm sitting in her car and we're listening and she's telling me, and she's excited, she wanted to show me this after church and she took me up to Twin Peaks way up there and I'm reading this and we're listening. And what was interesting about it, and I'll try to get more detail on this because it's something that needs to be documented, is that she was listening to "I Want to Talk About You," so the song came on and I said, that's my favorite song, it's the song that I heard John Coltrane talk to me on. And she said, "Bishop, this is the song that I was listening to when the Holy Ghost opened me up and revealed herself to me"... and it was the

same kind of experience where the Lord was telling her, "Erin, take care of yourself." Just as when I heard it and John came on and said, "Rama Krishna, take care of yourself."

After developing a prayer and meditation schedule, Coltrane later suggests topics for meditation on the recordings *Meditations* (1966) and *First Meditations* (1992). With compositions on both recordings titled "Love," "Compassion," "Consequences," and "Serenity," Coltrane urges rumination on some of the basic principles of Christ's teachings. Archbishop King comments:

> It's straight from the teachings of Christ, that you have to love one another ... love your neighbor as you love yourself, show compassion, clothe the naked and feed the hungry and house the homeless.

Many are Coltrane's teachings on meditation. Repeated listening of many of Coltrane's compositions for meditation, particularly those compositions on the album *Meditations* (1966), *First Meditations* (1992), and *Transition* (1993) also deal with the very nature of meditation, revealing a furious tone, an indication of great struggle. The force of much of Coltrane's music, particularly during his avant-garde period (1964–1967) teaches that meditation is not purely placid, but that through meditation lies the possibility for remaking ourselves and that the process of re-making can be a moment of great upheaval and arrest. Critiquing the music of *Transition*, biographer Eric Nisenson comments, "Although he uses repetitive phrases, there is never a moment of monotony in 'Transition'; it is a gripping piece of music. Listening to 'Transition,' it is hard not to hear confusion, frustration, and even rage, maybe at himself, maybe at God or at least the difficulties of the path to God. Yet the more one listens to 'Transition' the more one hears a diamond-hard beauty unlike anything else in music. That something so roiling can also have such beauty is one of the paradoxes of Coltrane's art" (Nisenson *Ascension*, 172)

Coltrane Consciousness is a mode of understanding the recordings of John Coltrane as meditations on God. At the time that *Meditations* was recorded in 1965, John Coltrane revealed in an interview with jazz critic Nat Hentoff that indeed his purpose was to meditate through the music. C.O. Simpkins, in his biography of John Coltrane, reveals, "He was asked by Nat Hentoff if *Meditations* was an extension of *A Love Supreme*: 'Once you become aware of this force for unity in life, you can't ever forget it. It becomes part of everything you do. In that respect, this is an extension of *A Love Supreme* since my conception of that force keeps changing shape. My goal in meditating on this through music, however, remains the same.

And that is to uplift people, as much as I can. To inspire them to realize more and more of their capacities for living meaningful lives. Because there certainly is meaning to life" (Simpkins 200).

Conclusions

In the view of the Coltrane Church, John Coltrane's personal and musical history of transformation and differential movement has yielded an enormity of concrete spiritual teachings and the incorporation of these teachings into the daily lives of believers has yielded miracles and manifestations that confirm their beliefs. The totality of John Coltrane's musical output represents an addendum to the New Testament writ in Sound. Coltrane Consciousness is about much more than experiencing jazz music in a church setting and feeling something vaguely inspirational in the music. For the Apostles of Sound, Coltrane Consciousness is about learning something concrete through the music and wisdom of John Coltrane about love, spiritual growth, and evolution. Like the Eightfold Path of Buddha, the advice of Lord Krishna to Arjuna in the Bhaghavad Gita, or the wisdom of the Gospels of Jesus Christ or the Epistles of Paul, members of the Coltrane Church believe that St. John Coltrane's teachings illuminate a way unto God and the Path to transcendence and redemption.

Such comparisons are neither purely rhetorical nor fanciful exaggerations for members of the Coltrane Church. The Apostles of Sound clearly articulate the notion that Coltrane Consciousness presents its devotees with a contemporary master teacher on par with the ancient divine mystics both in terms of form and content. With respect to form, Coltrane's spiritual teachings are considered revolutionary for the body of believers at the Coltrane Church because they are presented through the universal language of sound. With respect to content, Archbishop King and Mother Marina have endeavored to demonstrate that Coltrane's teachings recapture the revolutionary spirit of the teachings of Christ, Buddha, Krishna, and the Sufi mystics, focusing on love, grace, oneness, and selfless dedication to God. The founders of the Coltrane, the original Apostles of Sound, well understand that the purported evolutionary form and content of St. John Coltrane's teachings is fundamental to even the possibility of significant ideological differential movement in the arenas of culture, spirituality, and politics.

To embrace Coltrane's music and biography in both form and content as the substance of concrete teachings is to suggest a powerful counter-hegemonic spiritual pedagogy diametrically opposed to traditional Western spiritual pedagogy. Sound becomes a counter-pedagogical format to the traditional Western spiritual focus on the written and spoken word. With their investment in John Coltrane's teachings rendered in sound and music, Coltrane Church members suggest a path toward spiritual redemption that elides Western rationality and fundamentally challenges the colonial implications of using the master's tongue to experience spiritual salvation. This is further underscored by John Coltrane's persistent exploration of non–Western scales, harmonies, and rhythms. Coltrane's sound-text teachings, as understood by the Coltrane Church, emphatically integrate non–Western prerogatives, pointing to Eastern and African understandings of music, a differential relationship between God and man/woman. Indeed even those ideas that do emerge from Coltrane's Western Christian heritage integrate a unity of religious ideals and are suggestive of potential connections between the core beliefs of Christianity, Buddhism, Hinduism, and Sufism.

3

Jimbo's Bop City

You can play a shoestring if you're sincere.—St. John Will-
I-Am Coltrane

July 17, 1967. Franzo King sat in the back room of Jimbo's Bop City,
then located in the Temple Theater at Fillmore and Sutter streets, in the
midst of a gathering crowd at 2 a.m. Bop City was the place to be, where all
the great jazz musicians would try out new sounds after evening engagements at San Francisco's white owned clubs. Jimbo's had been the place
since Jimbo Edwards took it over in 1950 with the assistance of "The
Mayor of Fillmore," Charles Sullivan, from the flamboyant Slim Gaillard
(Pepin and Watts 138). Franzo took in the legends displayed on Harry
Smith's murals and the swirling shapes painted on the low ceiling. Franzo
carried himself like a modern man who listened to modern jazz. "You are
what you listen to," he would say, "and the music I listened to made me
progressive and modern and even avant-garde."

And Franzo brought his horn.

He found a space at a larger table, and asked one of the musicians
watching and waiting to jam if he could join him. He was there to talk
with other musicians about chords and playing through changes and about
other musicians. He would have ordered the chicken in the basket that
used to sell for only $5 but like so many who came to Bop City, his mind
was really only on the music. It was all he had been able to think about
for the past few years, especially since he'd seen John Coltrane at the Jazz
Workshop in '65 and '66. And as the night wore on into morning, he
decided maybe he'd get up the nerve to try out a few things he'd been wood-
shedding.

This was the house that bop built, at least according to the sign above the door. Known the world over. This place had hosted everyone from Ellington to Billie Holiday. There used to be a mural of Louis Armstrong on the wall. It was where the athlete and singer Johnny Mathis first cut his teeth in live performance. A sign bearing Billy Eckstine's testimonial was on the wall behind the bandstand. Duke Ellington feasted here with friends (Pepin and Watts 155). Teddy Edwards brought Bird here after hours. Dexter Gordon came up from Central Avenue in Los Angeles and played here. John Handy cut heads and made a name for himself here. This was where local hero Pony Poindexter got embarrassed taking on Frank Fischer in a head-cutting session on Bird's famous "Cherokee" (147).

Tonight a young, local tenor man, unknown to Franzo, fronted the rhythm section. He wailed through broken arpeggios, honks and shrieks, his eyes closed and his face tight, his body lurched awkwardly forward, bent at the waist, then stumbled backward almost into the drums against the exit door. He ran it down like John Coltrane *Live at the Village Vanguard* (1962) on "Chasin' the Trane" with endless variations and permutations, broken sentences, hollers, shrieks, moving inside and outside of chord tones, like an epic novel writ in sheets of sound. And Bishop looked around and felt a palpable tension in the air, a vibe like nothing else he'd ever experienced at Bop City.

Franzo spied a friend in the audience, alto saxophonist and local Charlie "Yardbird" Parker apostle Norman Williams.[1]

"Man," Franzo asked Norman Williams in the lingo of beboppers and black nationalists, "what's the matter with this brother?"

"Ain't you heard? Coltrane died today."

"Man, they done *killed* Coltrane?"

"They done *killed* Coltrane."

And between the two, holding alto saxophone cases tight to their chests, they understood how the drugs and the pushers and the cops who preyed on jazz musicians had once again conspired to rob a man of his life and rob his people of his music and spirit. They shared remembrances of how the drugs took Parker at 34, how Thelonious Monk got set up just sitting in Bud Powell's car, and how Gene Ammons was doing time for a similar set-up and whether he should have tried to outrun the pigs in his Fleetwood Brougham, and how Stan Getz had wound up in jail and how when he was released he'd gotten back on the junk, and what it was doing to Art Pepper's body and soul, and how it washed away Billie Holiday's voice, and how the list of jazz musicians on heroin or in jail for heroin was longer than the number of tunes many budding jazz musicians knew by heart, and how the list just kept going on. And now here was another

Mother Marina King sings the 23rd Psalm on February 8, 2008, at Cité de la Musique in Paris.

brother dead, a brother who had turned the corner on all of that and had gotten Jesus and religion and was like a priest or a saint or like a black god himself.

John Coltrane's death from complications associated with liver cancer on July 17, 1967, was actually far more prosaic. But what Franzo King and his companion that night at Jimbo's Bop City were talking about was what John Coltrane meant to them and to the community.

Franzo King first learned of Coltrane's untimely passing while attending this performance at Jimbo's Bop City. In similar fashion to the Sound Baptism of 1965, Franzo King was only hoping to catch a glimpse of one of San Francisco's many local jazz heroes or maybe a big name from out of town coming in for an after-hours jam around midnight or 2 a.m. But there was an unfamiliar solemnity in the air that night. A tenor player honked and wailed and grieved through his instrument on the bandstand. And Franzo King was again "arrested" by Coltrane, instantly and painfully confronted with the news of his untimely death at the age of 40.

His grief in that moment and in the months and years to follow would be as profound as his initial awakening in 1965. The death of John Coltrane would lend a sense of urgency to everything that he had been thinking and planning to do since the Sound Baptism. Specifically, Franzo King would begin to link the untimely death of John Coltrane with the untimely deaths of so many other black men and women in his community, and he would begin to interpret it as "murder," equating Coltrane's passing with the quotidian violence committed against black communities across America.

Franzo King walked out into a midsummer dawn, his slender hands clutching his alto saxophone case. He tugged at the bill of his stingy brim. It was the Summer of Love. Jimi Hendrix heralded in the new era with his appearance at the Monterey Pop Festival. Air battles raged in Vietnam over Hanoi and Haiphong and by early 1968 Vietcong commandoes would launch a series of 100 catastrophic shock attacks known as the Tet Offensive that would result in declining public support for the war. Muhammad Ali had been arrested in April for refusing to comply with the draft. Aretha Franklin's "Chain of Fools" and her version of the Rolling Stones' "(I Can't Get No) Satisfaction" were all over pop radio. Thurgood Marshall was appointed by President Lyndon Johnson to the Supreme Court. India's Indira Gandhi became the first woman elected to lead a democratic country. The Twenty-Fifth Amendment clarifying presidential succession was ratified. Race riots would break out in Boston, Detroit and Newark. The Biafra government of eastern Nigeria established an independent republic for the Ibo people. Sidney Poitier dominated theaters with appearances in *To Sir, With Love* and In *the Heat of the Night*. Model Naomi Sims' appearance on the cover of the *New York Times* fashion supplement signaled public acceptance of a "Black Is Beautiful" era. And of the most beloved and influential jazz innovators, John William Coltrane, died of liver cancer at age 40.

From Franzo's vantage point outside of Jimbo's Bop City, all of 1967 was fused together in the redevelopment of the Western Addition and the progressive removal of residents of color, the poor, and the elderly from San Francisco. It was immediate and tangible racial and class warfare. You could feel, hear, and touch the encroachment of corporatism and with it, forms of economic and environmental racism that would ultimately reshape a population. The future was here.

It was happening first in the Western Addition Area–2, a mere stone's throw from City Hall. Near Jimbo's Bop City, Geary and Fillmore had been raised and high-rise residential towers and modernist plazas that topped parking garages were being built, creating a new sense of urban modernism, a new look for the late '60s (Solnit and Schwartzenberg 49). Franzo read the articles in the *Sun-Reporter*, the newspaper for San Francisco's black population, decrying Justin Herman and his leadership of the San Francisco Redevelopment Agency as arch-villains in the conspiracy to remove African Americans from San Francisco (Hartman 18).

One by one the jazz, blues and rhythm and blues clubs in the Fillmore were falling to redevelopment along with other predominantly African American-owned businesses and houses in the Western Addition. Solnit and Schwartzenberg acknowledge, "Though blight was cited as grounds for razing the area, it was clear that expansion of commercial and civic functions was the real motive" (18). And earlier, citing Chester Hartman, historian of San Francisco urban renewal and redevelopment, Solnit and Schwartzenberg write, "the Redevelopment Agency 'became a powerful and aggressive army out to capture as much downtown land as it could.... The Agency turned to systematically sweeping out the poor, with the full backing of the city's power elite'" (18.).

It was also happening south of Market Street against the interests of white, retired union workers and with them a history of labor organizing and radical politics (Hartman 50). It was beginning to happen in the Bayview-Hunter's Point where Archbishop maintained his residence and where the early social listening clubs had been established by a nascent church of John Coltrane. There was a growing consciousness about all of the displacement and coalition building among divergent groups of increasingly dispossessed persons—in the end significantly marred by the racism of whites south of Market Street toward blacks in the Western Addition— and talk of residents getting organized to defeat redevelopment (50).

It was happening in so many American cities. While the lines would appear to have been clearly drawn between the cabal of real estate developers and long-standing members of the chamber of commerce, you couldn't be certain which of the various community leaders and organizations that had sprung up to combat urban renewal was legitimately working in the interests of the people. Archbishop King remarks:

> It was like you were being set up. I didn't know many people that were really telling the truth and that you could trust.

Franzo King knew the history and the moment in 1967. In that moment he used what he had and what he had was John Coltrane. At times John Coltrane would be all that he had. His devotion to Coltrane wouldn't be able to stem the tide of redevelopment. Not this time. There would be a forty-plus year evolutionary, transitional process. The church would slowly but surely insinuate itself within broader political processes and develop meaningful alliances in arts and education and audiences of mayors and congress members. And within the next twenty years Coltrane Consciousness would find itself allied with effective social justice movements for change.

It was after this night at Jimbo's Bop City, the night of Coltrane's passing, that Franzo and Marina King began reading the words of Coltrane in interviews and liner notes. They began to examine album covers and song titles with greater scrutiny. They read Frank Kofsky's articles that linked Coltrane with the more radical black nationalist movements of the urban north and west coast and contemporary Marxism. They read Amiri Baraka's *Blues People* (1963) and began to self-consciously understand the music of African Americans as black nationalist expression. They learned of Coltrane's spirituality and dietary practices. They studied Coltrane's biography and paid greater attention to those Coltrane had claimed as his influences. They even submitted Coltrane to numerological and astrological analyses.

There would be a host of minor and personal victories that would serve as an apprenticeship for activism down the road. Coltrane Consciousness would deliver Archbishop King from the precipice of depression and suicide. It would lead to food, shelter and clothing programs that would serve the homeless and downtrodden of the Western Addition. It would provide a space for alternative spiritual expression for those who couldn't find places for themselves within organized churches. It would provide a venue for musicians and a space for aspiring musicians to hone their skills. It would help to sustain a growing circle of devotees and launch a host of small-scale community-based activities against the ravages of redevelopment and the political currents of four decades. It would have a hand in monitoring the activities and proclivities for brutality of the San

Francisco Police Department. A culture of liberation in the name of John Coltrane would begin from the margins in San Francisco in the 1970s and continue into the present against the backdrop of an unprecedented urban gentrification made possible by historic displacements of African American and poor communities. St. John Coltrane would emerge as a champion and counter-hegemonic cultural force against the forces of capitalist expansion.

The second Sound Baptism at Jimbo's Bop City in 1967 has to be properly examined as a narrative that established John Coltrane as the quintessential black nationalist figure in jazz for this nascent community. Testifying to this early conceptualization in his Ascension Day[2] celebration sermon, July 16, 1998, Archbishop (then Bishop) King spoke to his congregation about the "assassination" of John Coltrane:

> I was in Jimbo's Bop City, a jazz joint, at 2 a.m. and there was a guy playing furiously on the bandstand. He was going from one corner of the bandstand to the next, playing, stopping, playing. I remember that I asked Bishop Norman Williams what was wrong with that cat and he told me, "Don't you know man? John Coltrane's dead." At that moment the first thought I had was, "Man, they done killed[3] Coltrane."
>
> I say Coltrane was killed because he did not ask to be born as a subcitizen. He suffered from everything that someone who has to live through the humiliation of ghettos suffers through. With Coltrane dealing with alcoholism and heroin addiction and then dying of damage to his liver, man, they done killed Coltrane. And I went home and just shut in and listened to Coltrane. I thought that the sun should not shine for three days or more, but God was merciful and allowed the sun to shine. And at the time I felt that the world had lost the greatest prophet and visionary of the twentieth century.

Archbishop King's recollections of that event locate Coltrane's tragic death within a broader history of the degradation and humiliation of persons of African descent. Coltrane's death by liver cancer due to the complications of drug and alcohol abuse makes Coltrane an urban American black everyman who shared the violence of racism and was killed as part of the broader and persistent assault on the lives of black men and women in twentieth century America. It is a starkly realistic portrait of Coltrane's life, deconstructing any illusion that Coltrane's artistic status rendered him oblivious or impervious to the horrors of racial hierarchy and white supremacy.

A politics of essentialized racial identity were constructed through Archbishop King's narrative at precisely the point where he conflated Coltrane's experience of racist degradation with his status as master musician and prophet/visionary. Implicitly, Coltrane's musical ability and meta-physical power obtain legitimacy because of his experiences with black poverty, racism, drug abuse, institutionalized violence, etc., within the black community. Only as a black man can he come to possess these powers. The movement of Coltrane Consciousness therefore begins within the black community where musical genius and spiritual awareness are produced within particular social, political, and cultural contexts.

This explains why the early years of the movement of Coltrane Consciousness were described by Archbishop King as fundamentally cultural and limited to the experience of black people in America:

> You see, I used to deal with the music as a strictly cultural thing. It is, after all, the only art form that the United States has produced; everything else comes from Europe and other places. When you start talking about the music that the people of African descent have produced, jazz is the only true art form that has been produced by this country. I think that a lot of it has escaped the community that produced it. And for whatever reasons, maybe the commercial aspects of it, the music is no longer in the community to hear. You have to leave the community to go hear the music now. At one time it was something that was in the community that the people could afford. It's expensive now. I think very few people can afford to hear this kind of music.

Those early years in the movement of Coltrane Consciousness were not without controversy. Here the Archbishop conveys a sense of the early challenges facing the church in establishing Coltrane and his music as "legitimately black" among increasingly younger and more skeptical populations as the popularity of jazz music declined:

> Black folks started saying that jazz was getting too white and Murray, David Murray out of the Church of God in Christ, and Art Blakey and them cats started saying, hey, we got to put the church thing back in here and that there was a whole movement to tie the so-called jazz music back to the church kind of freedom. Charlie Mingus was one. Because people were getting turned off with him, man, they said he wasn't black enough. When that whole '60s thing came out, that's when John Coltrane came out with Africa. My line was, brother, is that black enough for you? Is that black enough for you? You can't get no blacker than this.

The most poignant and revealing aspects of the association of black nationalism with origin narratives of the Coltrane Church are that it occurred in a black owned jazz club that would soon be subsumed by urban redevelopment, and that Archbishop King immediately interpreted Coltrane's assassination as another in the long series of state-sponsored assassinations of black leadership in the 1960s and 1970s. In addition to its importance with respect to local racial politics, Jimbo's Bop City had been known since its inception in the 1950s as a location that encouraged integration[4] and was on the vanguard of issues broached by the larger civil rights movement.

Writing for the *San Francisco Chronicle*, jazz critic Jesse Hamlin notes, "The Fillmore was the only area where blacks could go out and enjoy themselves and relax. They could feel they were accepted there because those were black clubs, regardless of the fact that some were backed or owned by whites. There were a lot of black owners, and they didn't want any trouble or violence. Our music was attracting white people, and they knew they could come and not worry about getting ripped off. After their regular gigs, musicians jammed at Jimbo's Bop City, the fabled after-hours club that opened on Post Street in 1950. Dropping in at 3 a.m., one might hear great players like Art Tatum or Dizzy Gillespie or Gerry Mulligan, or see Ellington or Brando relaxing with friends. A horde of young jazzers cut their teeth at Bop City, among them the esteemed saxophonist John Handy, who started jamming there in 1949 at age 16. A recent arrival from Dallas, he was plunged into an exciting new world. 'The place was totally integrated,' says Handy, who quickly became a regular, holding his own blowing bebop with stars like trumpeter Kenny Dorham. 'I was a kid right out of the South and here were mixed couples. It surprised me. But after a couple of looks, it seemed the natural order of things.' In the late '50s, Handy moved to New York and achieved acclaim working with Charles Mingus. When he returned in the early '60s, most of the Fillmore clubs had long since vanished because of tough economic times, shifting social patterns and urban renewal. Handy formed the racially mixed Freedom Band to perform at civil rights rallies. 'I felt the music was bringing people of different cultures together,' he said. Jazz was an avenue through which people were integrated. It was a spearhead for opening up minds.... It's democratic music" (Hamlin *San Francisco Chronicle*, 1998).

As a bulwark against racism, Coltrane Consciousness proved efficacious in the latter years of the civil rights movement precisely because Coltrane resonated the call to change of the 1960s. Archbishop King briefly reflects on feeling "right" about Coltrane Consciousness as a movement of radical change and rebellion against the dominant social order and on the relevance of Coltrane and his music in the civil rights era:

> John Coltrane's music could rightly be called the soundtrack for the civil rights movement of the 1960s. I mean ... "Alabama," about those four little girls being blown up in a church in Alabama. And the whole identification with Africa at that time.... I mean, you can't get any more African than *Africa/Brass*.

The three icons of the '60s are not Bobby, Martin, and John, not from a pure kind of sense. That was a manufactured icon for the people, a tri-con, and it turns out to be a big con. The real tri-con is Malcolm, Martin, and John Coltrane, and it really became clear to me. I get this feeling every time I get in a large African American gathering with the precepts of spirituality and righteousness and liberation and atoning and healing and it just strikes me in a very clear sense that somehow we have abandoned the most valuable of all the icons because John Coltrane is not present. And for me that's a great agony.

Black Nationalism and Coltrane's Philadelphia Years

Archbishop King's narrative construction of Coltrane's black nationalist identity as one among the oppressed black masses is also focused around his interpretation of Coltrane's musical and spiritual upbringing in Philadelphia, Pennsylvania, even before his experiences as a mature artist in New York City. Archbishop King's Philadelphia is the place where race, music, and spirit unite:

Philadelphia is a city of high musical development. John Coltrane, the masterful young musician, was initiated into the mysticism and power of Sound here. The Master came to experience and become a part of a deeply religious attitude amongst highly religious musical technicians, men who understood in a spiritually ritualistic way to: Sing all songs to God, and strove to: Live cleanly. Do right [Analahati 26].

Philadelphia was both the place where John Coltrane became a professional jazz musician and the place where he began using heroin. Philadelphia is in truth the place where Coltrane's status as black everyman is initially legitimated.

While John Coltrane was born in Hamlet, North Carolina, in 1926, his family moved to Philadelphia in 1944 after the deaths of his grandfather and father (1939) where Coltrane studied at the Orenstein School of Music and Granoff Studios and tutored in cocktail bars with the rhythm and blues bands of Earl Bostic and Eddie Vinson from 1945 to 1959, as well as the Dizzy Gillespie big band. Coltrane was also in Philadelphia when he was drafted into the Navy, where he played in the Navy Band in the Pacific (Cole 26).

Bill Cole describes Coltrane's Philadelphia experience as his "real musical center" (Cole 25). "It was in Philadelphia that he first began to know other musicians, other people who were actually involved in the vocation that he was beginning to embark upon. It was in Philadelphia that he began a simultaneous formal and social education of music" (26). Cole also writes, "However, this also was the period when Trane began using drugs; and slowly but surely his addiction to heroin preoccupied his mind," and details Gillespie's firing of Coltrane and Jimmy Heath because of drugs (27).

In an essay titled "War/Philly Blues/Deeper Bop," LeRoi Jones/Amiri Baraka contextualizes Coltrane's journey after high school to Philadelphia within the wider events of World War II and black participation in that struggle, the development of urban American rhythm and blues, the changing mores and family structures of northern migrating African Americans, the influence of "monopoly music manipulators" over black music forms, and racism and race rebellions in urban black enclaves (Jones *Selected Plays*, 231). Significantly, Jones/Baraka treats Coltrane as an African-American everyman, discussing his sojourn from North Carolina to Philadelphia in terms of the mass migration of African Americans from the south to the urban north during the Second World War. "John Coltrane had now finished high school and split for Philly with some friends, making the classic journey from the Afro-American homeland to the 'promising' North" (228).

In his opening sentence, Jones/Baraka links the biography of Coltrane with the war: "Around the time the Nazis were beginning to pay for the mistake of invading the Soviet Union, John Coltrane was coming out of high school" (228). Here Jones/Baraka effectively links Coltrane's biography with the common stories of African American experience, sculpting Coltrane as an archetypal African American and specifically as the archetype of a black urban American worker. "In Philly Trane lives and works as an Afro-American worker. He is in a factory job everyday, as are his mother and cousin. He goes to music school in the evenings, and now he is beginning to work playing music an occasional weekend" and further, "The factory work, living and playing among the Afro-American working class, provided strong ties with that culture and the depth of expression, particularly musically. The very method by which Trane continued to make his living, even after leaving the factory, still connected him deeper to the Afro-American working class through the blues tradition, through the contemporary expression of it" (228).

Jones/Baraka's depiction of Coltrane the consummate black proletariat is an important cornerstone for the class-consciousness and political philosophy of Coltrane Consciousness. This is a church of working people, a decidedly proletariat leadership and congregation. The musicians of St. John's African Orthodox Church approach the performance of their music in the same workman-like fashion of John Coltrane in Philadelphia, often earning the bulk of their incomes outside of music while continuing to perform and build their reputations. Most importantly this is a church of working people dedicated to serving the poor.

Jones/Baraka's depiction of Coltrane as the consummate proletariat is not without some acknowledged contradictions. Jones/Baraka acknowledges that Coltrane was from a black bourgeois background in Hamlet, North Carolina. "He was the grandson of a petty-bourgeois nationalist preacher and son of a musical small-business man connected to black people inextricably by the experience of national oppression, yet with a class background that was not that of the Afro-American masses" (Jones 241).

In strictly musical terms, Jones/Baraka discusses Coltrane's proletariat background and sojourn from the Southern black belt to Philadelphia as the archetypal biography of jazz, and particularly bebop, innovators. Jones/Baraka compares the biographies of Charlie Parker and Dizzy Gillespie with that of John Coltrane: "In looking at the principal innovators of bop, for instance: Bird, from Kansas City (a key area in the thirties for the origin of the big blues bands and the shouters, it was where Charlie Parker first mastered his instrument with the Jay McShann band). Bird's father was a vaudevillian and a Pullman car chef, his mother a domestic. Dizzy Gillespie, was born in Cheraw, South Carolina, the heart of the Black Belt, his father was a bricklayer who had musical instruments around because he led a band on the side. Dizzy's mother left Cheraw in 1935 and came to Philly, and as soon as Diz finished high school he came on up. Almost an identical tale to Trane's, just a decade before!" (240).

For Jones/Baraka, the most salient aspect of Coltrane's particular musical development in Philadelphia, and for the development and furtherance of bop in general, was Coltrane's exposure to urban black blues and rhythm and blues performances. While Coltrane attended the Orenstein School and then later studied at the Granoff Studios during this Philadelphia period, Jones/Baraka is concerned more with Coltrane's exposure to the music of big blues bands, from Bennie Moten to Walter Page and the Blue Devils (230). Jones/Baraka argues that at this time, traditional blues forms were metamorphosizing into rhythm and blues (R&B) styles, an evolution to which a young John Coltrane was being constantly exposed. Jones/Baraka notes "R&B emerged as the basic contemporary black blues style of the forties" (231).

Jones/Baraka eloquently expresses the development of R&B styles from an amalgam of diverse blues styles. Jones/Baraka includes in the evolution of R&B the rise of R&B shouters who were "hooked up directly to the field hollers and coon yells and blues shouts of the earlier country blues and work song era," the emergence of a blues-oriented Southwestern style that included "the constant use of the riff, heavy drumming, and unison screaming saxophones behind the singers," and the development of an instrumental style of "honkers" who ventured "in the direction of the ever wilder shouted R&B style" and which was typified by the likes of Eddie "Lockjaw" Davis and Illinois Jacquet, to name a few.

According to Jones/Baraka, Coltrane entered Philadelphia and began his apprenticeship as a musician in a period of profound development in black music." So that Trane entering into Philly entered into two developing streams of black music. The basic blues thrust was rhythm and blues— the most modern blues form, the standard speech of the ghetto." Further, Jones summarizes, "What Coltrane was exposed to in Philadelphia was the most contemporary urban blues style" (231–232).

What Jones/Baraka expressly accomplishes in his anlysis, from a musical standpoint, is an appreciation of Coltrane's music -an also of bop and post-bop- as the music of working black people in the urban north. Particularly when contextualizing Coltrane's development and the development of bop within the emergence of urban rhythm and blues styles, Jones/Baraka locates Coltrane's biography and musical resume within urban black proletariat settings. For Jones/Baraka, the strength of bop and indeed of John Coltrane is their grounding in the blues tradition. The music of Coltrane's formative years as a musician, bop music, anchored in the blues, is the music of the people.

Conclusions

The narrative of Jimbo's Bop City and the Second Baptism of Sound reinforces historically particular understandings of John Coltrane as a black nationalist icon and enforces counter-hegemonic ideologies rooted in essentialized notions of blackness and Black Power. These racialized, essentialist notions are supported in large measure by attendant narratives of Coltrane's developmental Philadelphia years. These representations did not enable effective counter-hegemonic action. The church remained on the margins, continuing to not only be critical of mainstream activists and insiders, but incapable of building coalitions with other similarly marginalized cultural, religious, and political groups.

The contemporary scope of Coltrane Consciousness is now far broader than purely racial parameters. This transformation began in 1969 in a political shift from black nationalism to class consciousness under the tutelage of Dr. Huey P. Newton of the Black Panther Party. And in 1971 the influence of Alice Coltrane confirmed the church's steady movement toward universalist spiritual practices. In the end, the embrace of a broader Marxist class-consciousness perspective via Dr. Huey P. Newton and Alice Coltrane's confirmation of their spiritual universalism marked important and necessary transitional moments for the Coltrane Church toward an ideological foundation that would yield more effective counter-hegemonic cultural, religious, and political action.

4

The Yardbird Club and the History of African American Jazz Entrepreneurship in San Francisco

Black residents frequented the night clubs on the Barbary Coast and danced to popular Afro-American rhythms. Some clubs, including the Acorn, Apex, Sam King's, Purcell's, and Lester Mapp's were particularly popular, and several were organized as cabarets, a popular form of entertainment. Amid the revelry and gay music, San Franciscans saw interracial couples and dancing by members of all races. The cabarets often featured an 'all colored revue,' to the delight of black and white San Franciscans alike.[1]

—Albert S. Broussard (*Black San Francisco: The Struggle for Racial Equality in the West, 1900–1954*)

The inspiration of the 1965 Sound Baptism first manifested as a gathering, a listening clinic. This event marks the "Coltrane Church's" first stage of evolution. Recognition of the spiritual power of John Coltrane and his music was borne in a unique moment of intermusicality and connection between two young lovers and listeners and the greatest jazz musician of his era (Monson). A sense of urgency about how to respond to the Sound Baptism came July 17, 1967, upon hearing the news of Coltrane's passing.

Franzo and Marina King first used their apartment in a Potrero Hills housing project in 1965 and now in 1967 with greater energy as a listening clinic, where 1 to 3 times weekly people were invited to bring new recordings and readings. This cultural movement began quite innocently as friends gathered to listen to new records and share knowledge about the music. This was an initial cultural experiment, a social gathering focused around the appreciation of black art. Joined by Franzo's older brother Landres King, affectionately called "Shanghai," these listening clinics were known as "The Jazz Club" and initially afforded opportunities for Shanghai to educate Franzo and Marina in the music and Marina to share some of the great contemporary African American literature.

Franzo and Marina King solved the riddle of how to respond to the Sound Baptism by focusing The Jazz Club listening clinic on the musical evolution of John Coltrane. This new listening clinic began to put the inspiration of the Sound Baptism into practice and marked the evolution of Franzo and Marina King's personal spiritual recognition to community recognition of John Coltrane and his music. In 1967 Franzo and Marina King doubled down on a vision that began innocently enough in 1965 and took the good news of the Sound Baptism vision back to their community in San Francisco's Potrero Hills neighborhood and engaged in a grassroots cultural movement aimed at resuscitating the influence of jazz music. The continuing history of the Coltrane Church suggests that this initial grassroots cultural activity would be repeatedly affirmed by every listener that they approached and that their efforts would ultimately become linked with a global audience.

> We were listening to modern jazz and in so doing we considered ourselves modern and carried ourselves as modern people. And Marina would read to both of us. James Baldwin. She read *Another Country*. That was really something.

These were listening parties and listeners could argue the merits of liner notes and offer critiques of the music even as they were building a substantial vocabulary of the music. It was part social gathering and part educational experience, a sort of "musical reading circle." These listening parties fundamentally re-created the cultural environments of the many black-owned jazz clubs in the Western Addition that thrived in the aftermath of World War II and the 1950s and were steadily being dismantled by urban redevelopment in the 1960s including Jimbo's Bop City, The Texas Playhouse, and The New Orleans Swing Club. There was a growing awareness among the participants of these early listening clinics that jazz music was declining in significance in the black community and that redevelopment threatened the survival of these black-owned clubs and there developed a grassroots commitment by these devoted listeners gathered in the Potrero Hills apartment of Franzo and Marina King to address that problem. Their solution was the community-owned "Yardbird Club."

The St. John Will-I-Am Coltrane Church at 351 Divisadero Street.

By 1968 Franzo and Marina were using the basement of a Bayview-Hunter's Point apartment on 1529 Galvez Ave. as an after-hours jazz club called the Yardbird Club where local musicians could play what they wanted to play and earn a fair percentage of the gate. This practice, that initially mixed spirits with cultural activity, was named in honor of Charles "Yardbird" Parker or "Bird" as most jazz aficionados and musicians called the late bebop alto sax innovator. Archbisop King:

> Charlie Parker came like John the Baptist before the coming of John Coltrane. And so we named it the Yardbird Club in honor of he who came before the mystic known as Sri Rama Ohnedaruth,[2] St. John Will-I-Am Coltrane.

The cultural movement known as the Yardbird Club represented an ideological shift as the Coltrane Church moved from an informal listening clinic to an underground jazz club. Franzo King negotiated with the operators of a local Bayview-Hunter's Point house party where people paid a minimal fee—50 cents to a dollar—for R&B music and liquor. According to the agreement, at 2 a.m. the R&B house party was turned into a jazz nightclub where local performers like Benny Harris, Billy Higgins and Norman Williams performed live. With hours of operation between 2 and 6 a.m., this club became known as the Yardbird Club, named in honor of jazz great Charles "Yardbird" Parker. The Yardbird Club was simultaneously an organic outgrowth of the initial listening clinics and an underground business venture for burgeoning musicians as Archbishop King and Mother Marina operated on the fringes of legality. The Yardbird Club was also an answer to white ownership of clubs and provided a place, not unlike Jimbo's Bop City in the Western Addition, where musicians could experiment and play for the love of the music and the love of the community.

The Yardbird Club was also a direct response to the prerogatives of John Coltrane, specifically, Coltrane's creation of JOWCOL to protect his ownership of his compositions and his involvement with community jazz organizations like the Coltrane-Lateef-Olatunji Triumvirate in 1967. However, the church's Coltrane-inspired efforts with community jazz organizations in 1967, like the contemporaneous development of Horace Tapscott's UGMAA in Los Angeles or the AACM in Chicago, must be contextualized within the broader histories of African American jazz club ownership in urban America. The Yardbird Club and subsequent manifestations of the Coltrane Church would in fact play a vital role in the development of jazz in the San Francisco Bay Area by supporting a dedicated jazz left[3] and communities of jazz musicians and listeners seeking a living music undiluted by the demands of commercialism and open to constant change and innovation.

Franzo and Marina King were now bringing the music back to the people.

The history of jazz music in the San Francisco Bay Area is in fact an integral part of the history of regional African American economic and political development. The popularity of the New Orleans jazz sound—which was the principal sound of San Francisco jazz—from the turn of the century through the 1920s provided an economic well-spring for black entrepreneurship and property ownership in some of San Francisco's most coveted neighborhoods. Swing, nascent bebop forms, as well as early rhythm & blues and rock sustained black clubs and businesses throughout the Western Addition during the 1940s and '50s in another golden era of San Francisco jazz music known as "Harlem of the West." By the emergence of the next native sounds of acid jazz in the 1990s, the music had moved from traditional African American neighborhoods and black-owned clubs. And by the dawn of the new millennium, the music would be relocated back to the historically African American Western Addition and Hayes Valley neighborhoods under the control of non-profits and corporate sponsored festivals and concert halls with the assistance and blessings of the San Francisco Redevelopment Agency.

Although the population of African-Americans in San Francisco at the turn of the twentieth century represented only a fraction of the city's total population, this was a most industrious class of people and jazz music played a central role in their activities. African Americans owned many of the places where the music of Jelly Roll Morton could be heard and dances like the Texas Tommy could be experienced. As northern California citizens of all ethnic backgrounds and social classes gathered for the hottest entertainment of the era, these places became the core of a booming African American economy.

Jazz was also at the center of many social and political debates about morality and legality in early twentieth century Barbary Coast society. Unfortunately, the music was hardly the most central commodity being sold in San Francisco's Barbary Coast, and the birth and association of the music with drugs, gambling, and prostitution –a relationship that is consistent in almost all regional histories of jazz music- spelled its eventual demise as well as that of the fragile black economy that had been built on a tenuous foundation associated with illegality. Ignited by the church and stirred up by the San Francisco press and, in particular, the *San Francisco Examiner* newspaper, the "good" citizens of San Francisco initiated a morality campaign that ended the black jazz clubs and community on the Barbary Coast, albeit leaving intact much of the illegality and immorality that thrives even now. It is not difficult to interpret the morality laws designed to curb the licentiousness of the Barbary Coast as part of a sophisticated racial project aimed specifically at closing every black-owned Barbary Coast establishment and limiting the entrepreneurial aspirations of San Francisco's African American citizens.

African American jazz entrepreneurship would re-emerge during World War II to entertain a growing population of largely Louisiana and Texas migrants working on the San Francisco docks and living in the Western Addition and Fillmore Street. In the wake of the removal and internment of Japanese-American citizens who had been the dominant population of the Western Addition, the Fillmore would burst with a new club scene that again provided spaces for African American musicians to entertain and experiment. However, under the stress of urban redevelopment, this second wave of black club ownership waned and ultimately the contemporary San Francisco jazz scene became marked by corporate ownership and the exclusion of indigenous black musicians. In short, after two significant historical periods of cultural entrepreneurship, San Francisco's black community has lost control of the production and distribution of its music and a historically viable source of entrepreneurship.

The history of jazz music in San Francisco suggests that jazz was an important vehicle for entrepreneurship that the city aggressively dismantled through propaganda in the Barbary Coast era and largely through the San Francisco Redevelopment Agency in the Harlem of the West era. The ownership of jazz music has always been a racially contested space and in San Francisco it has been marked by a gradual displacement from African American community control to the control of corporate-sponsored concert halls and festivals. The impact of this displacement has meant the creation of an effectively racialized two-tiered system that has dimmed the performative opportunities of local musicians, backgrounded the historical contributions of local artists, and limited the communal pedagogy of the music.

In the wake of the demise of African American owned jazz clubs on the Barbary Coast and the later Harlem of the West era of the '40s and '50s, the entrepreneurial promise of the music was never fully realized and African American jazz communities have never since had the opportunity to develop outside of European American and corporate ownership. Now, devoid of the entrepreneurial vitality of the early twentieth century, jazz music seems hardly the substance from which communities can be built and sustained. At the same time, the aura of illegality and "red-light-ism" that permeated the early history of the music in so many parts of the country has dissipated and transformed the respectability and profitability of the music. By the 1990s and the advent of San Francisco's acid jazz movement, there wasn't even a respectable minority ownership of the music in African American-owned clubs, and by the new millennium it had moved almost entirely away from clubs and community organizations to the control of corporate-backed festivals and multi-million dollar concert halls.

The Barbary Coast

The history of Bay Area jazz music in its heyday in the early 1900s is brilliantly conveyed through the first person testimonies of the Barbary Coast musicians of that era in Tom Stoddard's *Jazz on the Barbary Coast*. Barbary Coast is a term that describes the northern portion of San Francisco "comprising both sides of Broadway and Pacific streets, and the cross streets between them, from Stockton Street to the Waterfront (then Battery Street)" (Stoddard 158). It is an era specific term. Stoddard has included the narratives of the great composer and self-proclaimed father of jazz Jelly Roll Morton, Reb Spikes, Charlie "Duke" Turner, drummer Alfred Levy,

Harry Mereness, and the elegant pianist, trumpeter and band leader Sid LeProtti whose testimonies serve as the centerpiece of Stoddard's book. In addition to being a wonderful series of recollections of the great African American musicians who lived and worked in San Francisco's Barbary Coast, Stoddard's book reveals a great deal about African American society in that era, and the complexities of the jazz communities of the Barbary Coast.

The Barbary Coast was absolutely the center of San Francisco nightlife in the early twentieth century. New Orleans cornetist Bunk Johnson, who helped launch a New Orleans revival in San Francisco in the 1940s, first ventured westward to the Barbary Coast in 1905, and ragtime and the blues filled the air (Hamlin *San Francisco Chronicle*, 2010). Most clubs were open 24 hours a day every day except election day (Stoddard 13). Women were available for dances and each dance with a woman cost twenty cents (13). Sid LeProtti remains mum on the standard costs of other services yet the dance halls clearly doubled as houses of prostitution. Musicians played between twenty-six and thirty dances and hour when business was good and they played everything from marches and mazurkas to the blues (13). A bottle of beer was fifty cents. The crowds represented the ethnic melting pot that is San Francisco, immigrants from the Philippines, Armenia, Portugal, to the usual coterie of pugnacious American sailors who gave the Barbary Coast its name. Scattered amidst the dance clubs were Chinese gambling joints and "hop" joints and opium and cocaine flowed freely on these streets (20).

Among the many African American owned establishments was the "Portuguese-Negro boy" Louis Gomez' club called the House of All Nations, Charlie Coster's, Jelly Roll Morton's club called the Jupiter, the Dew Drop Inn, the Squeeze Inn. Perhaps one of the most famous of the many great clubs founded and maintained by African American entrepreneurs was Purcell's, founded by two ex–Pullman porters Sam King and Lew Purcell who later split and held two separate clubs. Sid Le Protti recalls, "Purcell's was one of the most famous Negro dance halls in the country and was located at 520 Pacific Street in one of the first buildings put up after the fire of 1906. They had started up on Broadway and then had moved down to Pacific Street. Pacific Street was the main stem of the Barbary Coast. We used to call it Terrific Street" (Stoddard 10).

And the money was good. As a band leader, Sid LeProtti recalls, "In them days, my salary was thirty-five dollars a week for playin' with the band and then playin' all night on the piano. The men in the band got twenty-five dollars a week because they cut out at one o'clock. Imagine, I averaged $465.33 a month over a period of twenty years. That's good money in them days, and that includes the seventy-five dollars—which was the most I made one night—on that one song" (Stoddard 61).

However, the black establishments of the Barbary Coast offered more than just black music for the white masses. These were black owned establishments that employed black women and catered to white men. European American establishments also prostituted black women. The Barbary Coast had its share of what were known as "crib bordellos." One, located at 620 Jackson Street, offered an international cast of prostitutes divided according to different floors. "There were several unique features about it—one was that it was owned by the city fathers and quickly became known as the Municipal Crib. Another was that Mexican girls served themselves up in the basement at twenty-five cents, Americans and other nationalities were on the first and second floors at fifty cents, French girls worked the third floor at seventy-five cents, and black girls held the fourth floor at fifty-cents. The girls rented cribs on an eight-hour basis and lived elsewhere because the rent, including protection, was sky-high. Chinese girls were available throughout the Chinatown-area cribs at the lowest rates. They were called "slave girls" but their condition of servitude was far worse than slavery and only a rare one survived past twenty-five years old" (Stoddard 165).

Sid Le Protti recalls the demise of the Barbary Coast: "The beginning of the decline of the Barbary Coast was a crusade started by the Reverend Paul Smith when he exposed all the doings that was going on. At that time, my band was playin' at the Porta La Louvre [circa 1916]. On the Barbary Coast they had to cut out the afternoon dancing –we used to play in the afternoon too- and then there was nothin' but evening dancing. Then finally in our travels around we finally come back to Purcell's. It started to get rough in 1915, it started getting rougher in 1916, and it got worse in 1917. It got to the place where they ruled out all of the sportin' houses. Then they got kind of rigid with us. They stopped all the dancin' in the boundary of the Barbary Coast. They let the dancin' go on across town in what they called the high-class tenderloin around O'Farrell Street where the Black Cat and Coffee Dan's were" (Stoddard 62).

Tom Stoddard editorializes, "The actual decline of the Barbary Coast began in 1913, led by the *San Francisco Examiner's* crusade to destroy 'the open market for commercialized vice' and replace it with 'wholesome fun.'" He continues: "To the voice of this powerful Hearst newspaper, whose owner had cavorted across the pages of history enjoying more than wholesome fun, was added the voice of a Methodist street preacher named the Reverend Paul Smith, World War I, and a changed social milieu" (Stoddard 207).

New morality laws were enforced through endless police raids, effectively closing many establishments. With the Red Light Abatement Law houses of prostitution were shut down for one year and, with owners unable to rent the premises and thereby pay taxes, properties were lost (Stoddard 65). Hard liquor was forbidden long before the national Prohibition era and establishments were raided and closed for providing hard liquor (64).

Harlem of the West: San Francisco Jazz in the 1930s, '40s, '50s, and '60s

The history of jazz in San Francisco between the end of the ragtime era of the Barbary Coast and the contemporary rebirth of jazz is poorly chronicled. According to Ted Gioia, whose seminal *West Coast Jazz* chronicles the history of the music in California from its earlier twentieth century roots to the present, jazz music in northern California in fact developed little from that nascent New Orleans sound of the Barbary Coast (Gioia 61).

Gioia and other established jazz historians have unfortunately missed the development of black community-centered jazz venues on Fillmore Street during the 1940s and '50s in what has been termed "Harlem of the West." Elizabeth Pepin and Lewis Watts have recently chronicled much of this history in *Harlem of the West: The San Francisco Fillmore Jazz Era*. Pepin and Watts testify to a dynamic environment where the likes of Billie Holiday, John Coltrane, Chet Baker, and Dexter Gordon experimented with their sounds in an after-hours community jazz setting. "During the musical heyday of the Fillmore District in the 1940s and 1950s, the area known as the Harlem of the West was a swinging place where you could leave your house Friday night and go from club to party to bar until the wee hours of Monday morning. For more than two decades, music played nonstop to more than a dozen clubs where Young Turks from the neighborhood could mix with seasoned professionals and maybe even get a chance to jump onstage to prove their musical mettle. Filling out the streets in the twenty-square-block area were restaurants, pool halls, theaters, and stores, many of them owned and run by African Americans, Japanese Americans, and Filipino-Americans. The neighborhood was a giant multicultural party throbbing with excitement and music" (Pepin and Watts 13).

Pepin and Watts introduce us to 31 African American clubs in the Western Addition, beginning with the 1933 opening of Jack's Tavern (aka Jack's of Sutter) that was the first club managed by and catering to an African American population (72). Coincident with the outbreak of World War II and the second great southern-northern migration of African

Americans, these new clubs included Club Alabam, the New Orleans Swing Club, the Long Bar, the California Theater, Elsie's Breakfast Nook, the Texas Playhouse, the Champagne Supper Club, Leola King's Blue Mirror, the Havana Club, Jackson's Nook, the Congo Club, Minnie's Can-Do Club, and Jimbo's Bop City (72). The 31 clubs in the Western Addition provided avenues for performance, experimentation, and earning a living for many native Bay Area African American musicians including but not limited to saxophonist Jerome Richardson, singer Sugar Pie DeSanto, saxophonist John Handy, pianist and singer Frank Jackson, saxophonist Bobbie Webb, guitarist Junius Simmons, bassist Skippy Warren, bandleader Saunders King, singer Johnny Mathis, bandleader Johnny Otis, singer Etta James, bassist Vernon Alley, and saxophonist Pony Poindexter. Many of these musicians as well as the history of Harlem of the West remained largely unknown until the Pepin and Watts book; a testimony to the destructive cultural power of urban redevelopment and black removal.

In light of Gioia's failure to document the internationally recognized phenomenon of the Fillmore's Harlem of the West, it's difficult to accept his conclusions about the static development of jazz music in the San Francisco Bay Area during the war years. Gioia writes: "Whatever pioneering spirit San Francisco captured in those early days of jazz disappeared in later years. Modern jazz musicians found San Francisco an inhospitable environment long after the music had made inroads in many other cities. In the late 1940s, when jazz had already undergone a revolution elsewhere, San Francisco was still holding on to the same New Orleans-inflected music—now played mostly by white enthusiasts—it had embraced after the Great War" (62).

Gioia's sweeping conclusions about the static development of the music are refuted in small measure by much of the oral testimony provided by Pepin and Watts. Speaking of opportunities for musical experimentation at Jimbo's Bop City, Federico Cervantes notes, "I played at Bop City for ten years straight, and then on and off. I got a chance to experiment with chord progressions and things of that nature, even when I was playing behind the other musicians" (Pepin and Watts 152). John Handy comments, "Nothing is like New York, musically speaking, but when you consider how small the African American population is in San Francisco, we did okay. There wasn't a Fillmore sound per se, but Dexter Gordon lived here for a while, Charles Mingus lived here. Vernon and Eddie Alley and Pony Poindexter were from here" (152.). Vallejo-born Johnny Otis speaks of specifically looking for talent in San Francisco at the Booker T. Washington Hotel & Cocktail Lounge: "I used to come up to the Fillmore from

Los Angeles, looking for talent. I found a lot of musicians and singers that way. It was fertile ground" (132). Jim Moore underscores the Fillmore as a center for a great musical education and contextualizes the downfall of jazz music within histories of urban redevelopment and corporatization: "Before redevelopment, the Fillmore was a neighborhood. When your musicians weren't working, they would go to jam sessions and create. And when you went to a session, if say, a trumpet player played a certain type of line, and you were a trumpet player, you'd want to do something better than he did when you'd go back. One thing would feed off the other. It wasn't about money—it was about creating. That's one of the things that caused the elimination of the art form. Now it's all big corporations. Corporations have come in and the bottom line is the dollar" (176).

What Gioia does accomplish, however, is outlining the differential evolutionary paths of heavily racialized and segregated expressions of jazz music. Gioia indicates how in the wake of the demise of the Barbary Coast, the San Francisco jazz scene of the '40s and '50s was heavily segregated, inhibiting the success of African American musicians and the growth of the new music. Gioia characterizes the San Francisco scene of the 1940s and '50s as "the last bastion of white traditional jazz," and notes the restrictive practices of the local musicians' unions "black musicians found a less than equal opportunity to make their names while staying in San Francisco" and further, "That modern jazz could survive in such a setting was for some time open to question. That it would eventually thrive there was something approaching a miracle" (Gioia 62).

Gioia argues that the San Francisco jazz scene of the '40s, '50s, and '60s was so limited for black innovators that even the sojourns of Parker and Gillespie—important "diplomatic" presentations of the new bebop sound—in Los Angeles and their all-too brief appearances in San Francisco yielded little toward the development of bebop and more modern sounds. Charlie Parker appeared in this period at such notable white-owned San Francisco clubs as the Blackhawk, and the Say When.

In light of the history of Harlem of the West, Gioia's characterization of the San Francisco jazz scene as limited to the New Orleans sound is clearly a characterization of the stunted progress of white and largely commercialized jazz being played in white-owned establishments. The same lack of experimentation and musical progress cannot be definitively said to have been characteristic of African American owned clubs in Fillmore and the growing Harlem of the West.

It's unfortunate that Gioia's narrative completely ignores the Fillmore in the 1930s, '40s, '50s, and '60s. In Gioia's narrative the Prohibition-era demise of the Barbary Coast seemed not only to be the death knell for African American owned clubs but also of the employment of African American musicians. However, Gioia's mention of the role of segregation in the differential development of jazz music in the San Francisco Bay Area proves invaluable because it is part of a legacy that continues to haunt African American musicians in the Bay Area in the present age.

The Acid Jazz Scene

In the mid–1990s a new jazz scene emerged in the San Francisco Bay Area with an infectious, danceable fusion of hip-hop, funk, Afrobeats, and jazz. "Acid jazz"[4] was an original and locally produced sound, a home-grown genre that featured an innovative fusion of jazz, rap, funk, and rock and such notable local artists as the Charlie Hunter Trio, Mingus Amungus, the Broun Fellinis, and Alphabet Soup. Acid jazz standouts T.J. Kirk, for example, a quartet composed of three guitarists Charlie Hunter, John Schott, Will Bernard, and drummer Scott Amendola, played what has been described as a "raucous and loose-limbed" fusion of Rashaan Roland Kirk meets James Brown-inspired funk jazz (Hamlin *San Francisco Chronicle*, 1995). The acid jazz scene notably focused on local musicians and was almost entirely supported by local clubs rather than corporate-backed festivals and foundations and featured a broader community of local musicians including Berkeley High graduate Charlie Hunter and Kevin Carnes, David Boyce, and Kirk Peterson, who founded Broun Fellinis in San Francisco in 1991.

Although it remained in locally owned clubs and small venues, acid jazz marked the relocation of the music from a traditional African American community—North Beach in the Barbary Coast era and the Western Addition/Fillmore in the Harlem of the West era—for the first time in San Francisco jazz history. Furthermore, acid jazz did not involve black entrepreneurship. The majority of nightclubs that featured the acid jazz sound were located in the South of market or SOMA district amidst its renovated industrial lofts, and specifically, Folsom Street. The Up and Down Club, the Paradise Lounge, Club DV8 and Bruno's were among the more popular acid jazz venues.

When the acid jazz scene fizzled, many local Bay Area musicians like guitarist Charlie Hunter and Alphabet Soup keyboardist Dred Scott left for New York. This exodus of a native born sound in effect reinforced the long-standing notion of the inferiority of San Francisco as a "jazz town" as the city's most innovative musicians of the era headed east to make a viable living with their sound. Certainly those invested in the possibility of developing San Francisco as a legitimate and competitive jazz marketplace, must have realized the need for greater infrastructural development and support. And in the new millennium, the confluence of corporate-sponsored festivals and opportunities presented by redevelopment in the Fillmore/Western Addition and contiguous Hayes Valley neighborhoods would spark a resurgence of this notion of San Francisco Jazz.

SFJazz Heritage Center and the New Millennium Jazz Scene

In the post-acid jazz era, the Bay Area experienced a revival of interest in jazz music that many have likened to the glory years of the ragtime clubs on the Barbary Coast and Harlem of the West. The new millennium popularity of jazz in the Bay Area has, however, not led to the development of African American owned and community-centered venues but rather the increasing corporatization of the music and culture of jazz. Not only has the music moved away from San Francisco's traditional African American communities, a move foreshadowed by the acid jazz era, but the local clubs that flourished under the acid jazz scene have diminished in their importance as venues for new sounds. The new San Francisco jazz scene, in spite of its relocation to the Western Addition and neighboring Hayes Valley neighborhoods, ironically finds itself alienated from communities that gave rise to the music, under increasing corporate control, and featured in elaborate concert halls and on the stages of corporate-backed festivals rather than locally-owned clubs or community organizations.

There were two primary corporate contenders in the early new millennium business of San Francisco Jazz: The coupling of Yoshi's and the San Francisco Jazz Heritage Center in the redeveloped Western Addition, and SFJazz in the adjacent Hayes Valley neighborhood.

Yoshi's, is a jazz and sushi supper club founded by Kaz Kajimura and Yoshi Akiba in 1974 on Claremont Avenue in Oakland[5] that opened an upscale club in the revitalized Western Addition as part of the San Francisco Jazz Heritage Center and the Fillmore Center in November 2007. Thanks to an initial $4.4 million dollar loan[6] from the San Francisco Redevelopment Agency, Fillmore Heritage Center developer Michael Johnson[7] created a 28,000 square-foot venue with a 420-seat nightclub and a 370-seat Japanese restaurant and lounge with "curving walls and soffits, big sculptural Japanese lanterns, and a mix of dark and blond woods" (Hamlin, *San Francisco Chronicle*, 2004). In similar fashion to the SFJazz Collective,

Yoshi's was launched by a super-group of out-of-town musicians including drummer Roy Haynes, vibraphonist Gary Burton, saxophonists Kenny Garrett and Ravi Coltrane, and trumpeter Nicholas Payton. Yoshi's itself is part of the larger complex of the Fillmore Heritage Center, "a $75 million redevelopment project that includes a 12-story condominium tower, a contemporary soul food restaurant and a 6,000-square-foot Jazz Heritage Center" (Hamlin, *San Francisco Chronicle*, 2004).

Concomitant with the corporatization of jazz performative spaces is the failure to properly preserve the local cultural history of the African American participation in San Francisco jazz. This is also a contested space characterized by increasing corporate encroachment. In 2008, one year after the launch of Yoshi's, the San Francisco Jazz Heritage Center was launched as a cultural centerpiece of the Fillmore Heritage Center and its partners, Yoshi's and the new corporate entertainment and dining in the historic jazz district.[8] The Jazz Heritage Center, funded by the Koret Foundation, with a distinguished board of former administrators from San Francisco State University, Stanford University, the San Francisco Botanical Garden Society, real estate development and corporate market research,[9] is primarily dedicated to elevating the national and international reputation of the San Francisco jazz scene and preserving the contributions to San Francisco jazz history of such legendary icons as Ella Fitzgerald and Duke Ellington, and *secondarily* "to recognize the numerous local musicians who developed careers alongside them," according to www.jazzheritagecenter.org/pages/about.html.

Located in the Hayes Valley neighborhood is SFJazz, founded in 1982 by Randall Kline as a year-long presenting organization that produced the San Francisco Jazz Festival that commissioned new music, ran educational programs, and put on shows in local theaters, clubs and concert halls. On January 20, 2013, SFJazz launched the SFJazz Center, a permanent home for SFJazz, and "the first stand-alone major facility in the county devoted to the swinging American art form" (Hamlin, *San Francisco Chronicle*, 2010). The center, itself a 35,000 square-foot glass and steel structure, boasts a $64 million dollar 700-seat distinctly urban concert hall located on the corner of Fell and Franklin streets, and sits on the edge of the upscale restaurant culture of Hayes Valley down the street from the Davies Symphony Hall and the Opera House with its "ethereal cool" where "translucent bars float in the darkness like abstract piano keys" (King).

SFJazz boasts an all-star performance ensemble, the SFJazz Collective, launched in 2004. In 2014 the ensemble featured Miguel Zenon, a Puerto Rican alto saxophonist; David Sanchez, a Puerto Rican tenor saxophonist; Avishai Cohen, a New York-based trumpeter; Robin Eubanks, a trombonist and Philadelphia native; Warren Wolf, a vibraphonist from Baltimore, Maryland; Edward Simon, a Venezuelan pianist; Matt Penman, a New Zealand bassist; and Obed Calvaire, a Miami drummer. Perhaps the most prominent of SFJazz's founding members was tenor saxophonist Joe Lovano, a native of Cleveland, Ohio.

The incredible success of the annual SFJazz Festival has drawn attention to the Bay Area as a new Mecca for jazz music, surpassing, in the minds of some critics, the contemporary New York jazz scene. *New York Times* writer Peter Watrous, in an article from 1996 titled "In San Francisco, Jazz's Friendliest Context Since the '40's," commented, "As the festival has grown, so has the jazz scene here. In the last four or five years, jazz and jazz-related music have surpassed rock and pop in the new clubs. To go to Bruno's, in the Mission District, or the Up and Down Club in SOMA, the South of Market area, is to enter a world where jazz has once again become part of the social fabric, the background music of choice" (*New York Times*, November 2, 1996). One of the things that Watrous appreciates is the lower cover price of Bay Area clubs.

The present resurgence of jazz music in San Francisco since the birth and death of acid jazz and the development of SFJazz and the San Francisco Jazz Heritage Center and Yoshi's have nothing to do with black entrepreneurship and ownership in San Francisco. In fact, given the history and the circumstances surrounding the demise of the Barbary Coast, one could argue that the resurgence of interest in the music is in part predicated on the lack of black ownership and control of clubs and venues; in other words, it's now "safe" to appreciate this great American art form. Indeed the music is no longer as socially challenging as it may have been in the 1950s, '60s, and '70s and has become in effect the new American classical music, wholly embraced by white and black bourgeois society, its red light district origins having been dismissed, its sounds now archived and taught by universities and institutes and arts foundations. There is a kind of mood of "imperialistic nostalgia"[10] surrounding the present "classicization" of jazz music as well as the modern San Francisco jazz scene, an ability to look back on it lovingly now that the social revolutions and racial uplift it once sparked have been long forgotten.

The new millennium of San Francisco jazz has so very little to do with African American empowerment in San Francisco that it is not surprisingly coincident with the flight of many African American families from the city as real property continues to rise to inhuman levels. In fact the rise of jazz in the Bay Area has been linked to a new class of young entrepreneurs, a class in large measure responsible for the massive gen-trification of traditionally black neighborhoods in San Francisco. The acid jazz movement was less centrally located than in the Barbary Coast era, although a number of popular clubs were located around the Upper Mar-ket Street area and the south of Market Street area (SOMA). None of the city's core jazz clubs during the acid jazz era, including also the Up and Down Club and Bruno's were located in traditionally African American neighborhoods.

The dislocation of the contemporary Bay Area jazz scene from tra-ditionally African American neighborhoods and ownership is coincident with its profitability and increasing corporatization. In a November 17, 1996, article in the *Chicago Tribune* in 1996, jazz critic Howard Reich noted that "the San Francisco Jazz Festival has a budget of $1.6 million" and furthermore receives its financial support from a diverse array of cor-porate interests including Citibank, Transamerica, The National Endow-ment for the Arts, the city's Grants for the Arts, Nortel, and the James Irvine Foundation. Sony and Starbucks have in the past, paid for adver-tising for the festival. The festival began in 1983 under the control of the nonprofit San Francisco Jazz Festival with a meager budget of $27,000, according to the *San Diego Union-Tribune* of October 30, 1996. In its early years the festival employed only local musicians, but the musicians it had to select from include such luminaries as Bobby McFerrin, Tony Williams, John Handy, Bobby Hutcherson, and Joe Henderson, according to the *San Francisco Chronicle*, November 24, 1996. By 1986 the festival began drawing from musicians outside of the Bay Area and has come to encompass a very international jazz perspective.

The growth of the SFJazz festival surely mirrored the growth of jazz in the Bay Area in the 1980s to the present, both in terms of its financial success and in terms of its increasingly diverse presentation of the music. As the festival has broadened to include tributes to avant-garde composer Don Cherry and performances of Bach cello sonatas, fusion groups, or klezmer musicians, so too has the local club scene become increasingly diverse. Don Heckman, writing for the *Los Angeles Times*, comments, "Beyond the festival are the far-ranging jazz styles and attitudes heard in dozens of local clubs, all existing comfortably in a city with a reputation for uncompromising receptivity to individual differences," and further, quoting a director of corporate relations for the festival, "People come here because they feel this is a safe place to be themselves" (October 30, 1996).

Writing for the *San Jose Mercury News* in 2003, Richard Sheinin links the growth of corporate-backed festivals and institutions with the demise of community arts organizations and the independent club scene in the Bay Area. "At a time when arts organizations are going belly up or bleeding red, Northern California jazz festivals are growing in size and prominence.... By marketing jazz as high art, promoters are tapping a new market and making a grand cultural statement. Right now, despite a struggling club scene, there is more jazz in the Bay Area than anywhere else in the country outside New York." Citing Berkeley-native Joshua Redman, one of the few local musicians with a broad national appeal, Scheinin views the rise of corporate-backed festivals and foundations as a national phenomenon that threatens to marginalize the voices of local artists.

In spite of the San Francisco Jazz Festival drawing almost exclusively on local talent in its early years, the Bay Area jazz scene in the 1990s remained plagued by racialism and a fundamental distrust of its local musicians (Gioia 111). Unfortunately much of this distrust is directed at African American musicians who are even now rarely courted by local companies. Referring to the 1980s and '90s, Gioia comments, "It is all too telling that, even with the preponderance of jazz record companies in Northern California, the two biggest black jazz talents to emerge from the area in recent years—Bobby McFerrin and Stanley Jordan—were ignored by the local record labels and had to go back east to be 'discovered.'"

The most contemporary symbol of the distrust of local African American musicians was represented by the controversy surrounding the 2007 Yoshi's anniversary album that somehow managed to omit any black performers. The Yoshi's anniversary disc included tracks from Marian McPartland, Joe Pass, Joey DeFrancesco, Poncho Sanchez, Madeleine Peyroux, and Robben Ford. The recording could have included frequent Yoshi's performers McCoy Tyner, Elvin Jones, Oscar Peterson, Anthony Braxton, Wallace Roney, Mulgrew Miller, Branford Marsalis, Taj Mahal, Sonny Fortune, or Bay Area native and favorite Joshua Redman. In Jesse Hamlin and Steven Winn's June 2, 2007, article from the *San Francisco Chronicle*, "Shamed, Yoshi's Pulls CD," Yoshi's owner Kaz Kajimura and artistic director Peter Williams attributed the omission of African American artists to "'haste and expediency.' 'This was done on the spur of the moment, and we didn't have a lot of time and research to put into it,' said Kajimura. Yoshi's began working on the project in late March to mark the club's 10 years in Oakland in May."[11] Yoshi's addressed the controversy by withdrawing the disc and issuing a public apology.

Perhaps the most personal egregious incursion was the decision to exclude the Coltrane Church from the 2005 SFJazz celebration of John

Coltrane's music. Adopting the Lincoln Center model, SFJazz committed itself to honoring one composer each year. Writing for the *San Francisco Chronicle*, David Rubien speaks of a band that SFJazz put together featuring Joshua Redman, Bobby Hutcherson, Nicholas Payton that will perform seven different shows, and along the way Rubien mistakenly alludes to a planned appearance by Coltrane's son "Ravi Shankar." One show featured seven Coltrane tunes.

John Coltrane and Community Jazz

I have made the argument that the history of San Francisco jazz is linked to the entrepreneurial aspirations of generations of African American migrants and, further, that the steady movement of the music from black-owned clubs and community organizations toward corporate-sponsored festivals and concert halls has been a consequence of the gradual disenfranchisement of African Americans in the city, much of which has been effectuated by the San Francisco Redevelopment Agency. Before examining the efforts of the Coltrane Church within this context, it might do to inquire about John Coltrane's position on the corporatization of jazz and the efficacy of community efforts to retain local control of the music.

George Lewis has argued that John Coltrane was a critical figure for community jazz advocates. Critiquing community jazz precursors to the Association for the Advancement of Colored Musicians (AACM),[12] Lewis notes, "According to the Nigerian musician Babatunde Olatunji, Coltrane and Yusef Lateef were working with him on plans to organize an independent performance space and booking agency. Olatunji portrayed the saxophonist as declaring in their conversation that 'we need to sponsor our own concerts, promote them, and perform in them. This way we will not only learn how to take a risk but will not have to accept the dictates of anybody about how long you should play, what to play and what you get'" (Lewis 91).

According to Lewis, Coltrane, Lateef, and Olatunji drafted a mission statement: "1. To regard each other as equal partners in all categories; 2. Not to allow any booking agent or promoter to present one group without the other two members of the Triumvirate; and 3. To explore the possibility of teaching the music of our people in conservatories, colleges and universities where only European musical experience dominates and is being perpetuated (91)."

The Triumvirate of Coltrane-Lateef-Olatunji ended with Coltrane's untimely passing in 1967, but the organization managed to stage a community-based performance as an exemplar for later organizations. "One of Coltrane's last performances, titled 'The Roots of Africa,' was produced by the new organization in April 1967 at Olatunji's Center of African Culture in Harlem. While Coltrane's subsequent passing apparently ended this collaboration, the need for change was evident to many musicians, and the efficacy of highly individualistic strategies for accomplishing their goals was very much in question" (91.).

Coltrane's Triumvirate was consistent with the general aims of what was termed by *Down Beat* magazine in 1964 as the "October Revolution in Jazz" (Lewis 92). The 1960s was a consciousness-raising moment for many jazz musicians that reverberated throughout the country, as musicians became increasingly aware of inequities in publishing, ownership of concert spaces, artistic control, the impact of commercialism, racism, and working conditions. For so many, from Horace Tapscott's UGMAA to Richard Abrams, Steve McCall, Phil Cochran, and Jodie Christian's AACM, the solution was to return the music back to the community in order to insure both economic and aesthetic control and combat the economic exploitation of largely white and corporate-owned clubs, studios, and publishing houses.

The Triumvirate continues to be an important precedent for the community musicians of the Coltrane Church. In a Winter 2001 church newsletter titled "Expression: A Publication of the African Orthodox Church Jurisdiction of the West," then Rev. Sister Wanika King-Stephens notes in a review of the compact disc release of *The Olatunji Concert: The Last Live Recording*, "It is believed that Saint John Coltrane wanted to study with Olatunji and when Olatunji had the idea to start the center, Coltrane helped fund the center. Upon completion, Saint John was the first to perform in the space. This album features that live performance and was recorded just three months before the ascension of Saint John Coltrane." Observing the power of Coltrane's performance in this community setting, she further notes, "This session is not for the typical dinner jazz connoisseurs. This is John Coltrane in the raw. There are no punches pulled in this session."

The Coltrane Church and the Contemporary Community Jazz Scene

By the 1990s the Coltrane Church was one of only a few remaining community-centered jazz organizations in an emerging context of corporate control of the production and distribution of jazz music. With the exception of the now defunct Upper Room, a juice bar and community

Archbishop King solos at an outreach performance at the Upper Room in the mid–1990s.

music scene for persons recovering from alcohol and drug addiction; the African American-owned Rasselas Jazz Club and Restaurant[13]; Sheba's Piano Lounge[14]; John Lee Hooker's Boom Boom Room; and the Savanna Jazz Club, to name a few, the landscape of specifically African American-owned jazz clubs became sparsely populated. With respect to the preservation of the history of African American musical forms in the Bay Area, organizations with deep community roots such as the African American Art and Culture Complex founded in 1989, the Ella Hill Hutch Community Center founded in 1981, Thomas Simpson's AfroSolo Theatre and AfroSolo Festival, Rhodessa Jones and Idris Ackamoor's Cultural Odyssey engage the space of preservation and performance of local, community artists.

For its part, the Coltrane Church had long followed Coltrane's support of community-centered jazz. From the Yardbird Club forward, the Coltrane Church provided a forum for instruction and community performance through Ohnedaruth, the Sisters of Compassion, and the reggae-inspired Mystic Youth. Such diverse local icons as Charlie Parker acolyte and alto saxophonist Bishop Norman "New Testament" Williams; and percussionist E.W. Wainwright (*Roots of Jazz*), a veteran of Horace Tapscott's community jazz organization, the Union of God's Musicians and

Ohnedaruth performs at the Upper Room in the mid–1990s. From left, the Rev. Franzo King, Jr.; Archbishop King; Fr. Roberto DeHaven; Jon Ingle; Bishop Norman "New Testament" Williams; Clarence Stephens.

Artists Ascending (UGMAA) in Los Angeles performed Sundays at the Coltrane Church. David Boyce of the Broun Fellinis spent many a Sunday in the early 1990s playing his horn at the Coltrane Church. Jack Boulware notes, "When David Boyce moved to the city in 1991, before forming the Broun Fellinis, he spent many memorable Sundays playing his horn at the church. 'They were steppin' out,' he says. "There must have been six saxes up there. Being in church, playing space music—it was great. If they happen to believe that one of the most intense musicians of the 20th century is a saint…" He shrugs, as if to say, 'So be it.'"[15]

Ohnedaruth has been a performance venue for pianist and drummer Frederick Harris (Albert "Tootie" Heath, George Coleman, Dizzy Gillespie and Billy Higgins, Bishop Norman Williams, E.W. Wainwright, Eddie Marshall, Eddie Moore, Jules Broussard, Margie Baker, Ed Kelly, Faye Carol); tenor saxophonist Roberto "Bluewater" DeHaven (Watermusic, Jungle Grooves, Drew Gardener Trio, Anthony Bryant's New Reign, Pearl Ubungen Dancers and Musicians, dancer JoAnna Haigood, E.W. Wainwright's African Roots of Jazz, Kaliedophone); tenor saxophonist Franzo King, Jr. (Wallace Roney, Carlos Santana and Wynton Marsalis); bassist Clarence

Stephens (Cecil Taylor, Don Cherry, Tony Williams, Eddie Henderson, Bobby McFerrin, David Garibaldi, Steve Turre, Michael Clark, John Lewis and The Modern Jazz Quartet, Ernie Watts, Rasheid Ali); bassist Wanika King-Stephens (Dream Forward), violinist Jon Ingle, drummer Anthony Bryant (Anthony Bryant's New Reign); flautist and alto saxophonist Ira Levin (Comfy Chair, Sun House, Uncle Eye and the Strange Change Machine, White People, The Levins), and drummer Rama John Lee Coltrane King (Ohnedaruth).

Most of the members of Ohnedaruth grew up in the church and as jazz musicians and picked up their instruments for the first time in the context of Ohnedaruth. Deacon Max Hoff, for example, lived a monk's life, residing in a basement beneath the Divisadero facility and immersing himself in the music. This tradition continues for vocalist Cartier King and saxophonist Franzo King III, both of whom learned the language of jazz and acquired their initial performance experiences during Sunday services.

Ohnedaruth has additionally been accompanied by such Bay Area legends as Narada Michael Walden, Carlos Santana and has appeared at festivals in Antibes and Paris, France. On February 8, 2008, Ohnedaruth performed at Cité de la Musique in Paris, France as part of a festival of spiritual music, accompanied by E.W. Wainwright on drums.

The Coltrane Church has also sponsored its own alternative, community-based festivals. Between 1995 and 2011 the Coltrane Church attempted a more focused engagement of the San Francisco Jazz Festival and greatly expanded its alternative community-centered jazz events. Among these was "A Night Called Freedom," a Saturday June 28, 1997, summer fund-raising concert held at St. Gregory's Episcopal Church in the Potrero Hills neighborhood featuring the voices of Reverend Mother Marina King, and Sisters Angela Dean-Baham and Deborah Wright. Many of the church's community arts partners were present for a benefit festival held March 17, 2000, at Bimbo's in North Beach to assist the church with relocation in the wake of rent increases imposed on its 351 Divisadero location. The concert featured percussionist E.W. Wainwright, a church ally, percussionist John Santos, the Ralph Carney Quintet, pianist Chad Wagner, and the Broun Fellinis (Sullivan). In the winter of 2001, Bro. Frederick Harris held a solo piano concert titled "From Mozart to Monk," and evening that was further complimented by a proclamation from the office of San Francisco Mayor Willie Brown proclaiming July 20 as the official Saint John Coltrane Day.

Under the leadership of a new pastor, Wanika King-Stephens, the Coltrane Church initiated a benefit concert series in 2011 that represented

Above and below: Ohnedaruth performs with guitarist Carlos Santana (clapping, second from left in beach photo) in Nice, France, in 1992.

perhaps the most organized and consistent use of the incredibly talented musicians among its congregation since the church's founding and incorporation. Featuring performances at local clubs (e.g., Rasselas), receptive churches seeking to integrate jazz music into their worship services (e.g., Calvary Presbyterian Church) and in their 1286 Fillmore Street facility, the early performances of the Coltrane Consciousness Concert Series featured Destiny Muhammad a.k.a. "The Harpist from the Hood" and the Destiny Muhammad Trio, and the Sacred Music Concert with Minister of Music Fred Harris, E.W. Wainwright, Ritchie Howell, Gary Brown, and Destiny Muhammad. Later in the fall of that same year the church launched an ambitious and highly successful three-day Equinox Festival of Sound and Dance in celebration of the 85th birthday of John Coltrane. Held at Calvin Hall at the Calvary Presbyterian Church, the festival included performances by the Frederick Harris Trio, John Handy, vocalist Ann Mack (sister of Mother Marina King), guest performances by Ohnedaruth saxophonists Fr. Roberto DeHaven and Fr. Max Hoff, tap dancers Toes Tiranoff and Megan Haungs, and spoken word by Marlee-I Hand, Archbishop King's youngest child.

On December 8, 2014, the St. John Will-I-Am Coltrane African Orthodox Church presented a free program at Grace Cathedral on San Francisco's Nob Hill, celebrating not only the 50th anniversary of John Coltrane *A Love Supreme* recording, but also calling for universal brotherhood and peace in the spirit of Coltrane work and life. This concert and prayer service was organized within the context of national attention to an epidemic of police murders of black men and women and the failure of grand juries across the country to indict police officers for obvious misconduct and racially motivated violence. The most notable of these incidents involved months of social protest sparked by the August 9, 2014, shooting of Michael Brown by Officer Darren Wilson in Ferguson, Missouri, and the failure to indict Officer Daniel Pantaleo for the murder of Eric Garner as a result of an illegal chokehold committed on July 17, 2014, in New York City as officers attempted to arrest Mr. Garner for selling "loose" cigarettes. As the concert and prayer service commenced, #BlackLivesMatter protestors in Berkeley, California, were shutting down access to the I-80 freeway in the East Bay.

The collaboration between Grace Cathedral and the St. John Will-I-Am Coltrane African Orthodox Church came at a critical time in Bay Area and national history, bringing the church back to an issue that it had long been involved in since the murder of Oscar Grant by BART (Bay Area Raid Transit) police officer Johannes Mehserle on New Year's Day

2009 at the Fruitvale Station in Oakland, California. The event was supported by the Rt. Rev. Marc Andrus, Bishop of Grace Cathedral, and among the notable activist San Francisco ministers in attendance were the Rev. Amos Brown, the Rev. Townsend, and Min. Christopher Muhammad (Nation of Islam).

Musically, in addition to the core members of Ohnedaruth (Archbishop King, Pastor Wanika King-Stephens, Frederick Harris, Max Hoff), the program also featured Destiny Muhammad (harp), E.W. Wainwright (drums), Richard Howell (tenor), Pascal Bokar Thiam (guitar), Dylan Jennings (baritone), and Tony Gil (harmonica). Among the Sisters of Compassion present were Supreme Mother Marina King, Marlee-I-Hand, Erinne Johnson, Cartier King, Desiree McCloskey, the Rev. Makeda Nueckel, the Rev. Mother Gloria Fisher, and the Rev. Mother Bonnie Lee. In an interesting transition, Marlee-I-Hand was the featured soloist for the church's rendition of Psalm 23 during the performance of "A Love Supreme: Acknowledgment," a central feature of the Coltrane Liturgy. The program also featured the Savannah African Jazz Dance Group and Minsters of Tap Percussion, Toes Tiranoff and Megan Haungs. Supreme Mother Marina King's sister Ann Mack sang a solo selection after the Archbishop's message of peace.

The Jazz Left

This contemporary cultural contestation between the local and national/international or the community v. the corporate, is best conceptualized as a struggle between the "Jazz Right v. Jazz Left," terms coined by Herman S. Gray in *Cultural Moves: African Americans and the Politics of Representation* (2005). Employing the late Stuart Hall's theory of cultural representation in order to tackle contemporary contestations of cultural production in American jazz music, Gray contrasts the "Jazz Right" politics of traditionalist Wynton Marsalis with the anti-canonical "Jazz Left" movement with its central figures of Ornette Coleman, Steve Coleman, Don Byron, Gerri Allen, Greg Osby, and Cassandra Wilson, to name a few. Gray articulates the relationship between Wynton Marsalis' unique blend of conservative and resistant cultural politics and his formalist and preservationist attitudes toward the jazz tradition. With respect to Marsalis, Gray notes, "jazz, according to Marsalis, must be formally studied, systematically codified, and practiced through performance, education, and institutional recognition" (37). Gray further comments, "I want to propose that Marsalis's canonical project at Lincoln Center, while an expression of one form of resistant black culture, is also fundamentally conservative. Musicians and critics alike view this as a project that constructs a classical canon by formalizing it into static texts and confining it to museums, conservatories, and cultural institutions" (47). Conversely Gray explains the Jazz Left's resistant and alternative cultural politics. "Taking a more transgressive approach to the tradition, the jazz left, by contrast, operates without, and hence beyond, the formal institutional, organizational, and financial infrastructure and resources necessary to get and sustain the recognition and stability enjoyed by the canon makers. I see the jazz left as a more amorphous, loosely structured, but no less important intervention in fashioning a public imagination and, more powerfully, an alternative understanding of jazz and black diasporic cultural formations" (71).

The critical "Right/Left" distinction for the contemporary San Francisco jazz scene revolves around the axis of the national/international jazz canon v. local cultural commitment and, in light of the Yoshi's debacle, possibly race. Gray's Right/Left distinction cannot be drawn merely in terms of for-profit v. non-profit nor in terms of private v. public, nor will it suffice to cast aspersions and draw lines around the corporate affiliations of board members. The fact remains that organizations as diverse as the Jazz Heritage Center and the African American Arts and Cultural Center are registered non-profit organizations who may at any time receive monies from public and private sources and may work collaboratively with a broad diversity of community and business partners to accomplish purportedly similar or compatible cultural goals. The critical difference lies in the Jazz Left's commitment to the local scene in terms of performance opportunities, historical archives, and teaching the arts versus the Jazz Right's commitment to a broader national and often commercial cultural scene.

Furthermore, this is not a glorification of the trope of the starving artist nor the demonization of commercial success. Few would question the economic necessity of a private jazz institution like Yoshi's, for example, promoting national artists with significant name recognition[16] in order to pay down its debt and survive in the high rent atmosphere of the redeveloped Western Addition. However, there are meaningful critiques to how this necessary pursuit of commercial viability is accomplished at the expense of the inclusion of local performers and histories.

Lacking corporate sponsorship, performing outside of the context of the major festivals and clubs in San Francisco, the Coltrane Church ran against the grain of the "right-leaning" new jazz establishment and foregrounded local artists and legends in its alternative festivals. The alternative festivals produced by the Coltrane Church, particularly since the 1990s, definitely locate the church in the cultural politics of San Francisco's "Jazz Left."

Conclusions

Since the early 1900s African American migrants to San Francisco have used jazz and other art forms as a forum for entrepreneurial activity. Although jazz certainly was certainly not among the primary factors motivating African American migration, local black jazz entrepreneurship became central to processes of building wealth and real political power as well as processes of ideological and cultural formation. Jazz was therefore central in many respects to African American community formation in San Francisco and provided burgeoning African American communities with visibility and legitimacy. From the Barbary Coast to the 31 clubs of the Harlem of the West, to the surviving handful of African American–owned clubs and community arts organizations, were institutions that provided visible expressions of black ownership, wealth, and cultural power; functioning materially and ideologically to legitimate San Francisco's African American community.

The St. John Will-I-Am Coltrane African Orthodox Church is fundamentally no different in this regard and should also be properly considered as local African American jazz entrepreneurship with the same implications for community building as the clubs of the Barbary Coast and the Fillmore of the West. Precisely because of the rising cultural value of jazz in San Francisco and its intimate relationship with corporate redevelopment in the Western Addition neighborhood, the material and ideological implications of the Coltrane Church as a jazz organization are comparable with those of the most storied entrepreneurial ventures in jazz music from the early 1900s to the 1960s and '70s.

Fischlin, Heble, and Lipsitz go as far as linking corporatization with censorship, critiquing censorship's impact on freedoms of expression, assembly, and access to "divergent forms of thinking" and force us to consider whether the contemporary corporatization of jazz music in San Francisco effects broader social and political movements by effacing "the music's association with resistant politics" (4). "Corporatizing music inevitably imposes constraints on freedom of expression. The market value of music is driven by other imperatives—especially profit. These imperatives are at odds with creative-commons musicking generated out of aggrieved communities in the name of resistance to oppression, community solidarity, and identity narratives" (4).

The rise of SFJazz and the San Francisco Jazz Heritage Center/Yoshi's complex and the new corporate profitability of jazz music are in fact contemporaneous with the triumph of the San Francisco Redevelopment Agency's plan for Western Addition Area 2. The corporatization and censorship of jazz in the Western Addition has seemingly dislodged the music from a now rapidly diminishing African American community. African American culture is presumably present and profitable without the actual presence of African Americans (Fischlin, Heble, and Lipsitz 4).

We cannot forget that the Apostles of Sound at the Coltrane Church are working musicians laboring within the context of growing economic, cultural, and ethnic inequalities of access and control over the production and distribution of jazz music, and that these inequities are rooted in a history that goes back to the Barbary Coast of the early 1900s. Many of the musicians of the Coltrane Church struggle to earn a living with their considerable musical skill and knowledge in small clubs and cafes and jazz workshops. In addition to their sporadic recording, increasingly sporadic appearances at Yoshi's, and invisibility at the SF Jazz Festival,[17] the virtual censorship of Ohnedaruth blunts its political impact and its relationship to community formation. It is for this reason that the Coltrane Church has sought to create its own community-based festivals as a means of remaining relevant and resistant. Any examination of this history of jazz and African American performance in San Francisco must respond to these inequalities as both cultural and political phenomena.

Ironically, by 2012 Yoshi's San Francisco, which had long operated in the red and received multiple bailout loans from the city, declared bankruptcy. By 2014 current owner Yoshie Akiba sold the interests in her club and restaurant to the Fillmore Live Entertainment Group who decided to offer pop, hip hop, and R&B.[18] The recent demise of Yoshi's certainly means that more attention will be focused on the SFJazz Center, but it may also foreshadow the demise of this most recent phase of corporate-backed jazz. And yet Jazz Left organizations like the Coltrane Church, continue to assert a cultural politics focused on community arts and artists, increasing the democratic accessibility and ownership of jazz music for performers, students, and listeners. In the long and very hopeful view, the history of San Francisco jazz may well demonstrate that the music can in fact *never* be taken from the hands of the people.

5

The Dr. Huey P. Newton
Experience

We have absolutely no reason to worry about lack of positive and affirmative philosophy. It's built in us. The phrasing, the sound of the music attest this fact. We are naturally endowed with it. You can believe all of us would have perished long ago if this were not so. As to community, the whole face of the globe is our community. You see, it is really easy for us to create. We are born with this feeling that just comes out no matter what conditions exist. Otherwise, how could our founding fathers have produced this music in the first place when they surely found themselves (as many of us do today) existing in hostile communities where there was everything to fear and damn few to trust. Any music which could grow and propagate itself as our music has, must have a hell of an affirmative belief inherent in it.

—St. John Will-I-Am Coltrane

In 1969, when the Yardbird Temple evolved into the Yardbird Vanguard Revolutionary Church of the Hour,[1] Archbishop King and his small family-centered flock developed a relationship with Dr. Huey P. Newton and the Black Panther Party for Self-Defense. Affectionately dubbed "Bishop One Mind," Dr. Newton embraced Franzo King as a student of Marxist philosophy and Franzo King adopted Dr. Newton as his mentor. It was here at the feet of the Servant that Archbishop King learned to move beyond the limitations of black nationalist politics and embrace a broader political vision and perspective that would merge with the political imperatives of black liberation theology, and the spirituality of John Coltrane:

105

Dr. Huey P. Newton would be sitting there, I would be sitting on the floor with a pen and pad. He would talk and I would take notes. I was his only student on that level that I was aware of, me and those that I brought with me.

The political story of the John Coltrane Church is fundamentally marked by an evolution from essentialist ethnic nationalisms to a more refined language involving a politics of fulfillment, transfiguration, universalism, and futurism. Narratives of Coltrane Consciousness in its pre–Dr. Huey P. Newton years affirmatively represent John Coltrane as an avatar of the black nationalism of the civil rights movement of the 1960s and as an avatar of an equally nationalistic history of black theological movements. In so doing they represent a more essentialist paradigm. By contrast, narratives of Coltrane Consciousness in the Dr. Huey P. Newton period and beyond reflect a growing and self-conscious religious and ethnic universalism and a move away from an essentialist racial politics. The Coltrane Church's ideological movement from essentialist to universalist politics –a move that mirrors its religious ideological evolution– is critical to understanding its growing ability to acquire power and relevance through efficacious coalition building with other subaltern partners in the San Francisco Bay Area and advocate a coherent program of political action in the face of ever-changing political circumstances.

1969–1971: Black Panther Party

This decidedly political and secular move marked an important ideological shift of the Coltrane Church away from a racially deterministic worldview towards a class and global perspective. Archbishop King studied under the direction of Dr. Newton. It was Dr. Newton, according to Archbishop King, who encouraged him to move beyond race and to consider his particular and seemingly racialized position and localized grievances amidst a context of global imperialism and anti-imperialist movements:

When I raised the question of race to him he very calmly and very coolly said, I can almost see him when I say this, "What's with the race thing? Comrade, it's not about race. It's not about race."

During these years the One Mind Temple became deliberately activist and engaged in the local politics of hunger and poverty. The One Mind Temple initiated a food program that was first taken to San Francisco State University to feed students engaged in social protest against the war in Vietnam and in favor of Ethnic Studies and Women's Studies programs.

Archbishop King solos during the Coltrane Liturgy at the Fillmore Street location.

The food program would later become an important adjunct of Black Panther Party activities, feeding activists and the poor at Black Panther rallies. Archbishop King remembers, "I would be down there with them bagging groceries for the people."

In fact, a critical aspect in the church's evolution away from a purely black nationalist racial politics and racialized spirituality was their involvement in outreach programs to feed, clothe, and counsel the poor—without regard to ethnicity—in the community of San Francisco's Western Addition neighborhood. Dr. Newton encouraged their growth in this direction and arguably influenced their shift toward a broader sense of community involvement. Archbishop King:

> Associating with Dr. Huey P. Newton kinda early, we went from the Yardbird Temple to the Yardbird Temple Vanguard Revolutionary Church of the Hour. We would say that as the hour changes, so do the needs of the people. I think that it was at that point that I started challenging the churches and saying that the churches are irrelevant to the needs of the people, they're not interested in the hungry, they're not interested in the naked, they're not interested in the homeless, and they're not interested in the real down-trodden.
>
> Then we had the idea of a free soup program. It was something that we had been doing before Dr. Huey P. Newton for the early membership of the church when we would get together and fast and break the fast with soup. So we said, if we're gonna be in this community then we have got to make some real significant and concrete contributions to the survival of the community in which we were based. So that meant that we had to have something going on here every day for the community and that's when we started having a seven-day food program.

The Yardbird Temple Vanguard Revolutionary Church of the Hour also initiated a police action committee and conducted a limited number of citizen arrests within the community, providing in effect a comparable but numerically limited self-policing presence to that of the Black Panther Party in Oakland. The intention of the Vanguard Revolutionary Police Action Committee, like that of the Black Panther Party, was to provide a counter to the criminal justice establishment with community self-policing.

This community would also form an emergency medical response service, a throwback to the Black Cross of Marcus Garvey's Universal Negro Improvement Association. In the event of a catastrophe, the Vanguard Police Action Committee could respond to assisting victims and helping people through the transition. Archbishop King:

> We weren't just about dealing with police violence with that committee either. Our committee could turn into the Black Cross or the Red Cross. I

can remember a sister's house burning down and pulling the police action committee together to solicit from the rest of the community and the community at large the things that they needed. I remember our whole thing was that we have to beat the Red Cross there. We can't be sitting around waiting on white institutions to help us in a time of disaster.

While Dr. Newton had a great effect on the racial and political perspectives of Archbishop King, he was also an important spiritual teacher. It is here where then Bishop King was duly re-informed of the inextricable link between politics, religion, and culture in building African American resistance movements:

And then I met the Servant and he brought that, I don't know what you call it ... spiritual ... political spiritualism or something. A lot of people don't realize how spiritual Dr. Huey P. Newton was because he was a communist. But when the Servant and I got together we opened up the Bible and he taught from the Bible that Jesus Christ, the Son of man, was an uncompromising revolutionary, and I sat and asked him a thousand and one questions.

During the time in which Archbishop King studied under Dr. Newton, the Servant was in fact affiliated with a number of spiritual teachers and had experienced the potentials of meditation while in solitary confinement:

There was time when the Servant was hanging out with Roshi Baker and Baba Ram Das, so you had the Hindi and the Buddhist and Roshi Baker was the head of a Zen Buddhist center and he viewed Dr. Huey P. Newton as the Buddha, that he had reached that kind of enlightenment that he was the Buddha. Dr. Newton told his story to Roshi Baker and Ram Das about being in prison and how he would have to be in solitary confinement and how his meditation would bring him to a certain level of realization when he had overcome or acquired a certain mastery over time and space.

The Black Panther years were not without difficulty. The relationship between Archbishop King and Dr. Huey P. Newton was in fact consistently threatened by the constant harassment and misinformation of the Oakland police department. Archbishop King was twice "arrested" by Dr. Newton and "put on trial" for conspiracy to murder the Servant. The fierce independence of the Yardbird Temple Vanguard Revolutionary Church of the Hour would predominate in this period. Embracing himself as a student rather than as a member of the Black Panther Party, then Bishop King would incorporate Dr. Newton's Marxist articulation of race as part of an oppressive ideological system that worked to inhibit poor people of different ethnic backgrounds from forming coalitions and upsetting the power of the ruling classes. He would incorporate Dr. Newton's activist engagement with the people. Although he was an insider, then Bishop King would never officially become a member of the Black Panther Party and the Yardbird Vanguard Revolutionary Church of the Hour would remain an independent force in the Western Addition and San Francisco. Archbishop King:

> I wasn't a member of the Panther Party, but I considered myself a servant of God under his teaching.

In light of police harassment and disinformation, "Bishop One Mind" would ultimately suffer the indignation and terror of two impromptu Black Panther trials for crimes deemed punishable by death. Bishop King would reach for John Coltrane in both instances, testing his faith in the midst of his darkest moments. And John Coltrane would deliver him.

The Trials of Bishop One Mind

Dr. Huey P. Newton was certainly critical in the Archbishop's development both politically and spiritually and would eventually outgrow his teacher. In the end, Archbishop King and the Coltrane Church remained steadfastly defined by a radically evolutionary nature, thus effectively limiting the influence of any one teacher or influence; the Coltrane Church would always outgrow its mentors because evolution was their most fundamental element.

Under the constant pressure of police harassment and in light of misinformation circulated by the Oakland Police Department, Dr. Newton held two trials for Archbishop King, accusing him of conspiring to kill him and later accusing him of theft and threatening him with a possible death sentence. In the first trial Archbishop King was accused of conspiring to murder the Servant based on the evidence of an unidentified car parked by Dr. Newton's apartment building. Archbishop King was able to defend himself by successfully convincing Dr. Newton that he did not own the car. But in the first trial the Servant had not assigned guilt prior to allowing Archbishop King to present his case. In the second trial Archbishop King and Dr. Newton found themselves in a labor dispute regarding the Archbishop's management of workers Dr. Newton had dispatched.

Archbishop King here speaks of the second trial when he was subjected to severe beatings at the hand of Dr. Newton and, faced with his death, Archbishop King called on the name of John Coltrane to save his life:

And as soon as they opened the door they drew pistols down on me. They took me in and searched me and they took me to the living room and then Dr. Huey P. Newton came out. As opposed to the first time they now announced to me that my trial was held last night and that I was found guilty and was condemned to death.

What the Servant wanted from me was a confession. And my thing was that if I lie in the face of fear then I lose my manhood and my manhood was still important to me. I'm in the middle and the Servant starts playing this Jimmy Cliff song on the record player, "pressure's dropping, pressure's gonna drop on you" and he's got that on and they've got a circle going and he was beating me. The Servant wouldn't let anybody else hit me but he had this little Japanese cane.

And I remember at one point I was bleeding, he had beaten me all over my knee. My knees are bad today because of that stuff. And blood was running all down my face. And I knew that the death sentence was that he was going to beat me to death. I was saying, thank God, just don't throw me off the 25th floor!

So I told him, "Well, Servant, if I'm a condemned man, can I have a dying man's wish?" And he said, "Yeah, what do you want?" I said, "I'd like to hear some JOHN COLTRANE!" I said it like we sing it to the rhythm of "Africa." And he said "Yeah, you can hear some JOHN COLTRANE!" and sang it back.

It came out like that for him. He said Coltrane's name as if singing it. So he goes and they get some Trane and I think that's when they laid down the guns and he didn't hit me anymore. They just went on talking. Pretty soon Dr. Huey P. Newton came out from the back and said, "We're not going to kill him now. We're going to kill him tonight." He ordered me taken to this motel that was near the penthouse.

So I remember getting on the elevator and thinking I got to break for it when we get down to the bottom but the spirit of the Lord was telling me to just cool it. We get downstairs and to this motel and I remember writing something to Dr. Huey P. Newton. I can't remember what it was. It was just a few words. I signed it with the blood that was dripping all over the place. I signed, "One Mind" with the blood. I told them to give that to the Servant. And I stayed there for a few hours. I remember some of the Panthers came over and left and then they turned me loose.

The narrative of the second trial that Archbishop King was submitted to by Dr. Newton is fundamentally a narrative of the miracle of the name power of John Coltrane. And it also affirms again the centrality of John Coltrane as an axis from which the evolutionary movement of the Coltrane Church continues to spin. As positive as the influence of Dr. Newton may have been with respect to Marxist teachings, the Dr. Newton experience also affirmed the church's fundamental desire to continue progressing and developing. Continued association with Dr. Newton at that time clearly meant possible death and the untimely demise of the Coltrane Church.

In spite of how Archbishop King suffered in the midst of the Servant's torture and trial, Dr. Newton continues to be reflected upon as a positive influence in the development of the Coltrane Church. It took a dream for Archbishop King to forgive Dr. Newton, and their brief reunion in San Francisco International Airport in 1977 after Dr. Newton's exile in Cuba offered the Servant an opportunity to apologize:

> In the dream there was this circle of Panthers and people from my circle and we were having prayer and they didn't want to let Dr. Huey P. Newton in the circle. And I am defending somebody again. I come up and say, his sins are no greater than anyone else's. If God forgives us then we must forgive him and make him a part of this circle. And I pulled him in the circle. I remember waking up and telling Mother Marina, I've forgiven Dr. Huey P. Newton. And I had done it in my sleep.

On their last meeting in San Francisco International Airport, Archbishop King recalls:

> He grabbed my hand. He kissed my hand and he apologized. He said, "It was all the Servant's fault. It was all my fault and I beg your pardon."

Conclusions

In *Small Acts: Thoughts on the Politics of Black Cultures*, Paul Gilroy persuasively argues that black cultural expressions of nationality are improperly essentialized and overlook the plural histories of a diasporic people who have experienced centuries of racial domination (120). "In my view, the problematic intellectual heritage of Euro-American modernity still determines the manner in which nationality is understood within black political discourse. In particular, it conditions the continuing aspiration to acquire a supposedly authentic, natural and stable identity. This identity is the premise of a thinking 'racial' self that is both socialized and unified by its connection with other kindred souls encountered usually, though not always, within the fortified frontiers of those discrete ethnic cultures which also happen to coincide with the contours of a sovereign nation-state that guarantees their continuity" (121–122).

Gilroy contrasts this troubling essentialist paradigm of black cultural representation –particularly black music—with a pluralist standpoint that appreciates "complex representations of a black particularity that is internally divided: by class, sexuality, gender, age, and political consciousness." He continues: "The difficulty with this second tendency is that, in leaving racial essentialism behind by viewing 'race' itself as a social and cultural construction, it has been insufficiently alive to the lingering power of specifically 'racial' forms of power and subordination. Each outlook attempts to compensate for the obvious weaknesses in the other camp but so far there has been little open and explicit debate between them" (123).

Searching for a "more refined political language" and dismissing modernist claims to racial authenticity of self-consciously hybrid cultural forms, Gilroy focuses attention on what he calls black music's commitment to the idea of a better future (a politics of fulfillment) and its critique of capitalism (a politics of transfiguration) (131–133). "In its simplest possible terms, by posing the world as it is against the world as the racially subordinated would like it to be, this musical culture supplies a great deal of the courage required to go on living in the present" (133).

What emerged through their tutelage in Marxist class-consciousness was more than reverence for a black saint but reverence for a man who overcame his oppressed status that was merely *symbolized* by his blackness. The post–Dr. Newton Coltrane Church emphasizes a kind of "universal blackness," thereby calling attention to broader global histories of oppression from which Coltrane's redemption and sainthood take flight. It is not uncommon to hear casual discussions amongst members that label any oppressed group as "black," whether that be historical references to the Vietnam War or references to European American church members who have clearly rejected the fruits of white privilege. Therefore, the most important impact of Archbishop King's tutelage under the late Dr. Newton is Dr. Newton's Marxist perspective, which de-emphasizes the importance of race in favor of a more sophisticated class analysis of historical oppression. Dr. Newton articulated race as but part of an oppressive ideological system that worked to inhibit poor people of different ethnic backgrounds from forming effective coalitions to upset and overthrow the power of the ruling classes. Archbishop King:

> When I raised the question of race to him he very calmly and very coolly said, I can almost see him when I say this, "What's with the race thing? Comrade, it's not about race. It's not about race." Dr. Huey P. Newton taught me that it wasn't all about race, but that it was about class.

Inspired by Dr. Newton's class and global perspectives, Archbishop King sought to push the envelope a bit farther and demonstrate how the parables of Coltrane's musicianship might help to transcend narrow ethnic boundaries and build a union of all people more pleasing to God. Indeed, this broad palette from which diasporic self-creation is drawn at the church also helps to fashion an inclusive ministry which ultimately brings diverse diasporic interests under its umbrella.

The broadest civil rights consequence of this aspect of the ministry has indeed been a remarkable shattering of ethnic boundaries and the embracing of a multicultural ethic among the dedicated and faithful members of Saint John's. Church practice and Coltrane Consciousness have effectively avoided becoming icons of racial authenticity. Indeed the furthering of the music in its rightful spiritual place has created at the St. John Will-I-Am Coltrane African Orthodox Church precisely the level of brotherhood and understanding that John Coltrane had hoped to effect. Coltrane Consciousness ultimately transcends both civil and human rights issues and reaches for what Archbishop King—citing Coltrane's view that "the whole globe is community" (Analahati).

6

The Yardbird and One Mind Temple and New Church Movements in the 1960s and '70s

All a musician can do is to get closer to the sources of nature,
and so feel that he is in communion with the natural laws.

—St. John Will-I-Am Coltrane

As the Yardbird Temple became the Yardbird Vanguard Revolution-ary Church of the Hour in 1969, and then the One Mind Temple, the spir-itual development of this small congregation began to flower. In the late 1960s and early 1970s, a fledgling congregation moved toward meditation, fasting, and prayer. Now they were earnestly seeking the enlightenment promised by the 1965 Sound Baptism and could count themselves among a host of new church movements in the San Francisco Bay Area.

With the One Mind Temple Franzo and Marina King initiated another ideological shift in their evolution as they grew in their appreciation of the spiritual aspect of John Coltrane. Archbishop King comments:

> I think we really began to see that this was more than just about saving the music for our culture, but that it was about opportunities for saving souls and bringing people back to God as we were being brought back to God under the inspiration of John's music. You could say it was an evolution of our thinking and that's why we quote John when he says that the music can change the initial thought patterns. John's music changed our whole way of thinking, not only about this music but about ourselves and our relationship to God." It was at this point, leading up to the 1971 lease of a building on 351 Divisadero Street, that the Yardbird Club became a church, and through these testimonies we witness the further evolution of their spiritual awareness.

115

Archbishop King's testimonies here definitively address the transcendence of Coltrane Consciousness beyond purely social and cultural parameters into an all-encompassing and transcendent spiritual phenomena. This is the moment when the church began. Archbishop King's testimonies are filled with references to the Holy Ghost and the notion of the experience of the music as more than cultural phenomena but instead as a Pentecostal Holy Ghost-inspired revival event. This is the moment when Archbishop King and Mother Marina began to perceive themselves as more than mere listeners and as mystics. This is the moment when Archbishop King and Mother Marina began to understand the music as a vehicle for spiritual transcendence. Once any music is experienced as such it escapes the constrictions of culture, time, space, and place, opening up for the listener a real glimpse at freedom and spiritual transcendence.

Archbishop King comments at length about what would become another evolutionary shift from the Sound Baptism to the cultural listening clinic to the Yardbird Club jazz bar to the spiritual practice of the Yardbird Temple, the political engagement of the Yardbird Vanguard Revolutionary Church of the Hour, and the Eastern spiritual practices of the One Mind Temple and its many manifestations:

> How did the church get started? I like to say that it was a movement of the Holy Ghost and that it manifested itself in the way that we began to identify it as a prayer circle. Many people want to know why we went to that point with it. Well, this was our sound baptism, it was a Holy Ghost-filled event.
>
> You see, I used to deal with the music as a strictly cultural thing. It is, after all, the only art form that the United States has produced; everything else comes from Europe and other places. When you start talking about the music that the people of African descent have produced jazz is the only true art form that has been produced by this country. I think that a lot of it has escaped the community that produced it. And for whatever reasons, maybe the commercial aspects of it, the music is no longer in the community to hear. You have to leave the community to go hear the music now. At one time it was something that was in the community that people could afford. It's expensive now. I think very few people can afford to hear this kind of music.
>
> So I think I was caught up with a re-education thing to bring the music back to the African community. However, after seeing John Coltrane, I realized that the music was beyond culture. That it wasn't just a cultural experience as much as it was a spiritual experience. And that it was also a global experience. It is like John Coltrane said, that the whole globe is community for us. So then the music became all-encompassing for me. Even though the history of the music was coming through the history of

African people, it was something that belonged to the world and with further investigation you find out there were other people who had contributed to the music from different levels, whether it was as a composer or as designers of instruments.

So the whole thing became something that wasn't identified with one community but I think the thing that I got the most out of it was a call to acknowledge God and to be in the service of God. The music was a way to worship God and to serve Him in a true sense of the fatherhood of God and to live clean and do right. John was just taking the music and he had said and one time that the music, it was changing into something else. "In my estimation it's rising. It needs another place to be played in."

I think that was the key for me. When I heard John say the music is rising and needs another atmosphere to be played in and with the struggle that I was having within myself to live out the hope of being a minister, a preacher, and a spiritual person, I think it was that statement that affected me more than anything else. I knew that there needed to be a religious and spiritual community around the music. I knew that John meant that the music needs a church. The first intent of the music as John Coltrane says is praising the Lord: "Let us sing all songs to God to whom all praise is due." Something was really driving us to God. I really felt that's what he was saying. He'd also said that he didn't think playing in clubs was good because he felt he had a lot of playing in him to get out but he didn't feel that the clubs were the best place for the music to be played. So, saying 'yes,' the music needs to be in church, has a lot to do with my first experience with hearing John Coltrane play and feeling like I was in church. There was one who was a holy man that was anointed and full of the Holy Ghost.

John Coltrane said that the music was an instrument that could change the initial thought patterns that would change the thinking of the people. So I saw music then as an instrument for making that change that would take peoples' thinking from prejudice and hate. We believe that through John's music we can change all of that and so introducing people to John Coltrane's music was also giving people an opportunity to be changed by that music. And as John Coltrane would say, "into a force for real good." He said there were forces that bring evil and forces that bring good. I want to be a part of the forces that bring good. I think those are some of the things that initiated and encouraged and supported in my mind what I was doing at that time in terms of seeing the healing properties in John Coltrane's music.

The radical theological voice of the Coltrane Church is in part the result of Franzo and Marina King's close and consistent study of the black liberation theology[2] of Howard Thurman (1899–1981) and James Cone (1938-) as well as the social justice mission and charismatic leadership of the likes of Elijah Muhammad (1897–1975), Father Major Jealous Divine (1876–1965) and Daddy Grace (1881–1960). Archbishop King:

Archbishop King takes a solo during the Coltrane Liturgy at the 1286 Fillmore Street location.

We had read Howard Thurman and we were reading about Father Divine and it was recently that I remembered how important Daddy Grace had been to us. But what most people don't know is that I was seeing myself as coming in the image of Elijah Muhammad. I was going to be the next Elijah Muhammad.

The Yardbird Temple and the Yardbird Vanguard Revolutionary Church of the Hour would evolve to the One Mind Temple concomitant with a move to 201 Sawyer Street in 1971. The One Mind Temple would subsequently become the One Mind Temple Vanguard Revolutionary Church of the Hour and later the One Mind Temple Evolutionary Transitional Body of Christ upon a subsequent relocation to 351 Divisadero Street in 1973 across the street from the famous Both/And Club where John Coltrane had played and inspired hip young white avant-garde musicians like Terry Riley. 351 Divisadero Street had also been the former home of the Theatre of Madmen Only, a 1960s San Francisco head shop.

These three manifestations of the One Mind Temple across two locations served as forums for increasingly radical expressions of the divinity of John Coltrane. Franzo King adopted the name "Bishop Ha'qq," signifying the Islamic term *al'ha'qq* meaning "ultimate truth." Mother Marina King would take the name "Mother Ha'qq." Here, John Coltrane was God, a sec-

Services in the mid–1990s at 351 Divisadero Street.

ond coming of Christ who had come with a gospel of sound. Church members made no bones about Coltrane as God and their cult of Coltrane's personality. Coltrane was openly worshipped and conflated not only with Jesus Christ but, as church members grew in their study of world religions, with the Hindu deity Krishna, enchanted player of the flute.

The One Mind Temple and its later manifestations as the One Mind Temple Evolutionary Transitional Church of the Hour and the One Mind Temple Evolutionary Transitional Body of Christ marked an ideological shift that was consistent with the popularity of new church movements and utopian cults of personality in the San Francisco Bay Area during the 1960s and '70s. This was an ideological concretization of the deification of John Coltrane as God. In 1971 the One Mind Temple Evolutionary Transitional Body of Christ accomplished the deification of an ex-heroin addict African American jazz musician and, in the midst of emerging dialogues of west coast urban black militancy, the Apostles of Sound were fundamentally worshipping a black man and exceeding the farthest limits of black nationalism and theology.

In later years the church would publish some of their original writings

The late Fr. Roberto DeHaven (Bluewater), left, and Archbishop King conducting the Coltrane Liturgy at 351 Divisadero Street in the mid–1990s.

from the One Mind Temple Evolutionary Transitional Church of the Hour period in a document entitled *Coltrane Consciousness* and originally included with the first publication of *John Coltrane Speaks* in 1981. Much of what is included in this document addresses the fervent nature of this church's devotion to John Coltrane and their understanding of his elevated spiritual position. The document is also tinged with references to Hinduism and bespeaks the important Hindu phase they would later experience prior to and with greater intensity under Alice Coltrane (1974-'81) as well as a growing openness to all forms of spiritual expression.

The first chapter of *Coltrane Consciousness*, titled "Equinox: The Promise Manifested and Fulfilled," begins with quotations from Lord Krishna, Christ, and the Gospel according to St. John. All of these quotations associate Coltrane with a Christ-like, Krishna-like presence, as he who is sent in fulfillment of God's promise to comfort. Lord Krishna speaks: "Whenever and wherever there is a decline in religious practice, O descendants of Barata (great Son from the Father), and a predominant rise in irreligion, at that time I descend Myself" (*Coltrane Consciousness*, 1981 p. 3). Christ is quoted: "And I will pray the Father and He shall give you another Comforter, that he may abide with you forever, even the Spirit of Truth.... At that day ye shall know that I am in the Father and ye in Me and I in you" (3). Finally, from the Gospel according to John: "There was a man sent from God whose name was John. The same came for a witness, to bear witness of the Light that all men through Him might believe" (3).

In the view of the One Mind Temple Evolutionary Transitional Body of Christ, that man sent from God, that Comforter, he who descended from heaven in a time of irreligion was John Coltrane. Coltrane was the second coming. His scriptures were written in sound, a universal language intended to pierce the artificial boundaries of race and nation. His experience as an African American born in the American south who came of age as an artist in Philadelphia and experienced the ravages of drugs and liquor, all spoke to his relevance. *Coltrane Consciousness* documents this fertile period of recognition where Archbishop and Mother Marina King begin uncovering layer upon layer of coincidence and significance revealing the true mystical nature of Coltrane and his music.

Attempts at uncovering the spiritual significance of John Coltrane yielded more than solidification of the belief that Coltrane was God. Franzo and Marina King undertook a thorough study of spirituality that would encompass Western and non–Western belief systems. They would read everything from Howard Thurman—the father of modern black liberation theology—to Sufi mystic Hazrat Inayat Khan[3]—a musician turned mystic who fundamentally believed that God is Sound. This activity yielded a deeply ingrained spiritually universalist position that Franzo and Marina King would take with them through future years of transition. Mirroring Coltrane's own interest in everything from Christianity, the Kabbalah, Sufism, Hinduism and Platonic philosophy, they too saw in Coltrane not only the reappearance of a Christian God but of gods and deities from many traditions.

With respect to Coltrane as the reincarnation of Christ, Archbishop King layers a re-telling of the birth of John Coltrane with the birth of Jesus Christ in *Coltrane Consciousness:*

> At the season of the autumnal equinox on September 23, the Day of Even, when Darkness and Light are equal and the world is held in perfect balance, to this age of decaying moral and religious duty, in the year of our Lord nineteen hundred and twenty-six, the Spirit of Truth appeared and manifested in a physical form and dwelt in a living temple. This temple, being filled with the Holy Ghost and that with fire, would be called "Gift of God," John, even John William Coltrane. He was to suffer and grow in Truth, to live a truly religious life, and express it in Music. Anointing souls in the Christ Spirit through this music, he would bring forth the spiritual fruits of the autumn harvest [*Coltrane Consciousness,* 1981 p. 4].

In another moment, Archbishop King conflates Christ with Krishna and the prophet Moses, and provides the signature element of *Coltrane Consciousness*, namely that Sound is divine or holy and that the sound of John Coltrane specifically represents a new spiritual dispensation following the law of Moses and the dispensation of grace ushered in by Jesus Christ.

> Dear Listener, Sri Rama Ohnedaruth, the mystic known as John William Coltrane, is the promise of scripture manifested and fulfilled. The signs and scriptures read and the Holy Ghost interprets: out of Christ or anointed consciousness, John Coltrane consciousness is, Coltrane is that one of the same love, being of one accord and one mind with the Father, of the same mind that was in the Anointed Savior, Christ Jesus. John Coltrane consciousness is Christ consciousness. It is Grace. Anointed of the Holy Spirit in the will of the Father, Lord John emanates the Holy Sound or Word of God; he is the evolved, transcended existence of anointed consciousness, the Word [4].

Calling John Coltrane the "Christ of the twentieth century" and referring to him by his Hindu name (Sri Rama Ohnedaruth), Archbishop King writes,

> In paralleling the Jesus of two thousand years ago, He was an artificer, a mechanic and a craftsman whose craftsmanship required skill and knowl-

edge of a particular kind, as a carpenter. Is not this the carpenter, the son of Mary in Mark 3:6? Jesus being born at a time and an age where emphasis was put on mechanics, craftsmanship, and skills enabled him to be armed in the science of mathematics. The Christ of the twentieth century, Sri Rama Ohnedaruth, may also be viewed as an artificer, a mechanic, a technician, a skilled craftsman and a scientist, one whose mastership required certain skills and knowledge of a particular kind as a musician [5].

These persistent conflations of Coltrane with Christ and Krishna present ideological challenges for any potential new members. On the one hand this spiritually universalist ideological shift creates the potential for a more inclusive ministry. On the other hand, the One Mind Temple simply didn't proselytize and its openness toward spiritual universalism was an expression of its institutional evolution and competition for relevance, not membership, in the marketplace of spiritual ideas in San Francisco. The One Mind Temple was neither concerned with whoever might be offended by its spiritually universalist practices nor its fundamental belief in the divinity of John Coltrane. Archbishop King:

> We would board up the windows and we wouldn't let anybody in. Bluewater [Fr. Roberto DeHaven] talks about that. How he kept coming back and I don't know how long it was before we let him in. We weren't looking for members.

This practice continues under the contemporary manifestation of the African Orthodox Church. While the church doors are opened for new believers every Sunday, and the church continues to minister to travelers in San Francisco International Airport and through its Outreach radio program and musical performances throughout the Bay Area, the Coltrane Church is not a church that is actively seeking new membership.[4] The Coltrane Church is still very much involved in the process of changing hearts and minds, the initial thought patterns, and welcomes people of different faiths to return to their original houses of worship and interpret John Coltrane within the framework of their faith. Archbishop King:

> We didn't solicit for membership. We didn't care what you were. When you leave, you can go to the Zen Center or the Church of God in Christ. And it was about seeing God in everything and being able to worship in any space that was dedicated for God whether it was in a field or in a housed space, but realizing that if you go to the Zen Center and somebody said that we're having meditation and we're getting in touch with our inner selves.... Well, who is in you but Christ? Get in touch. I've got no problem, I'm gonna get in touch.

And whatever the form of worship is, the ritual of it, I don't necessarily have to be familiar with that, but I don't have a problem with whether or not I'm going to fold my hands like this when I pray or whether I'm going to turn my palms up. All of it is a semblance of reverence to God, it's an obeisance. Maybe I want to prostrate myself. I don't have a problem with that.

So it just reminded me of so much of what we've been talking about in terms of not only the unity of religious ideas but it sounds like John Coltrane when he said, "I am a Christian, and my mother and father were Christians, my early teachings were Christian. But it's, Well, do you know the truth, brother?" Don't come in here talking about I'm a Christian and I'm a Roman Catholic and I'm an A.M.E. and all of that. Do you know the truth and is that truth your God, or is it just some information that you have logged somewhere?

Eschewing any commitment to spread the faith, Franzo and Marina King were free to explore the spirituality of John Coltrane against myriad traditions and to do so without committing Coltrane to any single faith perspective. In sum, the One Mind Evolutionary Transitional Body of Christ years were marked by the recognition of the divinity of John Coltrane as God, spiritual universalism, and a fierce independence that would always place limits on the degree to which the Coltrane Church could be influenced by any given religious or denominational association.

The black liberation theology of Howard Thurman and James Cone as well as the social justice mission and charismatic leadership of the likes of Elijah Muhammad, Father Divine and Daddy Grace would seem to be the most apparent spiritual precursors of the Coltrane Church, particularly given their shared African American cultural context. However, the origins and evolution of the contemporary St. John Will-I-Am Coltrane African Orthodox Church should also properly be contextualized against the unique histories of African American participation in new religious movements (NRMs) in the San Francisco Bay Area during the 1960s and '70s.

In spite of the location of both Archbishop King's family lineage within the history of black Pentecostalism[5] and the church's conscious study and incorporation of the influences of Father Divine and Daddy Grace, many of the specific ideological shifts of the Coltrane Church reflect significant moves toward incorporating Eastern (specifically Hindu and Sufi) religious ideas within Holy Ghost-inspired black Pentecostal worship. Because of its specific location within the histories of 1960s and '70s new religious movements, the Coltrane Church has long served as an important alternative to traditional African American worship traditions, specifically providing a forum for Eastern spiritual expression for San Francisco's

African American communities. Only within the context of the African American participation in new religious movements is it possible to understand the appeal and theological significance of the Coltrane Church in the marketplace of religious ideas in San Francisco in the 1960s and '70s.

The history of the Coltrane Church reflects a broader new religious movement towards the Easternization of religion and ongoing challenges to religious orthodoxy and establishment. The narratives of church founders and members reflect an awareness of "competition" in a marketplace of religious ideas that include ideas outside of the realm of traditional African American religious discourse.

Few, outside of Arthur Huff Fauset (1970), have written of the impact and significance of Easternization and challenges to orthodoxy on the black church establishment in particular. James S. Dorman's concept of a "Black Orientalism" is a step in the right direction. Dorman illuminates a sophisticated incorporation of heterogeneous "black Orientalist imaginaries" in African American expressions of Islam. "Black Jews, black Muslims, Rastafarians, and black Spiritual churches both generated and were generated by black Orientalisms that were contiguous with Euro-American Orientalism. Twentieth-century esoteric black sects primarily invented traditions not by retention of African pasts but through the invention of black Orientalist imaginaries constructed through performance, ritual, and commercial exchange" (Curtis and Sigler 117). And further, "Orientalism, in other words, means more than simply antihumanist essentialism that views the Oriental Other as hypersexual, violent, childish, and decadent. As Deutsch and Mazrui well recognize, Orientalism also describes those who study the Orient, admire the Orient, commercialize the Orient, and seek to embody the Orient" (120). Dorman in effect begs the question of whether John Coltrane as an exemplar and the Coltrane Church as followers were engaging in these kinds of heterogeneous "black Orientalist" improvisations within a broader and contiguous context of clearly less sophisticated European American appropriations in this broader marketplace of spiritual ideas that characterized many urban cities in the 1960s.

The foregoing sections in this chapter explicitly reference the many Eastern spiritual influences of the Coltrane Church. These are, broadly speaking, "black Orientalist" appropriations that come from an attitude of reverence and careful study. The ideological transformations of the Coltrane Church and concomitant shifts in the constitution of their core congregation also provide ample opportunity to examine "black Orientalist" phenomena within a competing and contiguous European American religious marketplace.

The Coltrane Church and the Marketplace of
New Religious Movements

What is a new religious movement? Does the Coltrane Church qualify as a new religious movement? Eileen Barker provides a pragmatic definition of NRMs in her essay "New Religious Movements: Their Incidence and Significance" in Bryan R. Wilson and Jamie Creswell's *New Religious Movements: Challenge and Response* (1999). Barker writes, "The definition from which I personally start—for purely pragmatic reasons—is that an NRM is new in so far as it has become visible in its present form since the Second World War, and that it is religious in so far as it offers not merely narrow theological statements about the existence and nature of supernatural beings, but that it proposes answers to at least some of the other kinds of ultimate questions that have traditionally been addressed by mainstream religions, questions such as: Is there a God? Who am I? How might I find direction, meaning and purpose in life? Is there life after death? Is there more to human beings than their physical bodies and immediate interactions with others?" (16).

The early manifestations of the Coltrane Church and the official sainthood of John Coltrane meet Barker's definition of a new religious movement—although the African Orthodox Church does not—in at least three significant areas: (1) the 1971 incorporation of the Yardbird Temple and the subsequent One Mind Temple meets the chronological requirement; (2) the Coltrane Church proposes a significant alternative to orthodox images of the Trinity that include significant overtures to Eastern spirituality; and (3) the Coltrane Church consistently integrates the words and music of John Coltrane with the Christian Gospels, Bhaghavad Gita, and Qu'ran as a means of advancing John Coltrane as a contemporary saint with universal spiritual continuities.

The context of New Religious Movements specifically locates the diverse and transitional spiritual practices within the Coltrane Church as part of a historically situated process that began in the San Francisco Bay Area during the 1960s and '70s. Rebecca Moore, in her critical history of the Peoples Temple, *Understanding Jonestown and Peoples Temple*, specifically links the Eastern influences of NRMs in the San Francisco Bay Area in the 1960s and '70s to the 1965 repeal of the Asian Exclusion Act. Moore, writes, "Another element that explains the rise of new religions was the repeal of the Asian Exclusion Act in 1965. Abolition of this act, promulgated in 1924 and aimed at limiting all immigration from Asia, enabled many religious leaders to come to the United States. These leaders brought with them a variety of new religions that attracted rebellious young adults who sought deeper meaning and a more involved spiritual practice than they had found in their parents' faith" (Moore 4).

To conceive of the Coltrane Church as a New Religious Movement is to locate it within a competitive marketplace of largely Orientalist religious ideas spurred by the 1965 repeal of the Asian Exclusion Act, that included the growth of Hinduism, the Hari Krishna movement, Buddhism, Islam, the Hippie Movement,[6] and a range of commercially available Eastern practices including vegetarianism, yoga, tantra, and meditation, to name a few. The Coltrane Church has a rich history of members who came in the midst of a conscious search for fundamental spiritual answers. Among the more noteworthy examples of this process are the late Fr. Roberto DeHaven and Bro. Max Hoff, both of who came to the Coltrane Church after substantive experiences in Buddhist practice.

Colin Campbell argues that the connection between NRMs and Eastern expressions of environmentalism, vegetarianism, etc., can be understood as part of a process that can potentially deconstruct and replace Western spirituality altogether. Campbell writes, "The thesis I would like to advance is that these developments can best be understood as constituting a process of 'Easternisation'. By this I do not simply mean the introduction and spread within the West of recognizable Eastern 'imports', whether these are products, such as spices, yoghurt and silk, practices such as yoga and acupuncture, or complete religious systems such as Hinduism or Buddhism" (Wilson 40). And further, "The thesis advanced here is that the traditional Western cultural paradigm no longer dominates in so-called 'Western' societies, but that it has been replaced by and 'Eastern' one" (40).

This process of "market shopping" a broad array of religious practices was a unique characteristic of the counter-cultural movements in the San Francisco Bay Area in the 1960s and '70s. Robert Wuthnow's[7] *Experimentation in American Religion: The New Mysticism and Their Implications for the Churches* specifically addresses the issue of religious experimentation in the San Francisco Bay Area during the 1960s and '70s. Wuthnow, a scholar who emerged from the Berkeley Studies of New Religious Movements in the 1970s,[8] defines four meaning systems within the New Religious Movements (theistic, individualistic, social scientific, and mystical) of the era and concludes that the dominant trend of religious experimentation was toward mystical faiths and practices and away from purely theistic or God-orientated perspectives.

In an interview for the online publication *Religion & Ethics*, Robert

Wuthnow, in similar fashion to Campbell, discusses the potential for Eastern religious practices to eclipse traditional Christian worship in America. "At this point, it's often easy, still, for churches to treat new religions with the 'out of sight, out of mind' principle governing. They just may be able to ignore the fact that there are large numbers of other religious people in their community, but that's changing very, very rapidly. You know, we're not in a situation where we can only look to some other country and say, 'Oh, well, there're Hindus,' or Muslims, 'living there.' They are living in our own neighborhoods, and in increasing numbers."[9]

Archbishop King has consistently decried differences in religion as mere "differences in form." He urges "freedom from religion" over and against "freedom of religion":

> In the call for the liberation from all these things that God hated: ignorance, deceit, darkness, oppression, etc., some are satisfied that the right to so-called freedom of religion in itself should be enough to deliver us from these sins. The term freedom of religion is more responsible for the lack and the liberalism in our churches today, and for the continual, perpetuating enslaving of the body and the soul in the minds of men. This term as so many are led to believe does not say freedom to determine our destinies, for what we are truly in need of is freedom from religion. There is a need to be free from that which religions are formed to deliver us from, free of religious principles that serve us rather than being enslaved to the Sabbath, for as Jesus says, "For the son is Lord even of the Sabbath day."[10]

Freedom *from* religion, for Archbishop King and the members of the Coltrane Church, means escape from religious denominationalism and an approach towards spiritual universalism. In this regard the Coltrane Church consistently reserves the right to appreciate the fundamental truths of every major religious tradition and the multiplicity of manifestations of John Coltrane within the context of those traditions. In the service of this freedom *from* religion, Archbishop King proposed an alternative vision of the Holy Trinity during the One Mind Temple years that effectively bridges Eastern and Western spiritual traditions.

The principal arguments of the mission statement of the One Mind Temple completed by Archbishop King, then known as Bishop Ha'qq include a powerful elaboration of the similarities between the lives of Christ and John Coltrane that underscore Coltrane's divinity as the reincarnated Christ; an anti-denominational statement; a comparison of melody, harmony, and rhythm to the Holy Trinity; a discussion of the spiritual potency of music; and a passionate argument for freedom of religious expression. In the statement, he wrote:

Above and below: **The altar and congregation at 351 Divisadero Street.**

With the realization that things are not merely related, nor are all things merged, but in fact are interconnected, we are able to understand the multiple meaning in this Psalm and with the further understanding that science teaches us that history does not move in circles but in cycles and things do not merely revolve but they do in fact evolve and transcend into being.

With respect to the analogy that Archbishop draws between the elements of music and the Holy Trinity, Archbishop writes further:

Where as we see the component parts of the Holy Trinity or the God head to be three in one, it is the same with the component parts of music: melody, being viewed as the Father; harmony, as the Son; and rhythm as the Holy Spirit.

In everyday church practice the words and wisdom of John Coltrane are integrated with Christ's teachings in the Gospels. Archbishop King's sermons frequently alternate between the teachings of Christ and Coltrane in order to demonstrate that there is much prophesized within the Scriptures about the spirituality of music, and to make the Scriptures comprehensible for a contemporary African American perspective. Coltrane's words often break the lesson of the Scriptures down even further, and provide a means for the faithful to understand how they can also integrate the word of God into their lives, as Coltrane has.

A Coltrane quote for the week is provided on the inside pages of the Sunday service program. This weekly quotation is read at the end of service along with the announcements and integrated into Archbishop King's sermons. The church has organized a collection of Coltrane quotes in a text titled *John Coltrane Speaks*. Church members can often be observed reading either the weekly quote or selections from *John Coltrane Speaks* even in the midst of the music service as a form of quiet meditation—particularly during the "Lonnie's Lament" segment of the service. I used to frequently observe alto saxophone player Ira Levin[11] drawing his copy of *John Coltrane Speaks* from his horn case and quietly reading for inspiration during the music, either before or after taking a solo.

The practice of integrating the words and wisdom of St. John Coltrane with biblical scripture is consistent with the historical black church traditions. In "Sources of Black Female Spirituality: The Ways of the 'Old Folks' and Women Writers," by Dolores S. Williams and collected in Gloria Wade-Gayles' *My Soul is A Witness*, Williams writes, "But the authority of the Bible was also determined by what the community added to the Bible and called "scripture" right along with the Bible as a scripture" (Wade-Gayles 188). However, the "Coltrane Church's" specific integration of John Coltrane inserts the non-traditional element of an extra-biblical commentator deeply influenced by Eastern spiritual traditions and, in particular, by distinctly Eastern notions of the unity of God and Sound.

Archbishop King's substantive integration of biblical scripture and the words of St. John emphasize an Eastern (Hindu, Sufi) conception of the inherent spirituality of music. In a sermon of December 4, 1994, Archbishop King managed to integrate the Gospel of Matthew, the Old Testament prophet Ezekiel, John Coltrane, and Elvin Jones. The specific message of using music to transform souls and "change the initial thought pattern" came right out of Coltrane's meditations on Eastern spirituality and resonated the extensive writings of the Sufi mystic Hazrat Inayat Khan.

> I like what Matthew says over in the 31st verse in the 24th chapter of Matthew, where he says, "And ye shall sing as angels with the clear sound of the trumpet." Wonder why I like that? "That ye sing as angels." I heard Elvin Jones talking about John Coltrane saying, he's an angel sent from God. Amen. The sound of the trumpet, Amen, with an awakening of the sleeping of mankind. They said they shall gather together his elect from the four winds, from one end of heaven to the other. Praise God Almighty. I want to thank God for that sound being trumpeted by one John Will-I-Am Coltrane and to the Lord using him to gather men and women from every part of the earth that they might give glory and praise to God, that even that the witness of the Scriptures might be fulfilled, Amen, and that all men can become brothers. Praise God Almighty.
>
> The angel is the Bible messenger and created spiritual being. Sometimes we have it fixed as men, Amen? That we like to think that John Coltrane, even St. John came as an angel above. Because one of the things that are attributes of angels is that they have strength and they have wisdom, Amen. And if you want to know something about strength then you need to get into the power of that wheel, the wheel we call the sound disc. And you'll find something about the power that is in this anointed sound of John Coltrane.
>
> Coltrane said that music was an instrument, one that could change the initial thinking and the thought patterns of the people. Some of us need our thought patterns adjusted. We need our thinking changed, and it takes the power of the Holy Ghost to do that, Amen. John Coltrane was a man of great wisdom, Amen. And my Bible tells me that if any man desire wisdom, may he ask of God, who gives to all men liberally, so that even you can be like angels.

Conclusions

In the One Mind Temple era, the Coltrane Church was a specific type of "Black Orientalist" New Religious Movement that had meaning within a local San Francisco Bay Area context in the 1960s and '70s that endeavored to deconstruct and replace Western with Eastern spiritual practices.

The significance of NRMs includes explanations for their contemporary growth as a response to a changing religious "marketplace." Barker writes, "One of the features of modern society which sociologists of religion, such as Durkheim, Weber and Wilson have frequently pointed out is that organized religion no longer has the kind of hold over social institutions that it has enjoyed in earlier periods. Religion has become increasingly a leisure pursuit that may be 'privatized' or 'individualised' or even, to borrow Luckmann's term, 'invisible.' Mainstream religious organizations have suffered significant losses of membership in most of Europe and, according to some, though not all, commentators in the United States" (Wilson 18). Barker credits this changing marketplace with the growth of religious pluralism (18).

Within the context of New Religious Movements (NRMs), the Coltrane Church's history of differential ideological movement may be understood as a series of responses to the ever-changing marketplace of religious ideas, including the evolving Orientalist Easternization of Western religious practice in the San Francisco Bay Area in the 1960s and '70s. Furthermore, as a new religious movement, the Coltrane Church must be understood as a potential threat to older, more established churches. Indeed the very existence of the Coltrane Church implies a critique of established church organizations and Western spirituality. Building on Fauset's ideas, Jacob S. Dorman suggests, "The alternative religious practitioners of the black metropolis appropriated the discourse of Orientalism for their own purposes, discovering political critique, spiritual illumination, and a recalcitrant position within an imperialist intellectual tradition through a sustained engagement with the Oriental Other" (Curtis and Sigler 133). Whether cultural, political, or religious domains, the Coltrane Church as a new religious movement continues to provide a fresh and exciting perspective in the marketplace of religious ideas that by its nature implies a sharp critique of the orthodoxy of established faiths.

7

The Alice Coltrane
Experience

*I understand that John Coltrane was a man, but you
ask me who John Coltrane is, and I'm not going to start
talking about him as a man without saying that he is a
man sent from God. And I'll talk to you in your own tradition. If you're a Christian, then I'll allow him to be a
saint. If you come in here as a Hindu then I'm going to tell
you that he's an avatar and that he's Blue Krishna reincarnated, a beautiful Black mind enchanter and player of
the flute. So my tie into John Coltrane is not just limited
to my personal experience or my sound baptism, but it's
got something that John initiated in me and that was to
study and search out the Scriptures. The rights that the
Vedas ordain and the rituals taught by the Scriptures, all
of these am I.*

—Archbishop Franzo Wayne King, D.D.

Narratives of the period in the church's developmental history that
begin with their association with Alice Coltrane, widow of John Coltrane,
and the formation of the Vedantic Center in 1974 testify to the continuation
of an important ideological shift from Christian influenced spirituality to
Easternization and spiritual universalism, a process that had already begun
during the One Mind Temple years in the midst of a growing marketplace
of new religious movements in San Francisco in the 1960s and '70s.
Although she did not bring spiritually universalist ideologies and practices
to the church, Alice Coltrane provided opportunities for further studies
in Hinduism and in this fashion helped the church to grow further in an
important Eastern spiritual direction that it had already initiated. This is

an ideological shift parallel to the movement from black nationalism to class consciousness. There is an important union in this phase of the church's development of religious holism and visionary futurism.

During this period many of the narratives of spiritual universalism in Coltrane Consciousness represent John Coltrane among the pantheon of Christ, Krishna, Buddha, and Muhammad, giving credence to his music as a spiritual text and affirming his ascension to heaven and place at the hand of God. Dr. Huey P. Newton's emphasis on class over race begins to take hold of the thinking of Archbishop and Mother Marina King. The church begins to incorporate non–African American members, ministers, and musicians. Further, most narratives of renewal in Coltrane Consciousness deliberately conflate Eastern and Western mystical traditions, presenting a belief in the universality of religious expression and a far broader expression of brotherhood than the black nationalist leanings of the church's narratives of origin.

The contemporary manifestation of the St. John Will-I-Am Coltrane African Orthodox Church is explicitly structured around Christian worship. Their evolution toward spiritual universalism has done nothing to diminish that Christ-centered perspective, but it has generated a powerful relativistic position toward spiritual revelation and truth. In other words, the Coltrane Church explicitly recognizes the possibility that other communities at other times and in other places have received spiritual revelations that are no more or no less true than their revelations of God through Coltrane and Christ. Although the testimony of the initial Sound Baptism experienced by Archbishop King and Mother Marina suggested no overt call to specifically Christian worship, the ministry and community have clearly evolved toward Christian worship as an outgrowth of their continued interaction with Coltrane's music. It is therefore also important to address the means through which Coltrane's music articulated a unique Christ-centered spiritual universalism.

Alice Coltrane, widow of John Coltrane, is an important part of this history and development of St. John's African Orthodox Church. Her association with what was then called the Vedantic Center supported this congregation in an intense period of Hindu worship and study and greater exploration of Eastern mystical traditions and texts.

1974–1981: The Vedantic Center

There were four important living teachers for Franzo and Marina King. Phyllis Proudhomme, Supreme Mother, encouraged the spiritual vision and practice of the early church in her letters. Dr. Huey P. Newton provided the core political teachings that rejected race thinking for class consciousness and further underscored the black liberation theological teaching of Jesus Christ as radical revolutionary. Alice Coltrane provided the living link the Coltrane Church needed to John Coltrane and supported the practice and discipline of Hinduism. Archbishop George Duncan Hinkson of the African Orthodox Church provided Franzo King with instruction in orthodox Christian practice, facilitated him earning his doctorate of divinity, and provided his church with an ecumenical legitimacy that would serve as a foundation for greater social activism.

Archbishop King's spiritual relationship with John Coltrane's widow began when the One Mind Temple community journeyed to one of Alice's Berkeley concerts. Considering themselves the original disciples of John Coltrane, they plastered a poster of John Coltrane on the wall of her dressing room and prostrated themselves at Alice's feet, praying John Coltrane's "A Love Supreme."

Here Archbishop King provides a narrative of the church's first encounter with Alice Coltrane. In the midst of his testimony, he provides a clearer picture of the depth of passion and devotion that the early church held for John Coltrane as God and for Alice Coltrane as the "Mother of the Royal Family":

> There's gotta be a section that deals with how we viewed Alice, how we experienced her and where we see things at now with her as being the Mother of the Royal Family and the consort of Lord John who is known as Sri Rama Ohnedaruth, the mystic known as John Coltrane, coming in that greater condition, Krishna and Rada, and all of that.
>
> But I remember before she came here there was a brother that was with the Transcendental Meditation people, and he had been in touch with her and we were all excited, and he used a word that I wasn't familiar with, "macabre," to describe her continence. I remember that was a new word for me and so I'm saying that to support that when I first met her she seemed very troubled. But we were still on 201 Sawyer and were the Yardbird Temple, the Vanguard Revolutionary Church of the Hour then. We became the One Mind Temple by the time of her second visit, and I think we still had that in all of our religious art, the Yardbird Temple, Vanguard Revolutionary Church of the Hour and she was playing at the Berkeley High School, community theater.
>
> I remember we went over there and they were telling us you guys can't come in, you don't have any tickets and I said, what you talking about, we're the first born out of sound. So we had to bless the dressing room where the Royal Mother's gonna be. Who are these cats man? We prayed and we hung the Love Supreme up in the dressing room, burnt incense,

prayed the Love Supreme, and just created an atmosphere that would be spiritually receivable of the Royal Mother, Mother of the Royal Family.

And I remember she came down the steps after the concert and she was coming down and we bowed and she bowed and I gave here this thing that I had written called "The Evolutionary Transitional Existence of Christ." And that John Coltrane was the incarnation, not only the incarnation but an evolved transcended incarnation, that he came with an even higher message in that it was universal, it was global, and not just for Jews and a few Gentiles that got in, John Coltrane came with a universal language and we were comparing Jesus and John, as Jesus a carpenter having to deal with numbers and John being a musician having to deal with numbers and the language of John being a musician, was the universal language, and breaking down the name "Jesus" meaning "Savior," "Christ" meaning "Anointed," "John" meaning "Gift of God" and "Ohnedaruth" was a spiritual name that I think we got from Alice from some of the albums that she put out, "Ohnedaruth" meaning "Compassion" and so I had worked all of that stuff together, and we proclaimed John as God.

And then she called me one day from New York 'cause she was still in New York, and she said that we had been on her mind and that the Lord had moved her to her heart so she called and told us that she was moving to California and that she would be looking us up when she came. And she came here and she said, she saw the church, and she told us, she said, "You all are fulfilling John's highest ideas." That he always wanted a place like this, she said, "not that he would have called it a church because it might have caused some people to stay away from the church but a center, like you have here, this is John's highest ideals."

And we were out then. Oh, Lord, we're fulfilling the master's highest ideals, it was truly beautiful. When Alice would come into the place, as she came in, we would get on our hands and knees. Like, you know, when your guru comes in.

The encounter with Alice Coltrane supported the One Mind Temple Evolutionary Church of Christ's major ideological shift towards Hindu spirituality and practice. In broader terms, the congregation's incorporation within Alice Coltrane's southern California-based (Agoura Hills) Vedantic Center confirmed a move towards spiritual universalism compatible with their political, racial, and cultural universalist evolution under the tutelage of Dr. Newton. The One Mind Temple became the Vedantic Center where, under the leadership of Alice Coltrane, this group of Coltrane devotees engaged in Hindu chanting, studied the Bhagavad Gita, and at least one member journeyed to India with her for further study and meditation.

Alice Coltrane provided a space of focused study for this small congregation, recognizing their uncompromising devotion to her late husband

and teaching written meditation, and helping them to understand John Coltrane as Blue Krishna. Her authority was well recognized by the church, and all members humbled themselves to her royal stature as the Mother of the Royal Family and "wife of God," who came clothed in the garb of John Coltrane.

In this period the Archbishop speaks of moments of profound syncretic practice, where the Hindu chanting issued forth under the rhythms of African American gospel music. Here Archbishop King provides direct testimony of the heady spiritual ideological movement that the church was undergoing toward Easternization and spiritual universalism and of their ability to incorporate one spiritual aesthetic into the practice of another spiritual form. It is noteworthy that in the midst of ideological transformation, church members never lost sight of their immediate ideological past, intricately weaving distinctly different ideological fibers into a broader tapestry of their experience. Archbishop King:

> There was a core group then of about 12 adults and then Wanika took the initiation too and became Sara Swati who is a Hindu goddess that played strings. She wasn't playing bass then either, it turned out like a prophecy, that name, and at the time I was reading a book called *The Gospel of Sri Rama Krishna* according to M. And, so I was really into that when she came up and then the initiation, on initiation night she gave us a mantra and new names. And before she had done that, before she came up I had taken a vow of celibacy and had shaved my head and was going for ultimate perfection.
>
> Strict vegetarian, very ritualistic in my practice, up every morning at 4 a.m. with *A Love Supreme* on, listen to "Acknowledgment" face the east, "Resolution," just go right through the circle you know, south, west, north, then back to the east in four movements. Studying my horn. I had also run into a problem with studying music. I'm not where I desire in terms of ministers of sound and that kind of stuff. A lot of cats were just trying to make a living and I had made them, set them up like tin gods and I'm disappointed when they, you know, didn't come to that point and I just got really disappointed because they weren't the kind of people that I wanted to play music with, they weren't coming in that spirit of John Coltrane, very few of them were, and you know a lot of them were, I mean not only were they just trying to make a living.
>
> So when Alice came up and she said okay, we're gonna do this, and she was teaching us some meditative skills and gave us all new names. So, she gave me the name Rama Krishna, and Rama Krishna's wife is Sharida Devi, she gave Mother Marina the name Sharida Devi. And Sister Lee was Brahma Johti, Sister Deborah was Maha Shakti, and Bro. Brown was Sri Dar and Bro. Carl was Bulu Shaktama, and we had all these Indian names and we were all dressing in white and tilling the beads and chanting Hari

Krishna and all of this stuff. She taught us some beautiful chants, took us from cover to cover through the Bhagavad Gita, and opened up that Vedic knowledge for us because I didn't know anything about the Vedas even though John Coltrane said, "The rites of the Vedas are ordained in the rituals of the Scripture, all of these are mine." Oh, that's deep.

But she opened up the Vedas for us. And she would come up from Los Angeles quite often and we'd have what they call saat sang, kiratan when the guru is present she taught and we were really enjoying it, I mean, it was just such a beautiful opportunity for us.

And at that time we referred to John Coltrane as the Master. Master. Master. You know John has an album called *The Master*. The Master. The Master. I mean I didn't think anybody would argue that he was in fact the master if not other than a master musician.

A Legacy of Spiritual Universalism and Post-Racialism

It's clear that Archbishop King appreciates a universal spiritual response to the divinity of John Coltrane. This acceptance of the universal potential of Coltrane is also what undergirds ethnic inclusiveness at the Coltrane Church. The eradication of racism is a clear agenda in many of the testimonies of Archbishop King. This agenda is also in part supported by the interracial history of jazz music, John Coltrane's emphasis on brotherhood, and the universalist agenda of St. John's which is in large measure a direct result of the church's intensive period of study of Hinduism in the Alice Coltrane years.

In the following statement, Archbishop King clearly links Coltrane's universalist spirituality and ethnic inclusiveness, and for him the connector between the two is the power of music, a universal expression that has the potential for destroying all boundaries, whether religious or ethnic.

> I understand that he was a man but you ask me who John Coltrane is, I'm not going to start talking about he's a man without saying he's a man sent from God. And I'll talk to you in your tradition. If you're a Christian then I'll allow him to be a saint. If you come in here as a Hindu then I'm going to tell you that he's an avatar and that he's Blue Krishna reincarnated, a beautiful Black mind enchanter and player of the flute.
>
> So my tie into John Coltrane is not just limited to my personal experience or my sound baptism but it's got something that John initiated in me and that was study and search, to search out the Scriptures. The rights that the Vedas ordain and the rituals talk by the Scriptures, all of these am I.
>
> And then he's talking about one thought can produce millions of vibrations and you say my goodness, John is talking about more than culture and a time period, I mean, African classical music in terms of the history

Iconography of John Coltrane and the Holy Trinity, from the One Mind Temple years.

of African people is very short lived, so to really tie in the whole experience of John, his life and his music, you've got to go all the way back to Lord Krishna, you know, you've got to understand that, you've got to go back to so of the mythical,... Orpheus and his experience of raising the sun with the strumming of a guitar, you know, and just understanding the mystery the power of the music, if you go to the Old Testament and you see where the musicians in wartime led the procession and even with Jericho the music tearing down the walls so they could be penetrated with the occupants of that city which God had proclaimed.

It's like using the music to tear down the walls of the heart so that the Holy Spirit can come in or so Krishna can come and sit on the seat of the throne that's in your heart, and to tear down the intellectual walls that we have in terms of race supremacy and all of these other kinds of things that are creating chaos in the world.

With respect to its multicultural agenda, the Coltrane Church most directly harks back to the Church for the Fellowship of All Peoples, America's first racially integrated church founded in San Francisco by the great liberation theologian Howard Thurman (Broussard 188). Thurman, a former dean and professor of religion at Howard University, was an integral part of San Francisco's growing black elite. "Fellowship Church established several multicultural programs, and these activities were a bridge into San Francisco's ethnic communities. The church sponsored weekly fellowship lunches with members of the congregation and monthly intercultural fellowship dinners, which celebrated the culture of different groups of church members. It also maintained a library, which collected and circulated materials about different races, religions, and cultures. Weekly forums, coffee hours, and intercultural workshops for children and adults were also part of Fellowship Church's multifaceted program. Howard Thurman believed that these experiences were absolutely essential if people were ever to learn respect for each other as human beings, irrespective of race, religion, and ethnicity" (188).

Further, Bishop Ida Robinson's—founder of Mount Sinai Holy Church of Philadelphia in 1924—celebrated rejection of American nationalism during World War II was an important historical reference for the kind of universal communities that Franzo and Marina King longed to build even before the 1965 Sound Baptism. Clarence E. Hardy III writes, "Few ministers were more committed than Robinson, Tate, Smith, and Horn to the new conceptions of religious community that would overtake boundaries of region and even nation. And perhaps no one of these expressed this passion more bracingly than Robinson did directly in the teeth of an American nationalist sentiment unquestionably at its height. Not long after the Japanese attacked Pearl Harbor and the United States and Japan declared war on one another, an FBI report filed in 1942 alleged that Robinson was an agitator because she had publicly stated that she had 'nothing against the Japanese.' For Robinson, sworn enemies of the United States were not enemies of the people of God" (Curtis and Sigler 27).

The differential movement that the Coltrane Church effectuated in moving from non-denominational Coltrane devotion to Hinduism was clearly enabled by Alice Coltrane. However, there is little evidence that her Hindu influence also implied post-racial inclusivity. It is the church's acceptance of the universalist potential of John Coltrane that has more definitive implications for post-racialism and only through John Coltrane are *both* spiritual *and* ethnic differences deconstructed for members of the Coltrane Church.

John Coltrane's relativism is clearly implied in the mission statement that appeared in church programs between 1994 and 1998:

> We are fully aware of the universality of John Coltrane's music and his philosophy, and that his spirit and legacy does reach and touch the lives of people of many different faiths, creeds, and religions. We however, in this time and place, are grateful for the opportunity to lift up the Name of Jesus Christ through John's music, knowing from personal experience and testimony, and from a great cloud of witnesses, that the Spirit of the Lord is in this Sound Praise as it is delivered from heaven through John.

These statements, like much of the initial philosophy of the Coltrane Church, are grounded in the church's interpretation of the liner notes to his breakthrough album, *A Love Supreme*. John Coltrane wrote:

> Dear Listener, All Praise Be To God To Whom All Praise Is Due. Let us pursue Him in the righteous path. Yes it is true: "seek and ye shall find." Only through Him can we know the most wondrous bestowals. During the year 1957 I experienced, by the grace of God, a spiritual awakening which was to lead me to a richer, fuller, more productive life. At that time, in gratitude, I humbly asked to be given the means and privilege to make others happy through music. I feel this has been granted through His Grace: ALL PRAISE TO GOD.

Eric Nisenson provides a passionate and convincing argument in *Blue: The Murder of Jazz*, that the jazz music scene is currently more segregated than it has ever been before. He savagely critiques the so-called neo-classicist movement in jazz which presently eschews any development in the music beyond Coltrane's modal period and whose scholars and performers (specifically Albert Murray, Amiri Baraka, and Wynton Marsalis) assert some sort of racial essentialism, claiming that jazz can only be played by black musicians. Critiquing Albert Murray's *Stomping the Blues*, which Nisenson claims to be the seminal work of the present neo-classicist movement in jazz, Nisenson observes, "Throughout most of *Stomping the*

Blues, Murray's racial views concerning jazz are implied rather than stated. To him, 'blues music' is by, of, and for African Americans, and only for them. Murray does not hedge, at least; he is up front, jazz can only be played idiomatically by black people, or, rather, American black people. He offers no reason why this would be so" (Nisenson 33).

Nisenson's work is of great importance because, in the face of critics like Murray, he provides ample evidence of the racial unity among musicians, a sort of brotherhood wherein the only thing that mattered was the sound of man's music. "The truth is that most musicians, despite what some may actually say, do not care about race when it comes to actually making music; they care about the sound created by the other musicians-everything else is irrelevant. Musicians have always loved to share ideas with each other, to learn from one another and jam together, regardless of race. This is the way jazz has grown and renewed itself. Musicians have always appreciated the actual music that was created, and have mostly ignored other, ephemeral considerations" (35).

Ohnedaruth at 1286 Fillmore Street. Kneeling from left, Deacon Max Hoff, the late Fr. Roberto DeHaven. Standing, from left, Master of Music and pianist Frederick Harris, bassist Pastor Wanika King-Stephens, bassist and church warden Clarence Stephens and the Rev. Franzo King, Jr.

The question is whether the jazz performance and spiritual practices of St. John Will-I-Am Coltrane African Orthodox Church mark an important return to the racial perspective of jazz musicians in the swing, bop, and post-bop eras, that multi-ethnic and inclusive spirit wherein the only thing that mattered was the quality of a man's sound. Clearly the spiritual agenda of St. John's brings even more to bear on the multi-ethnic agenda of the music, in effect demonstrating that not only can people of diverse backgrounds make wonderful music together but that they can also seek after God together. Interestingly, improvisation, which is the thread that effectively connects the music and the spirituality, is by its nature a process requiring openness to diverse sounds and influences. The Coltrane Church is radical in large measure because they truly take improvisation to task in not only forming the music but also in forming a post-racial community in Christ.

In an eloquent letter to Don DeMichael that appeared in *Down Beat* magazine in 1962, John Coltrane expressed both the desire to communicate to the world and his understanding of the inherent freedom message of jazz. Here Coltrane provides his critique of Aaron Copeland's book, *Music and Imagination* (1952). Coltrane eschews the word "jazz" and re-contextualizes the motivation and community of the "jazz" musician. Importantly, he acknowledges the legacy of slavery and the ongoing context of racism in America.

John Coltrane writes,

The "jazz" musician (you can have this term as well as several others that have been foisted upon us) does not have to worry about a lack of positive and affirmative philosophy. It's built in us. The phrasing, the sound of the music attests this fact. We are naturally endowed with it. You can believe all of us would have perished long ago if this were not so. As to community, the whole face of the globe is our *community* [Coltrane's italics]. You see, it is really easy for us to create. We are born with this feeling that just comes out no matter what conditions exist. Otherwise, how could our founding fathers have produced this music in the first place when they surely found themselves (as many of us do today) existing in hostile communities where there was everything to fear and damn few to trust. Any music that could grow and propagate itself as our music has, must have a hell of an affirmation belief inherent in it. Any person who claims to doubt this, or claims that the exponents of our music of *freedom* [Coltrane's italics] are not guided by the same entity, is either prejudiced, musically sterile, just plain stupid or scheming. Believe me Don, we all know that this word which so many seem to fear today, "Freedom," has a hell of a lot to do with this music [Analahati 65- 66].

What the Coltrane Church understands is that in his music John Coltrane attempted this universal communication of freedom through formal innovations in music that involved the integration of non–Western scales, tones, and rhythms. In discussing his contributions to jazz music, Eileen Southern writes, "He was notable for his innovative approach to improvisation, his unorthodox handling of rhythms and form, his use of African, Arabic, Indian, and other non-western elements in his music, and his deep spirituality" (Southern 481).

In an interview conducted in 1968, Alice Coltrane spoke to the universalism of Coltrane's music:

> I asked him what it was that he was doing in music. These are his exact words: he said, 'I am looking for a universal sound.' At the time I didn't quite understand him fully, but I think what he was trying to do in music was the same thing he was trying to do in his life. That was to universalize his music, his life, and even his religion. It was all based on a universal concept, all-sectarian or nonsectarian. In other words, he respected all faiths, all religious beliefs [Rivelli and Levin 123].

A great deal of attention has been focused on Coltrane's use of non–Western musical ideas and instrumentation in the critical literature of jazz studies. The importance of this aspect of the genius of John Coltrane to the post-racialism of the Coltrane Church is that it underscores his holistic, relativistic, and inclusive approach to world religions.

Coltrane's evolving identification with African and Eastern—particularly Indian music—teaches congregants that African and Eastern spiritual and aesthetic traditions are vital paths to redemption. As he opens the ears of his listeners to world sounds, he also opens the hearts of believers to non–Western spiritual traditions, encouraging a relativistic and holistic perspective of religion. Indeed Coltrane is far more spiritual than religious, for he explicitly shunned identification with any one particular religious organization. "I believe in all religions," is the quotation used most often by Archbishop King during his sermons. Lewis Porter notes, "It wasn't only the sound of world music that attracted him; Coltrane was interested in all kinds of religion, and in all kinds of mysticism. He knew that in some folk cultures music was held to have mystical powers, and he hoped to get in touch with some of those capacities. He told Nat Hentoff, 'I've already been looking into those approaches to music—which particular sounds and scales are intended to produce specific emotional meanings'" (Porter 211).

Evidence of such African and Eastern musical and mystical identification includes compositions such as "Africa," "India," "Kulu Se Mama,"

"Dakar," and "Om." For example, on the *Om* recording Coltrane and the quartet are heard chanting from the Bhagavad Gita at the beginning and end of this nearly thirty-minute piece. "The final words were: 'I, the oblation, and I the flame into which it is offered. I am the sire of the world and this world's mother and grandsire. I am he who awards to each the fruit of his action. I make all things clean. I am Om—OM—OM—OM!'" (Porter 265). There was more Hindu chanting on the posthumous release *Cosmic Music.* "On February 2, 1966, the group chanted 'A-um-ma-ni-pad-me-hum,' said to represent 'the seven breaths of life,' at the start of 'Reverend King'" (265).

In addition to the musical and mystical traditions of India, Coltrane also incorporated African musical techniques and instrumentation. Porter comments, "Coltrane also studied recordings of African music by Nigerian drummer Michael Babatunde Olatunji. Olatunji and Coltrane played opposite each other, alternating with a third band, Art Blakey's Messengers, at New York's Village Gate during the last week of August 1961. John wrote 'Tunji' for him in 1962. Coltrane seems to have applied some of the concepts he heard in the music of Olatunji and in folkloric African recordings to his own music. First of all was the use of ostinatos, with each instrument having its own rhythm that adds into the whole. African structural concepts may have influenced him too- West African drumming groups will repeat one section until the leader gives a cue to go on to the next, much as Coltrane does in 'My Favorite Things'" (212). Porter goes further, indicating that Coltrane's composition "Dahomey Dance" was inspired by a Folkways recording of two African singers, and that during the *Africa/Brass* recording Coltrane was listening to African recordings for "rhythmic inspiration" (212–213).

From the biography of John Coltrane it is important to note that his first wife, Naima, was a Muslim, and his second wife, Alice, would become a Hindu only two years after Coltrane's passing. John met Naima (Juanita Austin) in Philadelphia in 1954. According to Lewis Porter, Philadelphia was something of a Muslim stronghold (96). His introduction to Naima and their subsequent marriage was all a part of Coltrane's exposure to Islam, and in Philadelphia Coltrane was also introduced to a number of Islamic musicians, including Art Blakey, Yusef Lateef, and Ahmad Jamal (96). That early introduction to Islam may have marked Coltrane's initial thoughts about the validity of different religious beliefs. Recalling those days in Philadelphia, Coltrane remarked, "About two or three years later, maybe twenty-two, twenty-three [the late 1940s in Philadelphia], this Moslem thing came up. I got introduced to that. And that kinda shook me. A lot of my friends, you know, they went Muslim, you see. So I thought about that, anyway, it took me to something I'd never thought about –you know, another religion?" (257). Regarding Alice Coltrane, Lewis Porter writes, "Mrs. Coltrane has become a mystic, an advanced disciple of Swami Satchadinanda, whose name suggests the achievement of spiritual 'reality' in Hindu" (297). By 1975 Alice Coltrane had founded the Vedantic Center which is currently located in southern California, and had changed her name to Turiyasangitananda (297.).

It can be argued that Coltrane's relativistic perspective was a result of his being a musician, although few musicians have been as spiritually open as was John Coltrane.[1] It's important to remember that music was the chosen means of expression for John Coltrane, and that while he could surely have written his relativistic views on religion or given more inter-views stating his beliefs on this and other topics, Coltrane chose to pursue music as an avenue of expression. Indeed Coltrane deliberately eschewed manipulating music for any particular position or philosophy. Instead Coltrane remained true to the universalist and hybrid nature of music and sought to embrace that understanding in his life outside of music. While his music urged selflessness and unconditional love, it surely cannot be said to embrace any particular denominational perspective on these higher ideals.

Coltrane once remarked:

I think it's going to have to be very subtle; you can't ram philosophies down anybody's throat, and the music is enough! That's philosophies. I think the best thing I can do at this time is to try to get myself in shape and know myself. If I can do that, then I'll just play, you see, and leave at that. I believe that will do it, if I really can get to myself and be just as I feel I should be and play it. And I think they'll get it, because music goes a long way, it can influence [Analahati 36].

Coltrane's musical expression of a religious holism has important implications for Coltrane Consciousness. Archbishop King informs us, "John Coltrane for me in the Eastern tradition would be what they call a Saat Gura, he would be the true teacher that not only taught but lived it out and he had the knowledge of God."

Because Coltrane's teachings are expressed almost entirely through sound, and because they express above all a selfless devotion to God, they are as revolutionary in a contemporary context as the Socratic method of ancient Greek history, the teaching in parables of Jesus Christ, or Sid-dhartha Guatama's (Buddha) imperative for truth in South Asia in the sixth century BC. It is important to emphasize that Coltrane vigorously eschewed traditional Western pedagogy. Through music Coltrane was aiming for a language far more universal, more subtly expressed upon first contact and more profoundly felt through repeated listening and reflection.

Sunday worship services are certainly inclusive. The Coltrane Liturgy incorporates the Hindu chanting from Coltrane's recordings, "A-um-ma-ni-pad-me-hum,"[2] which often comes at the end of "Lonnie's Lament" and "Spiritual" while the Introit to the African Orthodox liturgy is sung. Many of the Hindu names derived from the Hindu past under Alice Coltrane are still used. The church has a long-standing relationship with the Nation of Islam mosque in San Francisco. Archbishop King has sought for many years to bring the music of John Coltrane into the Jewish synagogues in the Bay Area. The church has fellowshipped with Catholics, Baptists, Pentecostals, Episcopalians, and Lutherans in recent years. In practice, the church has fully embraced the holistic approach of John Coltrane and clearly regards this as an important teaching of the master's music.

In a rough six-page mission statement for the One Mind Temple Evolutionary Transitional Church of Christ, Archbishop King writes,

> For as there have been many nations of people, the Jews, the Muslims, the Buddhists, Hindus, Ha'qqs, etc. The central Truth of each of its prophets was unity.
> As the word "right" gives no justification to slavery, neither does the word "freedom" give deliverance to religion. There is not merely a need for freedom of religion, but a call for unity of religious ideals, and a greater need to be free from religion.

These statements go beyond the ability to equate differing spiritual truths. Read precisely, the differential ideological movements of the Coltrane Church through a variety of spiritual planes embrace a futurist, relativist, post-racial philosophy that moves the Coltrane Church into the 21st century. As the story of the Coltrane Church unfolds, it will be increasingly evident that their affirmative relativistic non-denominationalism afforded them the opportunity to make significant political, religious, and cultural alliances, not the least of which includes alliances forged in their later efforts against police brutality, environmental racism, foreclosure, and redevelopment in San Francisco.

Widow of God Sues Church, Church Rejoices

Perhaps the most widely publicized event in the history of the St. John Will-I-Am Coltrane African Orthodox Church, and surely the event that brought this small congregation to national attention, was the $7.5 million lawsuit brought against them by Alice Coltrane for improper use of John Coltrane's name.

The *New York Times* covered this story in 1981. In an article titled "Coltrane's Widow Sues San Francisco Church," Krebs Albin and Robert McG. Thomas, Jr., write that Alice Coltrane stated the church was illegally using his name "without family sanction and is misrepresenting us and infringing on copyright laws.... A spokesman for the One Mind church, when asked whether permission had been sought to use Mr. Coltrane's name, said, 'Did you ever think it was necessary to ask Mother Mary to use Jesus' name?'"

The lawsuit arose out of what Archbishop King refers to as "antithetical differences" and did not mark a complete break between Alice Coltrane and Archbishop King and his fledgling congregation. Up until the time of Alice's recent passing[3] they communicated through others including Sis. Lee, Sis. Deborah, and Sis. Erin, who continued to visit with Alice Coltrane.

The importance of Archbishop King's testimonial account of the events surrounding that lawsuit is that his love and respect for Alice Coltrane expanded his thinking about the leadership of women in the church. Archbishop King was devoted to Alice Coltrane because of her position as the mother of John Coltrane's children and his companion. He continues to regard her as an anointed and high spirit.

Archbishop King remarks:

> With Alice Coltrane we were an authentic discipline. In the Vedas as opposed to Ha'qqism we had become Hindus, a more established practice, one of the ancient religions. We were also revolutionary in having a woman as guru. We were emphasizing the power of women, which would lead to Pastor Wanika. The innovative move was having a guru coming out of the African American Baptist church and becoming a Saat Guru.

The lawsuit was dropped in 1982 after the untimely death of Alice Coltrane's eldest son, John Coltrane, Jr., in an automobile accident. Archbishop King and Mother Marina have always presumed a connection between the two events, surmising that the grief that she experienced over the death of John Jr. led to her reassessment and abandonment of the lawsuit.

In the end, their highly publicized rift with Alice Coltrane would cause a temporary controversy and necessitate a further ideological shift. Commenting on the controversy, Sister S. Elizabeth, who joined the church after Alice Coltrane's departure, recalls the implications of that period in 1984.

There were people that lined up on every side. We had camps of people that were for us, against us, there were people who could listen to our explanations of what we were doing with this and then there were people who said, well Alice Coltrane sued you guys so you must not be legitimate and you must be using John Coltrane's name wrong. And that's how it hit in the ministry. People used it as something that they used against us to not listen to us. We still get questions today, "well does Alice Coltrane support this work?" You know, there are some prejudices that kinda last forever.

Conclusions

With Alice Coltrane from 1974 to 1981, the church was affiliated with the established religious practice of Hinduism and the authentic discipline of studying the Vedas. However, the truly innovative aspect of this period involved their association with an African American woman guru. Alice Coltrane had emerged from the African American Baptist Church experience and became a Swami, a Saat Guru. It was as if the Coltrane Church was saying that if African Americans were to have a guru, it would need to be an African American woman coming out of the broader African American Church experience.

Furthermore, Alice Coltrane's leadership and the reverence with which she was treated foreshadow increasing gender equality and black womanist theological leadership in the St. John Will-I-Am Coltrane African Orthodox Church. In many senses, the Alice Coltrane years, in addition to Mother Marina's co-ownership of the church's foundational narratives and the influence of Dr. Phyllis Proudhomme, enabled the consecration of Wanika Kristi King-Stephens as Pastor in 2010. The lawsuit would threaten to leave the church with a significant controversy that might endanger its position in the Bay Area marketplace of spiritual ideas, particularly in the wake of the horror of the Peoples Temple in 1978.

By 1982 the church was ready for another significant ideological shift, and this time for the purpose of shedding any controversy that might affect its greater spiritual, cultural, and political work and agenda.

> When we went into the Vedantic Center it was all about studying the Gita and we went down from 7 to 1 day in our service. Jonestown happened. This made the African Orthodox Church a welcome invitation and now we are going to be coming into a Christian community. When we split with her we came back to being One Mind Temple and started out food program again.

The publicity generated by Alice Coltrane's lawsuit would provide the Coltrane Church with this much needed opportunity for ecumenical acceptance. Bishop Dr. Ajari, who claimed to be a descendant of the last Russian Czar) of the Old Russian Believers on Mississippi Street in San Francisco, sent his Vicar Dr. William H. Green (who referred to himself as "Sessaway") to investigate the former followers of the "widow of God" who had dared refer to their religious practices as "orthodox." They provided the church with information about "orthodoxy" and later suggested that the church needed to join the greater African Orthodox Church, further agreeing to pay for the flight of the Archbishop George Duncan Hinkson of the African Orthodox Church.

8

The African Orthodox Church

Indeed, the American Negro church, viewed historically,
provides numerous vivid examples of the Negro's capacity
to revolt.

—Arthur Huff Fauset

Alice Coltrane's multimillion-dollar lawsuit brought the church to the attention of a national media and that exposure brought them to the attention of the African Orthodox Church. In his statements to the local and national media, then Bishop King referred to his church as an "orthodox" church. Use of this term drew the attention of Bishop Ajari of the Russian Orthodox Church, and Bishop Ajari sent a representative, his vicar, Dr. William H. Green a.k.a. "Sessaway" (now a bishop in the African Orthodox Church), to talk to Archbishop King and his congregation about the African Orthodox Church. Bishop Ajari ultimately approached Archbishop King about becoming a bishop in the African Orthodox Church, and although Archbishop King countered with evidence of his legitimation as bishop from his mother, Dr. Phyllis Proudhomme, Bishop Ajari managed to convince him of the greater legitimation under the African Orthodox Church.

In these testimonies Archbishop King speaks of Bishop Ajari, Dr. Green a.k.a. "Sessaway," and finally Dr. George Duncan Hinkson from the African Orthodox Church, their reaction to Coltrane Consciousness, and their guidance and support. It's important to take notice of how Archbishop King locates his church as an avant garde movement even as they contemplated integration within the African Orthodox Church:

> The press came at us hard brother and what they asked us in the interview was, "Well, what kind of church do you have here, Bishop?" I said,

Orthodox. I didn't know any more about Orthodoxy than a jackrabbit does Easter Sunday. You dig what I'm saying? That's when Ajari, Bishop Ajari, looks in the paper and he sees 'Orthodox,' and he sends his vicar over to talk to us to find out what's going on and to tell us about the African Orthodox Church. Brought us books. Bishop Ajari is Russian Orthodox Old Believers. He was also a Buddhist monk.

We had operated independently as a non-denominational faith for many years and we were brought to the attention of the African Orthodox Church, and His Eminence George Duncan Hinkson in particular who at that time was looking for a means to deepen the roots and broaden the branches of the African Orthodox Church, and he was in California looking for candidates for ordination and churches for fellowship into his jurisdiction. We were brought to his attention by Bishop Ajari of the old Russian believers, and we were examined and ordained and consecrated into the African Orthodox Church.

Archbishop King's official affiliation with the African Orthodox Church began in 1982 when he was consecrated as Bishop and continued through 1986 when he and his family journeyed to Chicago for an intensive period of study under Archbishop George Duncan Hinkson. Dr. Charles L. James appointed Archbishop King—then Bishop—as Chaplain General of the UNIA at the request of Archbishop Hinkson. Archbishop's King's consecration as Chaplain General placed him in direct lineage with African Orthodox Church founder Archbishop Alexander McGuire, who had been the first and last man before King to serve as chaplain general of the UNIA. In Chicago, Archbishop King and Mother Marina became members of the local chapter of the UNIA. The former Vedantic Center was renamed the One Mind Temple Missionary Episcopate of the African Orthodox Church of the West. And on September 19, 1982, John Coltrane was formally canonized as a saint by His Eminence the Most Reverend Archbishop George Duncan Hinkson and the House of Bishops.

The St. John Will-I-Am Coltrane African Orthodox Church is now the westernmost congregation of the wider African Orthodox Church, founded in 1919 by African American Episcopalians disaffected by racism in the church. Arthur Huff Fauset addresses this critical historical moment: "Large groups of Negroes in the United States, after having accepted the basic tenets of European Christianity, almost exclusively in its Protestant form, broke away from the established white churches to form churches of their own. The chief reasons for these separatist tendencies were the reluctance of white Christians to accept Negroes in the already established churches on a plane of equality, and the desire of Negroes to worship in churches where they could feel free to express themselves along the lines which the general condition of their lives prompted" (Fauset 8).

The episcopate of the African Orthodox Church comes from Ignatius Peter III of Antioch and the church follows the Western rites. George Alexander McGuire, the first consecrated bishop of the African Orthodox Church, also served as chaplain of Marcus Mosiah Garvey's Universal Negro Improvement Association (1914-), and the church has consistently maintained a social activist, self-help Garvey ideology that embraces the fundamental tenets of black liberation theology.

In *The African Orthodox Church: A General History*, Archbishop Philippe Laurent DeCoster writes, "George Alexander McGuire was an emigrant to the United States from Antigua and served as a priest in the Protestant Episcopal Church until 1918. McGuire's experience in the Episcopal Church had been tainted with incidents of discrimination against himself and his fellow black clergy. He severed his ties with the church and decided that only in a denomination of blacks with a black administration would equality and spiritual freedom be attained. McGuire's search for black equality led him to Marcus Garvey and to Garvey's Universal Negro Improvement Association. Garvey reinforced McGuire's notion of a black denomination and once McGuire founded the African Orthodox Church, Garvey used his periodical entitled the Negro World to disseminate the news throughout Africa" (De Coster 12).

From the Sound Baptism to a more focused listening clinic to the Yardbird Club and the Yardbird Temple to the One Mind Temple and the One Mind Temple Revolutionary Vanguard Church of the Hour and the One Mind Evolutionary Transitional Body of Christ to the Vedantic Center to the One Mind Temple Missionary Episcopate of the African Orthodox Church of the West, the eventual St. John Will-I-Am Coltrane African Orthodox Church marked another ideological shift of the Coltrane Church which now embraced orthodox Christian worship and officially "demoted" John Coltrane from God to saint. Franzo and Marina King and an ever-changing flock would remain, playing the music of John Coltrane, worshipping God and feeding the poor.

For Archbishop King, the beauty of their unification with the African Orthodox Church lay in Archbishop Hinkson's willingness to accept the church's essential devotion to John Coltrane:

> On the whole Coltrane thing, they didn't make any big deal out of it. By the time it got to the East we had already been in the church ten years and we were bringing some notoriety to the church as well and I had already served as the rector and the dean of the Cathedral so that gave me another

kind of ... coming through the apostolic succession, you know. Didn't have any problem with that. Matter of fact is they said that we have modern day saints and that's when they told me about Martin Luther King and Marcus Garvey and Alexander McGuire are saints in the church. It's not something that they play up but they've been canonizing.

According to Mother Marina, their introduction to the African Orthodox Church was marked by mutual respect and love. And in Chicago, under the tutelage of Archbishop George Duncan Hinkson, then Bishop King and Mother Marina found further encouragement in the U.N.I.A. tradition of the African Orthodox Church. To a great degree what they learned of African Orthodox Church history resonated much of what they had learned during their affiliation with Dr. Huey P. Newton and the Black Panther Party:

> We were in Chicago to meet Archbishop Hinkson for two years around 1986 to 1988. It was a good experience for my son, Franzo. We didn't have to tell him to practice his horn, he just did. I think that when he saw the difficulty of getting into a decent school, a good school, he really had to bear down. He saw people of color running hospitals and communities, which is something that the kids in San Francisco don't get to see too much of. That was a good experience for him there.
>
> When we were there in Chicago, the U.N.I.A., Dr. Charles L. James, made Bishop King the Chaplain General. There had not been a Chaplain General since Archbishop McGuire, the Patriarch of the African Orthodox Church. But again, it was just a coming together, it was really a love affair. He was an encouragement to us and I think it was reciprocal. It was wonderful, hearing the stories and being taught by a living disciple of Marcus Garvey. And he was definitely a man that was full of the Holy Spirit. He was a race man.
>
> We studied a lot of the writings and thought of Garvey and also Father Divine. There was a book that we read about Father Divine. In the inner circle we read and studied and we were expected to adhere to a lot of those teachings, whether it was that or in our study of Sufism. Our thing was, yes, be saved, but also be mystics. That required a lot of study. With the Human Outreach programs, that came from Bishop King saying, "I do not want to be another church on the block that's not doing anything for the people." This came from reading about what Garvey did and reading about what Father Divine did. They were great inspirations in that area. I think the Panther Party and even the Muslims are trying to do things to be self-sufficient. We haven't arrived yet but we are still working towards that.

This ideological shift towards the African Orthodox Church also marked a reappraisal and reincorporation of many of the previous manifestations of the Coltrane Church. Having undergone substantial changes in membership, the African Orthodox Church signaled stability and a basis for possible growth. The stability promised by the African Orthodox Church and the duration of a 20-year journey from 1965 to 1986 ushered in a genuine reappraisal of this congregation's struggles and triumphs.

Archbishop Hinkson not only welcomed the incorporation of John Coltrane as a new saint, but under the auspices of the African Orthodox Church the church initially maintained the One Mind moniker; maintained a listening clinic; Sunday worship services became increasingly renown as venues for visiting musicians; members continued referring to one another with Hindu names given during the Alice Coltrane years; and the kitchen at 351 Divisadero Street was consistently open and feeding the poor and homeless hot vegetarian meals. All of these and many other developments were carried out in earnest under the African Orthodox Church and all represented earlier manifestations in the evolution of the church.

From the African Orthodox Church to Community Activism

Perhaps the most significant moment in the church's early relationship with the African Orthodox Church from 1982 to 1989 was centered around Archbishop Hinkson's recognition of the critical importance of community activism in the church's early history. Not only would Archbishop Hinkson embrace the church's fundamental adoration of John Coltrane, but he also clearly understood their pre–Alice Coltrane history as an underground cultural and political force, including their involvement with the Black Panther Party and the Yardbird Club as an underground community arts organization.

Upon the close of his theological training in 1989, Archbishop King recalls Archbishop Hinkson's clear directive:

> Archbishop tells me, Bishop, I think you need to go secure things in San Francisco and go back to San Francisco like the new kid on the block and make yourself known as the Bishop of the great African Orthodox Church.
> That was profound because we were always an underground movement. I didn't give a hoot who ran for mayor or who was on the school board. He told me to come back and make myself known.

Archbishop King returned to San Francisco at a most propitious time. The Loma Prieta earthquake of 1989 happened and San Francisco's diverse religious communities were coming together around a common cause to provide aid and comfort. Archbishop King made his presence known at the San Francisco Religious Council, introducing them to the city's African American ministers, many of whom were also unfamiliar with him, and creating a broader coalition with white Baptists and Catholics in need of diversification.

> When I come back I go to the Baptists, they had a group that met, and I give them my card with the "In Tenebris Lumen. African Orthodox Church. By favor of Ignatius Peter III of Antioch. His Excellency the Most Reverend."
>
> I was out here visiting once from Chicago and a nun from the Catholic Archdiocese stopped me and said, We don't have you in any of the ecumenical list of churches ... this is interesting.
>
> So when I come back to that little church, Lady of Lourdes, and the ecumenical father was there and he introduced me and told me that the nun had been singing my praises and that I needed to meet you and he takes me over to the Methodists and all over the place and introduces me to everybody.
>
> So the earthquake happens and the San Francisco Religious Council was going to do a memorial service, and I ended up joining them, and I'm the only black person there. So I ask if we are going to have any other representation from the other black churches. And I told them about some of the black churches in the area.

Once "in" with San Francisco's African American religious leadership, Archbishop King became acquainted with another perennial outsider, Minister Christoher Muhammad—then Christopher X of the Nation of Islam:

> Lefty Gordon calls a meeting about gangs. They were trying to pass a law that if there were five black men together it could be called a gang and it could come under the gang injunction act. So Lefty calls the Rev. Brazell who used to be at Hutch. They called a meeting on this. So that's how I meet him.
>
> And then I meet Min. Christopher and he's talking to me about Dexter Gordon and all that and I'm thinking this guy is hip. I was trying to be like Elijah Muhammad. So we had a natural relationship. He was Christopher X then. Around the time he was organizing for the Million Man March. There were people hating on the march, Farrakhan hating, and this is how I really found out how much Christopher loved his leader.

The Archbishop's meeting with Min. Christopher would ultimately lead to the Coltrane Church's involvement in a new leadership circle, what Min. Christopher would refer to as "watchmen" for the black community:

> Minister Christopher came by and asked where are the watchmen. Who's really looking out for the community? Not the so-called leadership, but who are the real watchmen?

He wanted to put a leadership circle together. He wanted to know who would I suggest to be a part of that circle, that I trusted. I said, I don't know anybody, the line stops with you. I don't know anybody that I can say in this town that I trust with leadership that's ready to do real battle and that's not cowing and bowing and willing to go along to get along.

And he said, well I know a few people. That's when he brought Jim Queen and Wendell Adams. He pulled folks together. Richard from the Panther 8, San Francisco 8. Min. Christopher initiated this.

In the 1990s this would develop into an African American Community Police Relations Board that would engage San Francisco's political leaders and the San Francisco Police Department on the level of public policy. And in the new millennium, this leadership circle would continue to mature as the Caravan for Justice, a platform for fighting police brutality, advocating for environmental justice through ballot initiatives, and leading an anti-foreclosure movement against predatory lenders and big banks.

Conclusions

The significance of the African Orthodox Church is that it not only signaled another ideological shift but one that gave ideological cover, institutional and historical protection, and retrospective meaning to a seemingly ragged history of differential ideological movements. The 20-year history of the Coltrane Church up to this point was now fully legitimated by the institutional history of the African Orthodox Church that originated in 1921. A new religious movement was now fully incorporated within the institutional structure of a traditional religious organization. The Coltrane Church's mandates for social justice and serving the community were legitimated by the African Orthodox Church's association with Marcus Garvey's U.N.I.A. The post-racial politics and spiritual universalism that the church had learned under the tutelage of Huey Newton and Alice Coltrane, was affirmed by the anti-racist agenda of African Orthodox Church founder Archbishop Alexander McGuire. The desire to see God in their own image through the likeness of John Coltrane was reinforced by the African Orthodox Church's mandate for African iconography and cultural representations of Jesus as African.

This move toward the African Orthodox Church would fully legitimate the Coltrane Church as a Christian organization and mark an important step from the margins closer toward the center. Archbishop King indeed made his presence felt upon his return in 1989 and would thereafter be recognized as a significant religious, political, and cultural force, even if many of his new acquaintances within the broader network of churches, African American and otherwise, viewed him with suspicion and would oppose him on a variety of civil rights positions in the future. That legitimacy would only grow when more than a decade later on March 10, 2001, Archbishop George Duncan Hinkson would proclaim then Bishop Franzo Wayne King, D.D. to be Archbishop of the Jurisdiction of the West.

The question from 1989 forward was simply how the newly organized St. John Will-I-Am Coltrane African Orthodox Church would use its "legitimated" status to begin effecting real cultural, religious, and political power for its community, constituents, and partners within the San Francisco Bay Area. The answer lay in Archbishop King's enduring relationship with Min. Christopher and the Nation of Islam and the manifestation of Min. Christopher's vision of being "Watchmen for the People" and creating a protective circle around the community.

9

Anatomy of a Miracle

My music is the spiritual expression of what I am—my faith, my knowledge, my being.... When you begin to see the possibilities of music, you desire to do something really good for people, to help humanity free itself from its hangups.... I want to speak to their souls.

—St. John Will-I-Am Coltrane

Although there was much political and cultural promise, the early years of the new St. John Will-I-Am Coltrane African Orthodox Church were not without spiritual challenges. Archbishop King and Mother Marina often speak of members who did not accompany them on their transition to orthodox Christian practice, and of others who remained with Alice Coltrane. Their faith would be tested, and in these moments church leaders and members would come together around the occurrence of miracles indicating that they were being led in the right direction. These narratives of miracles in the Coltrane Church testify to the spiritual efficacy of Coltrane Consciousness and speak to significant moments in which the faith of Coltrane Church members was greatly tested and their extraordinary journey was validated.

In the years that I regularly attended the Coltrane Church (1994–2004) I heard hundreds of testimonies attesting to the power of religion and, specifically, the music of John Coltrane. Bro. Reggie was delivered from drug and alcohol abuse and ultimately met his wife at the Coltrane Church. Archbishop King would often speak of how Coltrane came to him in visions and quelled suicidal paranoia. Sis. Mary Deborah once spoke of how the Lord intervened to prevent her from a terrible automobile accident and how a tape of John Coltrane was playing in her car during the incident. And certainly the church's ability to meet its rent and monthly

159

expenses during the course of the past forty-three years has been miraculous.

One of the most dramatic miracles in this music includes the healing
of Shahada, Archbishop King's third cousin and one of the many children
raised in the Coltrane Church. With his soprano saxophone in his hand,
Archbishop speaks of miracles in the music, of little Shahada, as she lay
near death, suffering from severe burns as a result of child abuse that
afflicted the entire lower portion of her body. He tells the story of how
they went to the hospital and put a picture of John Coltrane on the wall
above her bed, and played "A Love Supreme" and the Coltrane liturgy and
prayed until she was healed:

> And the way the mind works in my mind in particular and the way that
> I seem to identify everything that I do with this work or everything that
> happens around me with this work.... I was thinking about little Shahada.
> She got burned. At that moment, at that time period when she was going
> through that suffering, it was like she was suffering for the whole church,
> and that ... the symbolism of being burned from the waist down as
> opposed to up and dealing with that lower energy as being some kind of
> purifying experience, an opportunity for us as a body of believers to be
> purged through that experience, through not just the experience of the
> injury itself alone but also the healing process and what it did for this
> community in terms of us being more acutely aware of the need for God
> and our need and dependence on Him and the whole idea of being struck
> very clearly with the thought that it is all with God, we have no control
> over a lot of things that are happening.
>
> Even in the process of her injury, Sister Lee—Shahada was with her bio-
> logical parents then—had this intuition and this drive to try to get this child
> and the parents having this resistance to it and not really born out of a pure
> affection either. I think it had a lot to do with welfare and stipends and
> things like that and also maybe to try to prove or maintain their authority as
> parents. And just before it happened Sister Lee had told me that she felt like
> we needed to go see about this girl. And when she said it to me, I mean it
> wasn't the first time she had said that, but the last time that she said that to
> me, I said, let me know when you want to go. There was an urgency in it.
>
> However, that has been my sorrow as the Bishop to find myself lying
> back and waiting from an initiative from the body, rather than when that
> intuitive thing comes through the member to just be able to act on some-
> thing, or even when it comes to me. To not halter, to just move, like when
> the Lord says "Move," move. So then you have to wrestle with that. Well,
> what if we had went when we said we were going to go, well this wouldn't
> have happened. But this whole pleading with them, leave the children with
> us, you can have the welfare check, you can have the welfare check, we
> don't want it, we want the children and when you get situated in Modesto,
> we will bring the girls to you.

So for me, there's some great joy in there because there's some victory in it in that it was announced at least three or four times during that process, the burn creating pneumonia, and all of the other kind of things that happened with a burn that bad, including seizures, and being told, "Get ready, this is it, she's not going to make it," and then watching the Lord work, again through the music.

Because we would go to the hospital, take the tape, play Coltrane, sing the liturgy to her. We were doing this around the clock and it was as much of an aid for us as we credit it to being a part of her healing process. It was something that helped me to stay sane and others in the community and it seemed like it was also an extension of the work in terms of "Who are these people?" and having John Coltrane's image over the bed, playing his music, and singing the liturgy and all of that ... "Who are you people and what is this all about?" And then so you feel like, "We're not here to exploit this child to further the ministry," but, at the same time, there was an opportunity that spoke for itself, and so I don't remember what all I had said, there was one Wednesday night when the Lord had really given me that she was a representative of the church and that the gates of hell could not prevail against the church and in that she was the symbol of the church, of Christ's church, that she would survive this and in doing so we would also survive it but not only survive it but come out the stronger.

The tragedy that Shahada suffered was not only symbolic of the travails of the church as a community, but it offered an opportunity for a young church to test the music of St. John Coltrane, test their faith, and test their travels through a wealth of cultural, religious, and political ideologies. The Coltrane Church clearly needed confirmation of its core mission and validation of its complex history. Were they in the midst of a meaningful evolution? Through a confluence of coincidences and "signs," it became evident to this young congregation that they were on the right path. Archbishop King speaks further of this confirmation:

When I start thinking about sorrows and joys and disappointments and victories ... what a great victory it was that her therapist was a listener. It was somebody that I knew casually from being in and out of the listening scene in the clubs and things, and knowing about the church and being a Coltrane devotee. He had the most painful part of her therapy of changing the bandages and so he had the witness and the testimony of the music and how it aided her.

So, those kind of things, you feel good about it and you feel the idea of being of a champion is the kind of thing that motivates me, to be a champion for the suffering, for the people, making a contribution for the liberation of the suffering, liberating the suffering of the people, that whole kind of thing, and I'm pretty well convinced that if it had not been for the personality of myself and this church and other community members in this church, that child would have died.

And not just with our prayers but the way the Lord was leading us and the authority that we had to take, because being a distant relative they didn't want to give me the privilege, or Sister Lee, that the parent would have.

The father's being charged with a criminal act of assaulting a child like that. The mother's pregnant six, seven, eight months with another child, and having some real difficult times with seeing her baby suffer like this and not really equipped in terms of her youth and her wisdom to put the kind of pressure on that medical staff.

Because at one point I just say "Hey, I'm this child's godfather, I'm this child's Bishop and priest" and you know they're trying to limit when I can come in, because when we go in we start jamming people up and I had to pull the whole staff that was working there with them into a meeting from the nurses to the doctors to the therapists to the assistant head of the hospital and the surgeons.

We had to call a meeting and let them know that we're a faith believing community and we are convinced in our faith that the wellness of this child is not going to just be through prayer but through the diligence and attention that we felt that we needed to do and we also felt that we had the right to criticize what we saw as being inconsistencies with good health care.

So that whole feeling of through that suffering and having that feeling of being a champion for that baby, being a comfort to her, I mean they couldn't get her to eat but I could, and so I think that's the same thing with the church, there's always that thing where the church is being assaulted and then you have to come in and you have to be that champion for the ideas and the thoughts that we all hold in terms of Coltrane Consciousness as something precious to be a defender of an ideal and of an ideal manifested.

A Religious Phenomenology of Sound

What are the terms and conditions that make it possible for music to serve vehicle for the effectual and miraculous transmission of the Holy Spirit? How is it that the music of John Coltrane as practiced by the Apostles of Sound effectuated the miracle of Shahada? Or, for those more skeptical, how is it that the music of John Coltrane effectuated the *appearance* or *perception* of a miracle for Shahada? I've called these terms and conditions, which define the power of sound, a *religious phenomenology of sound*.

"Phenomenology" is a useful term because it deals with the appearances of consciousness, and it is through sound that the appearances of the spiritual consciousness of St. John Coltrane in communication with the Holy Ghost are made manifest. Consistent with the tenets of phenomenology, the awareness of these appearances is not to be grasped by logical principles but by intuition. Coltrane Consciousness in this sense can be defined as that intuition through which the faithful are made aware of the presence of God in the music of St. John Coltrane.

I have chosen two principal avenues to explain the power of music and the phenomenon of religious healing within a conception of a religious phenomenology of sound: (1) the presence of sound and its intimate relationship with human consciousness; and (2) the performative power of sound to call something into being and set actions into motion. While the categories of *presence* and *performance* are drawn from Western philosophical studies of language,[1] I have drawn on far more esoteric Eastern mystical sources in order to fully explain this phenomenon; unfortunately, the power of sound that we encounter in this ethnographic context almost completely elides contemporary Western science and philosophy. Sufi mystic and musician, Hazrat Inayat Khan comments, "It seems that what science realizes in the end, mysticism reaches from the beginning" (Khan 39). Specifically, very little in the Western canon explicitly approaches the mystical issues of the manifestation of the soul in sound, nor the Coltrane Church's notion that sound is creation and God is the Supreme Musician.[2]

First of all, for the Coltrane Church, the power of music lies with its ability to be more than merely representational, but to have a *presence* of its own in unity with the thoughts of the producer of that sound. Hazrat Inayat Khan also comments, "The voice is not only indicative of man's character, but it is the expression of his spirit" (Khan 88).[3] Khan further elaborates how even Old Testament Biblical Scriptures connect voice and consciousness: "The very use of the words 'tongues of flame' in the Old Testament is a narrative of that voice and word which were warning of coming dangers. It was alarming for people to awaken from their sleep, to awaken to a greater consciousness, to a higher consciousness" (89). New Testament scripture also posits a relationship between the utterances of the tongue and the contents of an individual's heart. In Romans 10:9, the apostle Paul remarks, "That if thou shalt confess with thy mouth the Lord Jesus, and shalt believe in thine heart that God hath raised him from the dead, thou shalt be saved. For with the heart man believeth unto righteousness; and with the mouth confession is made unto salvation." From the standpoint of the experience of St. John, in a passage from his "A Love Supreme" testimony, Coltrane implies the same relationship between the heart—indeed the whole of human experience and expression—and music or sound: "Well I think that music, being an expression of the human heart, or of the human being itself, does express just what is happening.

I feel it expresses the whole thing, the whole of human experience at the particular time it is being expressed" (Analahati 1).

Within the tradition of Western philosophy, the arts are understood metaphorically in terms of language, and music and dance in particular are made comprehensible through the same de-coding processes through which we imbue the sounds and symbols of spoken and written language with meaning. Eastern mysticism begins from the other end, considering language to be ancillary to art and music in particular. "Hazrat Inayat Khan writes, "Language may be called the simplification of music; music is hidden within it as the soul is hidden in the body. At each step toward simplification the language has lost some of its music" (Khan 159). Khan also provides a brief history of man that posits the development of music prior to language: "In the beginning of human creation no language such as we now have existed, but only music. Man first expressed his thoughts and feelings by low and high, short and prolonged sounds. The depth of his tone showed his strength and power, and the height of his pitch expressed love and wisdom. Man conveyed his sincerity, insincerity, inclination, disinclination, pleasure or displeasure by the variety of his musical expressions" (158).

Consistent with the history, beliefs, and practices of Coltrane Consciousness, I have chosen to privilege the Eastern mystical valuation of music over language.[4] In the end, Khan's understanding of music provides us with the means to understand that Coltrane's thoughts are *present* in his music, and his music therefore has *presence*. Because of the presence of Coltrane's thoughts in his music, his music, as his speech, has an intimate relationship with his consciousness. The faith perspective of the Coltrane Church takes this a step further and urges that the Holy Ghost is in communication with Coltrane as he becomes more and more aware of God in his playing, the very consciousness of God is said to inhabit this music as God speaks through John Coltrane. Hazrat Inayat Khan urges that consciousness and will belong to God's own being: "It is God's own Being that in expression is will, in repose consciousness. In other words: in action it is will, in stillness it is consciousness" (Khan 219). In that sense, the practice of repeated listening that is upheld in Coltrane Consciousness is ultimately a devoutly spiritual practice of communicating with God.

There are also a number of important Eastern mystical, Biblical and Coltrane-inspired precepts for the *performative* power of sound. Perhaps the greatest example of performative speech in a biblical context lies in the account of God's creation of the earth in Genesis 1:3:"And God said, Let there be light: and there was light." In *Coltrane Consciousness*, Archbishop King cites other biblical precedents and explains the transformative power of Coltrane's music in terms of the horn of Joshua that tumbled the walls of Jericho, the parting of the Red Sea, and the healing of King Saul: "The Music of John Coltrane has the same nature and sound as the music which tumbled Jericho's wall, turned the course of rivers, and healed Old King Saul" (King and Analahati 34).[5]

1 Samuel 10: 5–6 is also considered the foundation of all the practices and teachings of Coltrane Consciousness on prophecy and healing:

> That's a scripture we really need to talk about because in that scripture there's a sound baptism that takes place if I remember correctly you know because I think it was Saul and he was going and he said, Hey, look, you know when you go up the hill you're going to run into these musicians or something or he goes up the hill and he runs into the musicians and after you meet there he begins to prophecy, he has the gift to prophecy after encountering these musicians, and to me, I don't know how that scripture has escaped me for so long. I mean, it seems like that would have been the scripture that I would really be clinging to shed some light on what we've been trying to do here with Coltrane.

An important theme in the arena of healing is the transformation of men and women through music into higher, more committed spiritual beings. This is the theme of spiritual renewal. Often the message of renewal is carried through the prophets. One important Christian connection between the music and spiritual renewal is made in Old Testament scriptures. 1 Samuel 10:5—6 links music and the power of prophecy and paints a picture that closely resembles the order of service at the Coltrane Church as the procession of musicians descends from the upper room to the altar.

> After that thou shalt come to the hill of God, where is the garrison of the Philistines: and it shall come to pass, when thou art come thither to the city, that thou shalt meet a company of prophets coming down from the high place with a psaltery, and a tablet, and a pipe, and a harp, before them; and they shall prophesy: And the Spirit of the Lord will come upon thee, and thou shalt prophesy with them, and shalt be turned into another man [1 Samuel 10: 5–6].

The power of music to heal is provided for in 1 Samuel 16:16 when Saul requests a skillful harp player in order to ward off evil spirits and restore health. That skillful harp player turns out to be David, who would distinguish himself as a great warrior and king of Israel: "Let our lord now command thy servants which are before thee, to seek out a man, who is a cunning player on an harp: and it shall come to pass, when the evil spirit from God is upon thee, that he shall play with his hand, and thou shalt be well" (1 Samuel 16:16).

Later, in 1 Samuel 16: 23 David utilizes his skill upon the harp to heal Saul: "And it came to pass, when the evil spirit from God was upon Saul, that David took an harp, and played with his hand: so Saul was refreshed, and was well, and the evil spirit departed from him" (1 Samuel 16: 23).

From the standpoint of Coltrane's own words and testimonies, perhaps the most important quotation included in *John Coltrane Speaks* has Coltrane stating, "I think music is an instrument. It can create the initial thought patterns that can change the thinking of the people" (Analahati 1). In the context of Coltrane's *A Love Supreme* testimony, it is clear that Coltrane intends that music and sound should transform the world by ushering forth the reign of peace, brotherhood and love. In *Coltrane Consciousness*, Archbishop King alludes to this, stating,

> It [the music] is transcendental, spiritual; it has the trans-cultural quality to create brotherhood, to create unity among all people, to create a society without war. There is healing power in the Name and Sound of John Coltrane. There is cosmic power in this evolved, transcended Sound [King and Analahati 34].

Hazrat Inayat Khan addresses the *performative* power of music primarily in terms of its ability to have a particular effect upon the spirit and to transform the natural world. Khan writes, "An ancient legend tells how the angels sang at the command of God to induce the unwilling soul to enter the body of Adam. The soul, intoxicated by the song of angels, entered the body, which it regarded as a prison. All spiritualists who have really sounded the depths of spirituality have realized that there is no better means of attracting spirits from their plane of freedom to the outer plane than by music" (Khan 160). Addressing the power of music to transform the natural world, Khan cites examples of ancient mystics: "There are instances in ancient tradition when birds and animals were charmed by the flute of Krishna, rocks were melted by the song of Orpheus, and the Dipak Raga sung by Tansen lighted all the torches, while he himself was burned by reason of the inner fire his song produced" (162).

The performative dimension of Coltrane's sound has as its aim nothing less than the effectual transformation of the souls of listeners. The power of music to wash away sins is nothing new within black church contexts. Eileen Southern recounts a popular Negro hymn from 1801 first published in Richard Allen's hymnal. The final stanza is:

> O then the music will begin
> Their Saviour God to praise
> They all are freed from every sin
> And thus they'll spend their days [Southern 173]

According to the religious phenomenology of sound that I have defined, Coltrane's music amplifies for the listener the consciousness of a man in constant prayer and meditation with God. Coltrane's music is his testimony of the power and beauty of God working in his life. Coltrane expressed the intimacy of music and consciousness and particularly a spiritual consciousness when he remarked, "My goal is to live the truly religious life and express it in my music. If you live it, when you play there's no problem because the music is part of the whole things. To be a musician is really something. It goes very, very deep. My music is the spiritual expression of what I am—my faith, my knowledge, my being" (Analahati 4).

An apparent flaw in my discussion of a religious phenomenology of sound is that I have collapsed thought, intention, and consciousness. An argument could be made that the *appearances* of consciousness seem to actually *be* consciousness within the definition of a religious phenomenology of sound. Are intention and thought the defining substance of consciousness or merely the appearances of consciousness?

What I am actually suggesting by leaving the borders between thought, intention, and consciousness gray and unresolved is that moments of religious ecstasy within Coltrane Consciousness or any system of spiritual awareness are precisely moments in which consciousness, thought, and action are all collapsed or experienced as collapsed, indeed where men and women experience God with such immediacy and closeness that one is said to be filled with the Holy Ghost. To be filled with the Holy is to experience joy through a sense of unification of all senses, and a belief in the unification and consistency of all that is real with all that is perceived.

The ecstatic experience of Coltrane Consciousness indeed involves a powerful union of thought, intention, and consciousness. It is the moment when, as Archbishop King says, "It all comes together like John said, 'all heat waves, thought waves, etc.' all one in the spirit of God." This is the enabling moment for the believer; it is the moment in which the believer experiences transcendence and views as if from high atop a mountain the landscape of possibilities. Within the discourse of Western European metaphysics, this Holy Ghost feeling of transcendence comes across as some sort of facile tautology: transcendence is the moment in which the believer has the feeling that his or her feelings are coincident with the actual presence of God and His Holy Spirit. However, transcendence can only be approached through faith. It is an experience that elides objective inquiry, but the miracle potential of "walking with the Holy Ghost" does produce tangible results.

This principle of one-ness and the possibilities for a transcendent experience indeed take us far beyond the *presence* and *performative* power of sound as elaborated in Western philosophy and into the landscape of Eastern mysticism. When speaking of transcendence I am arguing that sound has its relationship with the soul, and indeed with the origin of all creation; music is a manifestation of God, the Supreme Musician.

The complex history of the Coltrane Church, including its involvement with the mystical traditions of Hinduism, Christianity, and Islam are relevant. These traditions provide context and support for belief in the mysticism of John Coltrane and the miracle potential of music that is relied upon in faith at the Coltrane Church. It is not my aim to deal exhaustively with these traditions, but rather to deal with them at the level at which they are discussed and manipulated in everyday church discourse. In short, the relevance of the mystical tradition of Hinduism lies with the performative power of chanting that church members engage with on Coltrane's recordings and the Vedantic chants of their experience with Alice Coltrane. When dealing with Islamic mystical traditions I focus on the teachings of Sufi mystic and musician Hazrat Inayat Khan. Khan is regarded as one of Archbishop King's great teachers—even though that instruction is limited to reading the collected works of Khan—and his books have been widely read by the active members of the Coltrane Church. When dealing with the mystical traditions of Christianity, I have limited myself to a set of scriptures provided by Archbishop King and also widely shared among the active members of the congregation.

Conclusions

The miracle of Shahada's healing was made possible through the church's belief in the *presence* and *performative* power of sound to call things into being. The narrative of Shahada reflects possibilities for meaningful metaphysical experiences through sound, and it further confirms the mystical path undertaken by the Apostles of Sound. In many senses, the miracle of Shahada confirmed the evolution and differential movement toward the African Orthodox Church that enabled the continued survival of the Coltrane Church. The healing of Shahada was representative of the broader healing of the church and its members in the wake of their breakup with Alice Coltrane. The immediate future would challenge their commitment to the spiritual power of sound, and specifically the sound of John Coltrane. But the healing of Shahada would serve as a beacon in moments of irresolution that would ultimately guide them back home to their core mission of Coltrane Consciousness.

10

The Oscar Grant Movement

This session is not for the typical dinner jazz connoisseurs.
This is John Coltrane in the raw.
There are no punches pulled in this session.

—Pastor Wanika King-Stephens

In the early morning hours of New Year's Day 2009, a 22-year-old African American male, Oscar Grant III, was fatally shot by Bay Area Rapid Transit (BART) police officer Johannes Mehserle at the Fruitvale station in Oakland, California. BART officers were responding to reports of a fight on a crowded train returning from San Francisco and Grant was detained with several other passengers on the platform. According to officer Mehserle's attorney, Mehserle and another officer were attempting to restrain Grant who was lying face down and allegedly resisting arrest when officer Mehserle stood and proclaimed "Get back, I'm gonna Tase him," at which point Mehserle drew his service pistol and shot Grant once in the back. According to Mehserle's court testimony Grant then exclaimed, "You shot me!" Grant, who was unarmed, was taken to Oakland's Highland Hospital and proclaimed dead the next morning (Muhammad).

The events of the Oscar Grant shooting were captured by other BART passengers on digital video and cell phone cameras and disseminated to media outlets throughout the Bay Area, California, and the world. Alameda County prosecutors charged Mehserle with second-degree murder and voluntary manslaughter but when the verdict was returned July 8, 2010, Mehersle, who claimed that he was intending to use his Taser when he saw Grant reach for his waistband, was found guilty of involuntary manslaughter. Mehserle was sentenced to two years minus time served. He was eventually released June 13, 2011, to serve parole. The day after the verdict, the U.S. Justice Department, led by U.S. Attorney General Eric Holder, opened a civil rights investigation against Mehserle, and Oakland civil rights attorney John Burris filed a $25 million dollar wrongful death claim against BART on behalf of the Grant family. BART settled with Grant's mother and daughter for $2.8 million (Simmonds).

It was no surprise to any who were paying attention that Minister Christopher of the Nation of Islam and Archbishop Franzo W. King were at the forefront of a movement to bring public attention to the murder of Oscar Grant, a movement that would result in California's first prosecution of a white police officer for the murder of a black man:

> Oscar Grant would have been a secret. We started that. First time I heard about it I called Min. Christopher. He hadn't heard about it. He called me a couple of days later. He said, "Archbishop, do you know that boy's been dead six days and nobody has raised a voice?" That's when we started organizing over there and we got the phrase, "I am Oscar Grant."
>
> Nobody had done anything. The D.A. wasn't going to meet with us. We brought 300 people and crowded the place out and made him meet with us and just started that whole movement.

As the Coltrane Church continued in the 1990s and beyond to find greater denominational legitimacy through its incorporation in the African Orthodox Church, it began cashing in its social capital, aligning itself with more and more with the civil rights agendas of the community, and strengthening its relationship to the Nation of Islam. The Coltrane Church's engagement with police brutality was the product of alliances stemming from Archbishop Hinkson's 1989 directive to then Bishop King to "make himself known." It began in the 1990s with the African American Community Police Relations Board that would later serve as the foundation for their involvement in the Caravan for Justice, the Oscar Grant Movement, and the Stop Lennar Action Movement (SLAM), all of which continued to serve as a protective circle around the community. And so from 1989 to 2009 the Coltrane Church would become a recognizable political force, aligned with the Nation of Islam, and serving as watchmen for the community.

The African American Community Police Relations Board

In the wake of their post–1989 San Francisco earthquake meeting, Archbishop King and Minister Christopher Muhammad developed the African American Community Police Relations Board. It was a response to the city's attempts to criminalize black youth through targeted gang injunctions. Both Min. Christopher and Archbishop King understood the city's proposed gang injunctions, which would have criminalized African American youth merely for gathering in groups exceeding five, as part of a broader interest in land and property in the Bayview-Hunter's Point. The groundwork for the board was thus focused on the collusion of local business and police interest in many of San Francisco's traditionally African American neighborhoods. Archbishop King:

> We did a whole lot of police work before Oscar Grant. We came out against the gang injunctions. We showed where gang injunctions are geared to create a certain attitude in the local community that would cause them to invite more police in the community. But the idea was to criminalize the youth, villanize the community and then the police have a right to come in and when you look at the key places where the gang injunctions were being established it was like Palou Street that was the gate to the shipyards where they had plans to start development and move people out.
>
> We were already dealing with the circle of protecting the Bayview and we had meetings with the gangs of Sunnydale and Hunter's Point. We were educating the youth on the agenda that was laid out for them including the privatization of prisons and mass incarceration for the purpose of breaking up the leadership.
>
> When you put all the guys who are 21 to 30 in the penitentiary then you have a void that has to be filled and the youngsters try and fill the void and that's how you get all of this uncontrolled violence. Back in my day you had the elder brothers that were doing real crime and had their own thing going and they would tell you, Hey youngblood, you got to take that some- where else, you're making it hot. Or they could look in the group and pull that youngblood there and you could grow into the ranks. Now, with the proliferation of firearms, everybody is the king. If you are 13 and you can pull the trigger you've got a voice. So we were doing all of that kind of stuff with the Police Relations Board.

The board had its specific origins in the wake of a violent clash between police and Nation of Islam members. In light of the injuries sustained by the police, the San Francisco Police Department and the community found themselves with a shared interest in stemming the violence. Archbishop King:

> The African American Community Police Relations Board came into being after there were some brothers from the Nation in the Tenderloin collecting alms for charity and they got into it with an Arab group and the police were called and they came out strong and some of the police got injured. So they got locked up. So Willie Brown is Mayor at that time and we helped get him elected. So when Min. Christopher called Willie about

it, Willie got on top of it and the D.A. dropped the charges and let the
brothers out.

That incident in itself sparked Min. Christopher to come to me and say,
we can Mau Mau over this or we can take it and make something that will
benefit the community. And the African American Community Police
Relations Board would be a bridge between the police and the community.
There was a lot of resistance to it. Lau was Chief at the time and he was
game for it. The NAACP, the Nation, the Coltrane Church, and the Officers for Justice were for it and we met every two weeks unless there was
an incident. I remember there was something at Marshall School. There
was a killing.

Because it operated in much more than an advisory capacity, the
African American Community Police Relations Board maintained unprecedented authority, and was empowered to be present at crime scenes within
an hour of the police and to make policy recommendations, including recommendations for promotions. On one level the board functioned as a
fact-gathering unit whose presence at every crime scene insured the verac-
ity of police reporting, particularly in the area of officer-involved shootings, and on the other hand it functioned as a sort of office of Affirmative
Action, pressing SFPD to diversify its hires, empowered to make policy and
recommendations regarding administrative police personnel. Archbishop
King:

> So we had somebody on the board whether they were on the board or they
> were community workers at large and we were in Bayview, Lakeview,
> Potrero Hills, so if something happened we had an arrangement with the
> Police Department where we could go on the crime scene, we didn't have
> to wait for a police report. We had a commitment to meet within an hour
> of the incident. We would find out what was happening and give the police
> some guidance on how to deal with it.

Among its more notable personnel suggestions was the appointment
of the first African American Police Chief, Prentice Earl Sanders, in 2002.
Archbishop King:

> A lot of people said they weren't going to let me and Christopher run
> the Police Department. But we weren't trying to run the Police Depart-
> ment. We were being watchmen for the community. And it was a relation-
> ship and not an advisory committee so we had the power to make policy.
> We took Sgt. Johnson and told them we needed a black lieutenant and
> they made him a lieutenant. We had Marian Jackson of the Officers of Jus-
> tice so they could give us the inside workings of what the Police Depart-
> ment could and couldn't do. Willie Brown was very cooperative.... One of
> the most important things was having access to the chief and the crime
> sights where it was happening.

It was almost inevitable, particularly in light of its successes, that the police relations board would be dismantled. Archbishop King specifically cites the efforts of Mayor Gavin Newsom (2004–2011) and the usual crowd of African American insiders motivated in this case by their own jealousies and anti–Nation of Islam sentiment:

> I can tell you how it got busted up. When Gavin Newsom became Mayor he busted it up. After he had a big press conference and said what a great program it was he started breaking it up. Gavin really broke it up but he couldn't do it by himself. He needed some lap dogs and some slave chasers from within the community. It's the same old characters. The feeling was that we had too much power.
>
> The police union changed presidents, because the guy that was in there was supportive. It was the changing of the guard. The mayor, the police union, and all of that helped it and people in the community that were envious of the power we had established because Christopher is from Los Angeles and the Nation and the whole globe is community for me and I am not from the Fillmore or Hunter's Point. I remember someone from the *Chronicle* was trying to ascertain where I was from ... was it Mars? Come to find out I was born in St. Louis. I ain't set trippin'. It's like I say, we aren't theologically gang-banging.
>
> And then the whole thing against the Nation and the Nation really being the only army we have in this nation. So there was some jealousy there and people wanting to keep their old seats and the work we did pulled the cover off of a lot of folks. People in leadership really don't have any pride. They really need to be arrested for the way they've sold out the community. And then there was the funding and people want money and they'll do anything to get the funding, so that ended up tearing that up.

The Caravan for Justice

There are significant San Francisco Bay Area histories of police brutality and the wanton murder of young black men at the hands of the police in the aftermath of the demise of the African American Community Police Relations Board. Among these are the storied murders of Gary King, Jr., in 2007, Lovelle Mixon in 2009, James Rivera and Ernest Duenez, Jr., in 2010, Raheim Brown in 2011, and in 2012 the four murders of Alan Blueford, Kenneth Harding, Luther Brown, and Derrick Gaines.[1]

The historical pattern of these and many more incidents suggests a broader "open season" law enforcement policy on African American males which erupted in national protest movements in 2014 in the wake of the deaths of Eric Garner in New York City and Michael Brown in Ferguson, Missouri. Writing in 2010, Yussuf Simmonds of the *Los Angeles Sentinel* reminded his readers, "In 2005, the Los Angeles Sentinel ran an editorial titled 'This Is the Problem'—The Police Officer's Bill of Rights (California Law). The editorial went on to state, in part, 'According to our investigation, all of the police beatings and shootings, and the lack of justice received by the African American community, in large measure are directly tied to the 'policy' that is stipulated under the 'Police Officers Bill of Rights' which is also California law. Whenever an incident occurs: a shooting, beating, or any violation of a black person's rights at the hands of a police officer, the threshold of protection for the police officer appears to supersede the fundamental rights and protection of black citizens/victims. Everything that is done thereafter is about protecting the rights of the police.'"

The Caravan for Justice was a broad multicultural movement concerned with a range of community justice issues including police brutality, mass incarceration, environmental justice, foreclosures, and real estate development. It was a movement that recognized that all of these developments were intended to drive people of color and the poor out of the city of San Francisco. It was a movement in three stages during 2009, including mass rallies in Sacramento on February 19, April 8, and May 26, 2009. It was in large measure focused on issues of reforming California's Three Strikes law under Proposition 184 in 1994; police brutality; mass incarceration; the racial inequality of sentencing; the manipulation of gang injunctions in order to remove people of color and the poor from their land and housing; and the San Francisco 8,[2] former Black Panthers and associates being retried by then Attorney General Jerry Brown for a 1971 police killing based on evidence extracted by torture in 1973. They also garnered support for Assembly Bill 312 to form a BART Office of Citizen Complaints in light of the murder of Oscar Grant. Seth Sandransky of Truthout.org writes, "On that note, Assembly Bill 312 is before the state Legislature now. Assembly Member Tom Ammiano and state Sen. Leland Yee, San Francisco Democrats, are cosponsors of AB312. This legislation would compel the BART district to form an Office of Citizen Complaints to administer civilian grievances about the misconduct of police officers."[3] Quoting Keith Muhammad of San Francisco's Nation of Islam, Sandransky writes, "'The law enforcement approach to urban America is not working,' he said most recently. 'We have come to challenge unjust laws that imprison African-American, Latino and other minority people.'"

Archbishop King speaks of his experiences with Caravan for Justice:

> We started going out to Redwood City and Sacramento. We took three or four bus loads up to Sacramento.
> On the Caravan for Justice it dealt with mass incarceration and police

profiling and economic empowerment and all of those things were on the agenda.

That was the most powerful movement since the Mission Rebels with Jesse James. They had charters all over the city. Not just the Oscar Grant movement but the Caravan for Justice.

Writing for the *San Francisco Bay View* newspaper in 2009, an independent voice for the African American community in San Francisco, Crystal Carter speaks of the Caravan for Justice as a broad multicultural coalition up and down the state of California that included Latino and Asian American citizens united around police violence and mass incarceration: "Signs reading 'Justice for Oscar Grant,' 'Abolish the Three Strikes Law' and 'Demandamos Justicia Ya!' floated above a sea of ralliers of different ages, religious beliefs, genders and ethnicities. From Bakersfield up to Sacramento, activists, teachers and family members came together to rally against laws that have failed to serve the betterment of their communities." The Caravan for Justice thus formed a coalition of prison reform activists including Families United for Prison Reform, the Dream Builders, and Challenging Their Destiny.

Archbishop King also highlights the ethnic inclusivity of the Caravan for Justice: "We had a coalition that represented a broader spectrum than we had with the police relations board. We had the Latino community and even Shrimp Boy was involved. He came to one of our meetings. We had the Chinese community involved."

The ethnic coalition building of the Caravan for Justice was focused on eliminating tools of ethnic division that Archbishop King and Min. Christopher understood as central to the exploitation of communities of color. In an interview with Bay Area hip hop mogul JT the Bigga Figga in his magazine, *Mandatory Business*, Min. Christopher Muhammad explains, "So it's important for the brothers to understand much of the beef that the brothers have with the different neighborhoods or different sets, off times [*sic*] are encouraged by the police. They're off times are encouraged by law enforcement who literally causes the brothers through rumors, through innuendo, through all kinds of slander and gossip. It's designed to set the communities at each other. It causes the brother to feel like that because he heard that this happened from another neighborhood. He doesn't realize that maybe at the root of the rumor is a snitch or some kind of provocateur or some kind of person that's made a deal with law enforcement, that literally causes the brothers to fight and kill one another to the delight of developers like Lennar who literally take advantage of the confusion in the community" (JT the Bigga Figga).

The significance of the Caravan for Justice rested in its ability to specifically link police brutality with redevelopment and the urban removal of the poor and people of color. Min. Christopher further comments, "The police policy towards black brothers is being driven by the business community that has already determined that the land that the people live on is to be redeveloped. So they have all kind of schemes that they use to do this. The number one scheme is a gang injunction" (JT the Bigga Figga).

Archbishop King recalls the Caravan for Justice and its initial battles against the twin forces of predatory policing and redevelopment and its early successes against developers seeking to construct so-called "above market" housing that would threaten to remove people of color and the poor:

> When the development first started in the Bayview and they were building these above market houses and they were meeting at Dr. Walker's church and recruiting. Some of the home owners up there on Jamestown were complaining. The pitch was, we build this and the value of your property will go up.
>
> My thing was, that's not why I bought this house, for the value of the property. I bought this house because I want to live in the African American community. And I want young people that grow up to see people like myself living in the community and others.
>
> So we fought against I think it was some Irish developers that was coming in and we stopped that. So this was before the Oscar Grant movement, before the African American Community Police Relations Board, and before Lennar. It was to encourage people to realize that in building these houses, they are not building them for us.
>
> This is the same story as today. It's about property value going up and the value of black people going down. And we're against it. So we were instrumental in busting that up. The line that Min. Christopher had coined was to build a line of protection around the Bayview.

The Caravan for Justice was also involved in the revival of prison reform interests that had lost a hard fought battle in 2004 over statewide Proposition 66 to reform California's 1994 Three Strikes law and address racial and class inequities in the California criminal justice system. Then Governor Arnold Schwarzenegger along with former governors Jerry Brown,[4] Pete Wilson, Gray Davis, and George Deukmeijian and Broadcom Corporation founder and CEO Henry Nicholas led the charge for a dramatic come from behind defeat of Proposition 66 at the polls.

Contrastively, the mass movements of the Caravan for Justice would prove largely successful in many of their battles against gang injunctions and it won a hard fought victory for a BART Office of Citizen Complaint with AB 312. Crystal Carter notes the successes of the Caravan for Justice:

"Their last visit to the Capitol on April 8 caused two legislators, Tom Ammiano and Leland Yee, to initiate a bill promoting 'civilian oversight' to handle complaints against the Bay Area Rapid Transit (BART) police in the wake of Oscar Grant's death. The protest has also focused on issues involving gang injunctions and succeeded in prompting Sen. Roderick D. Wright and Leland Yee to inject a bill to combat them" (Carter).

In a pattern that would be predictably repeated against future community activism, the Caravan for Justice was opposed by the collusion of political leaders and an ingrained opposition of establishment black churches and black political insiders. There was perhaps no greater evidence of this collusion than in the aftermath of the police murder of Kenneth Harding in 2012 which found establishment religious leaders, even in the wake of four highly publicized murders of African American men in 2012, arguing in favor of an increased police presence in their communities.

> Now the other thing is when Kenneth Harding got killed on the light rail on 3rd Street it was the Nation that brought his mother down from Oregon and SLAM that organized the community and raised a few thousand dollars for them.
>
> When it happened I called up the police chief. They said they were going to be having a press conference. I told him we didn't roll like that. Tell me what's going on, we don't have to wait until a press conference. He told me that the kid was running and he shot himself. He asked me if I knew Bishop Birch and I said I knew him. He told me to talk to him because they were in touch with him and they were going to have a press conference. Birch was going to come and talk to me and Min. Christopher. So we crash the meeting.
>
> I'm sitting there and when one of the preachers is saying that brothers are selling dope down there and they need more police. I told him I was glad to be there but I'm having a problem with the things I'm hearing about more police. I don't think we need more police, I think we need more fearless men of God that can go and talk with our young people. I'm really saddened that we have to wait this long to hear from the chief of police about a man that has been murdered. We had an organization that dealt with this stuff and some of our so-called leadership was involved in breaking that up. They were yelling, what leadership are you talking about? Call some names! I said, Brother, I'm not here to call names and don't think I know what atmosphere I'm in. But now if anybody can tell me that the side of the fence that I was on wasn't tied to the truth, I'll back up off of it. But other than that, anything I've said over the last five to ten years about the police or the mayor or any slave chasers, I still stand on it.
>
> We would have ushered that rail into the community and we would have made sure the youth were educated. What happened to Kenneth Harding would have never happened.

To be sure, the Caravan for Justice was a significant political threat and in spite of its opposition, the Caravan for Justice continued and evolved and served as a foundation for a host of other community rights movements. Perhaps the most spectacular political victory for the Caravan for Justice was the gubernatorial defeat of Mayor Gavin Newsom—running as a "green candidate"—who between 2006 and 2009 had supported the Lennar Corporation's development in the Bayview- Hunter's Point in spite of significant questions raised about environmental poisoning.

> With Lennar, we had the Caravan for Justice and we took people down to City Hall and had people on every floor and when I saw Gavin Newsom, we followed him all the way to Marin County when he was running for governor. We told him, if you're running for governor, you're not running as a green mayor.
>
> We followed him. L.A. Everywhere he went there was someone from SLAM. And when I'm in Marin somebody comes over and asks who are you, and I say, I'm Archbishop King. They ask why am I there. I say, my mayor is here.
>
> Gavin comes out and I tell him, I'm going to bust you up man. He said he wanted to meet with us. I told him to talk to Min. Christopher. He already knew where I was coming from. When I got up to talk, I turned it into stand-up. I called him a pretty boy and everything.
>
> We accomplished California not having to put up with Gavin Newsom as governor. And he is never going to forgive us for that. He told me, when you guys camped those men outside of my office and took over City Hall like that ... well that was it for my campaign.

Conclusions

The Oscar Grant movement marked the culmination of over a decade of activism by the Coltrane Church and its partners, particularly the Nation of Islam, that was motivated by a desire to create a protective circle around the black community in San Francisco, and initially sparked by Archbishop Hinkson's directive for then Bishop King to make himself known within the community. The Coltrane Church's activism against police brutality, mass incarceration, and gang injunctions, whether within the context of the African American Community Police Relations Board or the Caravan for Justice had memorable successes that could be built upon in the future.

The African American Community Relations Board brought unprecedented community involvement into the management and day-to-day business of the San Francisco Police Department. The requirement for sensitivity training, the hiring of San Francisco's first African American

Chief of Police, and the community oversight of crime scenes all fulfilled Min. Christopher's vision of being watchmen for the community.

As for the Oscar Grant movement, the murder trial of BART police officer Johannes Mehserle was wholly unprecedented in the history of California law enforcement. As Archbishop King notes, "This is the first time in California history that a policeman has been held accountable. It never would have happened without that movement."

The Coltrane Church had traveled a great distance since Archbishop Hinkson's 1989 mandate to "go and make yourself known." But there were still new battles that lay ahead. While the Caravan for Justice initiated movements against real estate development in the Bayview-Hunter's Point, it had not yet begun to explore related issues of environmental justice that were killing the community. The Great Recession of 2008 would find San Francisco's traditional African American communities overwhelmed by the impact of perhaps 20 years of predatory lending practices. And the community would need, perhaps more than ever, a cultural presence and a symbol of its historic significance in the city of San Francisco, even as African Americans were being forced to re-locate from the city in unprecedented numbers.

And so the Coltrane Church, buoyed by its leadership in the Caravan for Justice and the African American Community Police Relations Board, would engage in a vicious political battle against the Lennar Corporation, San Francisco Mayor Gavin Newsom, and black community insiders over the issue of environmental racism. The Coltrane Church would take aim at the San Francisco Redevelopment Agency in a comprehensive proposal to renovate a historic and formerly black-owned property in the Fillmore/Western Addition and launch a community university. And, as if foretelling future battles, it would settle for once and for all the issue of gender inequality within its own leadership ranks.

11

The St. John Coltrane University
of Arts and Social Justice

Jazz ... if you want to call it that, to me, is an
expression of higher ideals, to me.
So, therefore brotherhood is there and I believe
with brotherhood there would be no poverty.
And also, with brotherhood, there would be no war.

—St. John Will-I-Am Coltrane

In July 2009, Frederick Harris, M.M., and I were enlisted along with Campbell and Associates Developers, Path Merker Architects, Garavaglia Historic Architects, and Nibb Construction to create a proposal for the San Francisco Redevelopment Agency to restore the historic Leola King Center property on Fillmore Street and create a St. John Coltrane University of Arts and Social Justice.

The Leola King story is one of the darker chapters in the history of redevelopment in the San Francisco Bay Area and perhaps, as G.W. Schultz of the *San Francisco Bay Guardian* has suggested, "a demonstration of why so many African Americans in this town will never trust the Redevelopment Agency." In the 1940s Leola King, an Oklahoma native, operated a series of restaurants and nightclubs in the Fillmore/Western Addition neighborhood including Oklahoma King's BBQ at 1601 Geary Street, where she served buffalo, deer, and quail meat; the Blue Mirror at 935 Fillmore Street; and the Birdcage Tavern at 1505 Fillmore Street (Schultz).

Buoyed by Title 1 of the Housing Act 1949, a federal law that gave cities had the right to seize property by eminent domain in order to deal with urban blight, the Redevelopment Agency launched its project to remove the so-called "blight" from the Fillmore during the height of King's

The church performs at Cité de la Musique in Paris on February 8, 2008.

business accomplishments, and was one of thousands of residents who were forced to give up their properties in return for a "certificate of preference" or promise that they could return when new buildings were constructed (Schultz). Some 5,500 certificates were issued in 1964 but over 50 years later few had been honored, with the agency admitting having lost contact information and redevelopment commissioners openly admitting that the certificate program was a joke. Leola King was personally issued two certificates but attempts to redeem these "devolved into costly legal wrangling with the agency that lasted more than two decades. She has never regained what she lost" and was paid a mere $25,000 for the Oklahoma King's BBQ property. George Schultz notes that after decades of struggle, "except for an apartment building of 12 mostly low-income units where she lives today, she lost all that she owned, including an Edwardian landmark home on Scott Street near Alamo Square and a half-completed bar she called Goldie's" (Shultz). The Leola King Center proposal was another battle in Leola King's long war to reclaim her property and cash in on the defaulted promises of the SFRA certificates.

The St. John Coltrane University of Arts and Social Justice had been a long time in the planning. Indeed since its 1982 incorporation into the greater African Orthodox Church and movement towards ecumenical legitimacy, the Coltrane Church had been steadily seeking avenues for expansion as a religious, cultural, and political organization. Almost immediately upon the departure of Alice Coltrane the church would re-launch the food program and begin serving hot vegetarian meals to the poor every Sunday. In the 1990s it would expand its outreach programs to include Christmas and Thanksgiving Day feasts for the poor, a toy and clothing giveaway during the Christmas holidays, airport ministry, coun-seling services, and its offering of public performances and concerts for the community. The new millennium would witness continued growth. On September 20, 2000, Fr. Roberto DeHaven and Fr. Max Hoff opened services of the Zion Trane Church of the Promise as a Missionary Epis-copate of the St. John Coltrane African Orthodox Church at the Cayuga Vault in downtown Santa Cruz. On March 10, 2001, Bishop King was appointed Archbishop by Archbishop George Duncan Hinkson and the senior clergy of the African Orthodox Church. And through its involve-ment in the 1990s and into the new millennium with the Caravan for Jus-tice, and the African American Community Police Relations Board, the church found itself at the forefront of community political activism.

The question now remained, how would the Coltrane Church, with the ecumenical legitimacy of the African Orthodox Church, evolve as a *cultural* force?

In 2002 Archbishop King called Bro. Frederick Harris and me to begin formulating a Coltrane-inspired pedagogy of arts instruction for a possible John Coltrane University. And in 2009, as a culminating event of its grad-ual post–1982 expansion, ecumenical credibility, and long-standing respect within the Western Addition and Bayview-Hunter's Point as agents of change, the Coltrane Church would, for the first time in its history, join a coalition of community *and* corporate partners, propose a community-based university, and adopt the strategies of corporate jazz institutions for the purpose of enlarging its vision of community-centered jazz culture.

I was involved with the St. John Coltrane University of Arts and Social Justice project in my capacity as Ph.D. in residence for the Coltrane Church, and I worked closely with Frederick Harris in the development of a vision for a Coltrane pedagogy of music and African American Stud-ies, which were to become the initial academic offerings of the university. Archbishop King selected Bro. Fred and me because of our academic cre-dentials and graduate degrees as well as our experience in developing pro-grams. I had just co-authored a queer of color academic option for the Department of Ethnic Studies at California State University East Bay, the first of its kind in the state. Bro. Fred, a pianist, composer, drummer and educator who received his B.A. and M.M. degrees in piano performance from the San Francisco Conservatory of Music, performed with Dizzy Gillespie, Regina Carter, and Kurt Elling, and held academic positions at San Jose State University and the Stanford Jazz Workshop. Bro. Fred additionally created and managed a jazz education program for young people in San Francisco's Bayview-Hunter's Point neighborhood through a grant from the Mayor's Office of Children, Youth, and their Families (MOCYF).

We drafted the following vision statement:

A Vision for the Future:
The Saint John Will-I-Am Coltrane
African Orthodox University

During the course of the present year, 2002, our Most Eminent Archbishop Franzo Wayne King, D.D. outlined a vision of the Saint John Will-I-Am Coltrane University, and the possibility of creating an institution of higher learning based on the principles of our patron saint and spiritual avatar, one John Will-I-Am Coltrane.

In faith we remain open to the visions communicated to us by God and only in faith are these visions made manifest. By the grace of God, even as we are in the midst of seeking a new sanctuary for our worship services and outreach ministries, members of an Executive Committee have been regularly meeting, gathering information, and planning for the eventuality of a St. John Will-I-Am Coltrane University. We have gathered from our midst a diverse committee of scholars and professionals, consisting of persons who hold advanced degrees in Divinity, Music Theory and Practice, Fine Arts, Anthropology, English Literature, Rhetoric, Speech Therapy, Occupational Therapy, Architecture, Culinary Arts, Nursing, and Holistic Healing.

In recent months we have begun to conduct preliminary studies and gather data. At this time and in this fashion we find it appropriate to share the vision and the work of this committee with the community of baptized members and believers. We naturally seek the assistance and input of all those motivated by the Holy Spirit to contribute to these efforts.

As it is presently conceived, the Saint John Will-I-Am Coltrane University would be the first institution of higher learning founded by a predominantly African American community on the west coast of the United States of America. Its mission would be to revitalize and extend a progressive pedagogy of the arts, utilizing creative expression as a means of facilitating the evolution and transcendence of students to achieve "richer, fuller, more productive lives."

In the spirit of St. John Will-I-Am Coltrane, the University would seek to propagate the beautiful and living arts and an affirmative philosophy of the inherent power of creative expression to change lives and communities. The University would embrace art and creativity as forums for the expression of the whole of human experience and as modes of abstract analysis and synthesis of the relationship of human beings to the universe. It would advocate an artistic/creative praxis, engaging the arts in the struggle to alleviate human suffering caused by ignorance and inspiring the pursuit of truth, love, cultural revitalization, community service, and leadership. The University would offer unique and highly specialized degree programs that integrate Liberal Studies with the Creative and Performing Arts, and it would seek to instill beauty, dignity, wholeness, self-respect, self-discovery, and academic excellence.

The University's vision, as conceived by Archbishop King, is fundamentally rooted in the life, music, and philosophy of St. John Will-I-Am Coltrane, eminent musician, composer, and innovator of African American Classical Music. The University would affirm that the life, music, and philosophy of St. John Will-I-Am Coltrane represent an innovative paradigm shift in western philosophy, art, and pedagogy, providing a means for individual and social transformation in a new millennium. St. John Will-I-Am Coltrane believed in the spiritual possibilities of the music to "create the initial thought patterns that can change the thinking of the people" and lead listeners to a commitment to "live clean and do right." St. John Will-I-Am Coltrane urged that there was an intimate relationship between free creative expression and the awakening of critical human consciousness; the arts serve to bring people to an awareness of truth. His life is an example of a disciplined pursuit of moral and intellectual excellence and the loving dedication of creative talent and expression to the service of humanity.

The University would also support the moral and spiritual growth of its students as a natural outgrowth of creative endeavor. We believe that the creative and performing arts are a means for expressing beauty, love, truth, and for awakening body and soul. In this regard, the University would seek to uplift the whole of human personality and help people realize their capacities for living meaningful lives. St. John Will-I-Am Coltrane said, "My goal in meditating on this through music, however, remains the same. And that is to uplift people, as much as I can. To inspire them to realize more and more of their capacities for living meaningful lives. Because there certainly is meaning to life."

In its appreciation of the spiritual possibilities of creative expression, the University would seek to promote inter-faith understanding and open-minded communication and draws upon St. John Will-I-Am Coltrane's theology of the unity of religious ideals. "I believe in all religions. What is important is whether a person knows the truth." The unity of religious ideals embraces traditions at the point that they intersect. There is little doubt that love, service, the pursuit of wisdom, compassionate understanding, peace, joy, and freedom, etc., are worthy of human attainment. The goal of the University would not be to dogmatically propagate religion nor proselytize, but to use the idea of the unity of religious ideals to guide its students toward moral and ethical character building. The University would seek to support its students in achieving their personal potential, be they Muslim, Buddhist, Christian, Jew, Hindu, Agnostic, or Atheist. We believe that an improved world is created by improved persons and by people understanding their common ideals and working together in service to uplift each other.

For those who have little exposure to the evolution of this ministry and of Coltrane Consciousness, the University is conceived as an organic outgrowth of 33 years of visionary leadership and institution building by Archbishop Franzo Wayne King, D.D. of the African Orthodox Church, who called together artists, priests, scholars, students, and devotees in the investigation, meditation, and application of the prophetic value of the found treasure and revelation of the true legacy of John Coltrane as an avatar of a noble and dignified personality in African American spirituality and art. St. John Coltrane anticipated such a gathering: "Yes, I think the music is rising, in my estimation, it's rising into something else, and so will have to find this kind of place to be played in."

Archbishop Franzo Wayne King, D.D. has an important social, political, and cultural leader in the San Francisco Bay Area. He has organized the provision of food, shelter, clothing, skill training, and counseling programs for those in need. Archbishop King has been a partner and advocate for social welfare and justice, providing forums for dialogue between different ethnic, class, gender, religious, and community perspectives. He has brokered communication between the mayor, police, housing authorities, and community groups and grassroots organizations. St. John Coltrane remarked, "...when there's something we think could be better, we must make an effort to try and make it better. So it is the same socially, musically, politically, and in any department in our lives."

The beauty of the St. John Will-I-Am Coltrane University is that it seeks above all to be a force for good, to promote unity, beauty, and love through creative and critical expression. "Everywhere, you know, I want to be a force for real good. In other words, I know that there are bad forces, forces out there that bring suffering and misery to the world, but I want to be the opposite force, I want to be the force which is truly for good."

If the vision of the St. John Will-I-Am Coltrane University has in any respect touched your heart, we ask for your input and assistance. At present, a simple statement of how the university as conceived might meet your educational needs would be an important contribution to our present investigation and planning. Further, any monetary contribution that you can make for the continued planning and eventual implementation of this project would be appreciated.

The vision statement for the proposed Coltrane University expressed many of the church's core values learned over its long history of evolution and transition. Specifically, the university would embrace a "progressive pedagogy of the arts," a post-racialist ethic, and a spiritual universalism.

All of these core principles were drawn from the life, music, and words of St. John Coltrane and the Coltrane University would have an ongoing engagement with the community about arts practices aimed at creating the very alternative social and political ideas espoused and exemplified by John Coltrane. Fischlin, Heble and Lipsitz note, "And creative, improvised musickings that reflect on and exact the formation of alternative communities have a great deal to tell us about how successful, meaningful encounters not predicated on violence, oppression, or inequity can be achieved" (31).

With respect to its "progressive pedagogy of the arts," the Coltrane University would place central importance on the ability of the arts to form communities and counter-narratives to discursive formations and practices in other social domains:

Progressive Pedagogy of the Arts

The Saint John Coltrane University is the first institution of higher learning founded by an African American community on the west coast of the United States of America. Its mission is to revitalize and extend a progressive pedagogy of the arts, utilizing creative expression as a means of facilitating the evolution and transcendence of students to achieve "richer, fuller, more productive lives."

In the spirit of St. John Coltrane, the University seeks to propagate the beautiful and living arts and an affirmative philosophy of the inherent power of creative expression to change lives and communities. The University embraces art and creativity as forums for the expression of the whole of human experience and as modes of abstract analysis and synthesis of the relationship of human beings to the universe. It advocates an artistic/creative praxis, engaging the arts in the struggle to alleviate human suffering caused by ignorance and inspiring the pursuit of truth, love, cultural revitalization, community service, and leadership. The University offers unique and highly specialized degree programs that integrate Liberal Studies with the Creative and Performing Arts, and it seeks to instill beauty, dignity, wholeness, self-respect, self-discovery, and academic excellence.

This progressive pedagogy of the arts that embraced "the while of human experience" was a specific attempt to incorporate what John Coltrane referred to as the "life side of music," and to teach improvisation as a cultural act that could inform all social domains including politics and spirituality. Citing Eric Nisenson, Fischlin, Heble, and Lipsitz note, "Coltrane represents a high-order example of throwing off the shackles of slavery and oppression, while recognizing global communities of otherness that destabilize limiting and degenerative notions of cultural purity. The music, highly improvisatory in its formulation and execution, enacts creative hybridities that point to musical freedoms, what Coltrane called 'the life side of music'" (23).

With respect to viewing the entire globe as its community and standing as a bulwark of post-racialism, the Coltrane University would specifically reject war and seek to build peace through artistic communication:

The Whole Face of the Globe Is Community

The St. John Coltrane University of Arts and Social Justice is an advocate for peace on earth. The University affirms the ideals of a global community. St. John Coltrane advocated, "...the whole face of the globe is our community." The ideals of global community find direct expression in the University's commitment to and practice of nonviolence and conscientious objection to war. "Well I dislike war period, you know. So therefore, as far as I'm concerned, it should stop."

As an outgrowth of its post-racialism, the University would also promote Coltrane's notion of the unity of religious ideals. It would be an interfaith university, practicing the very same spiritual universalism that it had learned through its One Mind Temple and Vedantic Center years.

An Inter-Faith University

In its appreciation of the spiritual possibilities of creative expression, the University seeks to promote inter-faith understanding and open-minded communication and draws upon St. John Coltrane's theology of the unity of religious ideals: "I believe in all religions. What is important is whether a person knows the truth.

Unity of Religious Ideals

The unity of religious ideals embraces traditions at the point that they intersect. There is little doubt that love, service, the pursuit of wisdom, compassionate understanding, peace, joy, and freedom, etc., are worthy of human attainment. The goal of the University is not to dogmatically propagate religion nor proselytize, but to use the idea of the unity of religious ideals to guide its students toward moral and ethical character building. The University seeks to support its students in achieving their personal potential, be they Muslim, Buddhist, Christian, Jew, Hindu, Agnostic, or Atheist. We believe that an improved world is created by improved persons and by people understanding their common ideals and working together in service to uplift each other.

Post-racial globalism and spiritual universalism were conceived as new and definitively counter-hegemonic ways of conceiving of self and community consistent with the thinking of John Coltrane. In the course of developing the pedagogy of the Coltrane University, we thought that could use a program in African American studies to explicitly link the musical instruction to these new ideas of self and community, and thus more effectively use the music to, as Coltrane suggests, "change the initial thought patterns." We proposed courses titled the African American Religious Experience, African American Social and Ethical Thought—19th Century and 20th Century, Freedom: The History of a People—19th Century and 20th Century, the History of Jazz, Jazz on Film, and African American Literature. These courses would provide substantive cultural support for the musical instruction so that the university could produce truly informed citizens. As Fischlin, Heble, and Lipsitz also note, "Now if we think of pedagogy in terms of 'the complicated processes by which knowledge is produced, skills are learned meaningfully, identities are shaped, desires are mobilized, and critical dialogue becomes a central form of public interaction' (Giroux xi), then to what extent (and in what ways) might improvisational musical practices be understood as vital (and publically resonant) pedagogical acts that generate new forms of knowledge, new understandings of identity and community, new imaginative possibilities with direct implications for social justice outcomes?" (44).

Finally, it did not escape our attention that within the context of local San Francisco jazz, the Coltrane University would have strengthened itself as a community jazz organization providing alternative performance opportunities and pedagogies of the music in the contested cultural spaces of the Fillmore/Western Addition and Hayes Valley neighborhoods. Our Coltrane-inspired and community-engaged jazz pedagogy would have almost immediately provided a methodological counter to the way that jazz theory and performance have been taught in the academy. Frederick Harris conceived of a far more immersive pedagogy in which students could learn the language of jazz by speaking it to one another and with their teachers in communal settings not unlike those that John Coltrane experienced in his Philadelphia years or with Miles Davis, Thelonious Monk, or Duke Ellington. This immersive pedagogy was in fact consistent with the prerogatives of the AACM or Horace Tapscott's UGMAA, notable exemplars of Frederick Harris' pedagogy. The proposed auditorium would have provided an alternative concert space for local musicians neglected by Yoshi's and SFJazz and for community jam sessions. In all, the Coltrane University would have created an alternative musical community from which we might reasonably have expected to hear a host of new sounds and ideas.

My bullet points and notes for the presentation included not only the mission statement and overall vision, but clear emphasis on the university as a community organization and a coherent and realistic plan of how we would build a student body from a core group of 90 Western Addition and Bayview-Hunter's Point K-12 students with whom Frederick Harris had already worked under a MOCYF (Mayor's Office of Children, Youth, and Their Families) grant. We further provided a timeline for WASC (Western Association of Schools and Colleges) accreditation, and justification of the experience and expertise of members of the Coltrane Church community supporting and leading the development of the university.

Redevelopment Project Bullet Points—Baham

- Philosophy of the University
  The whole face of the globe is community; Progressive pedagogy of the arts; Pedagogy of immersion—classrooms and multi-use space; Community engagement; Unity of religious ideals
- Proven/tested musical pedagogy—beginning with MOCYF grant for MUI; Stanford Summer Jazz Camp; Mercy High School jazz program
- Program begins with 90 k–12 students from MUI, some of whom have already worked with Frederick Harris in MOCYF project
- Program includes adult education throughout the day and weekends—consistent with prerogatives of St. John Coltrane outreach programs
  Food, clothing, shelter, counseling, music lessons
- Listening Library/Archive—offering walking tours; will approach Harlem of the West project
- Return of the spirit of the community/neighborhood

The final proposal that we delivered to the San Francisco Redevelopment Agency included $3.5 million in soft costs, $10 million in hard construction costs and $5.5 million in furniture, fixtures, and equipment costs. Funding would come from $3.5 million in historic preservation tax credits, $5 million in solar power credits, and $11 million in approved funding from Chase Bank. Working with Leola King LLC, the Coltrane Church joined a coalition that included developer Janet Campbell of Campbell and Associates Developers, and San Francisco supervisor for the Fillmore/Western Addition Ross Mirkarimi. With the demonstrable equity built into Janet Campbell's plan and the expertise of Garavaglia Architects in the preservation of historic sites, Chase Bank approved a loan for the project even before formal meetings. It was the vision of Leola King to restore the property and bring in community organizations like the Coltrane Church as well as facilities for technical education to help local businesses and residents. The facility would house an auditorium, recording studios, divisible classroom space, dining hall and kitchen, and a museum celebrating the history of the neighborhood including the jazz history of the Fillmore and the history of the many jazz clubs owned by Leola King during the 1950s, '60s, and '70s. The Coltrane Church was to be allotted day use for the purpose of Coltrane University activities.

Armed with the aforementioned ideals, a community-centered jazz pedagogy, a progressive liberal arts pedagogy, and an impressive architectural plan for the restoration of an historic structure from Garavaglia Architects, the Coltrane Church's team of developers, architects and intellectuals argued their case before the San Francisco Redevelopment Agency. Because of the history and racial politics of redevelopment, it was never my impression as a co-writer and co-presenter of the proposal that we had even the remotest chance of winning the bid. It was an impressive and comprehensive proposal and the Coltrane Church had certainly raised the level of its engagement in San Francisco politics. They were playing with the "big boys" at this point and they came armed with impressive bona fides. I was hardly surprised by the feigned enthusiasm with which we were greeted. But I was, in the end, quite surprised by the Redevelopment Agency's rejection of a proposal rooted in the needs of the community.

Campbell Architects launched a blog that made specific allegations about the process. They alleged, "The San Francisco Redevelopment Agency (SFRA) turned down all proposals and took the Proposal above on as their own, requesting the Church of Coltrane to become their tenant. The Archbishop declined. Later, it was determined that the SFRA had negotiated in bad faith by allowing developers to expend thousands of dollars on proposals to get work that was not going to be let. The SFRA had instead taken the funds dedicated to this project, during the submittal period, and quietly rescued the developer of The Fillmore Center a block away, who was facing ruin without the $3.5 million dedicated to this project."[1]

Conclusions

The John Coltrane University of Social Justice and restoration of the Leola King Center was an effort to openly confront the San Francisco Redevelopment Agency with respect to its 40-year history of lies and broken promises and its specific treatment of Leola King; enlarge the Coltrane Church's presence in the Western Addition as a community jazz organization; and counter the corporatization of San Francisco jazz by Yoshi's and the Fillmore Jazz Heritage Center. Their efforts were a clear demonstration of "differential ideological positioning," as they adopted the very same strategies of Yoshi's and the Fillmore Jazz Heritage Center and put together an impressive coalition of community activists, developers, architects, and intellectuals and obtained full funding from Chase Bank.

At the same time that the Coltrane Church employed many of the same strategies of its corporate competitors, it did so without reproducing similar forms of social and cultural domination. As Fischlin, Heble, and Lipsitz have noted, "As creative practitioners historically excluded from vital economic resources are redefining the way listeners and critics understand what counts as jazz history, as new initiatives are enabling the development of an infrastructure to support underrepresented and unheard voices (or 'unsung,' to borrow from Tapscott), the challenge remains for these initiatives not to duplicate —by virtue of being 'institutions' and formulating 'policies' themselves—the same cultural domination that they seek to abolish (54).

The Archbishop's refusal to accept tenant status was consistent with the Coltrane Church's long-standing reputation as a fundamentally counter-hegemonic community organization and emblematic of their refusal to participate in SFRA's structures of domination. There was simply no way that the Coltrane Church could ever have accepted such an offer. To do so would have ultimately meant forsaking their commitment to the community and with Leola King, the most well-publicized example of redevelopment exploitation.

There was a clear difference between petitioning SFRA for the purchase and restoration of the Leola King Center and accepting tenant status under SFRA control. At the end of the day, the Coltrane Church was interested in helping to right a wrong and assist Leola King and her family with redressing decades-old grievances. The Archbishop's refusal signified the church's prioritization of community of the individual interests of the church.

Although the St. John Coltrane University of the Arts and Social Justice remains an un-realized vision and the proposed Leola King Center on the corner of Fillmore and Turk Streets remains empty in 2015, the progressive pedagogy of the arts that was central to the project continues through Frederick Harris who still provides a community-based music instruction to vocalists and instrumentalists through the Coltrane Church. Furthermore, the university represents the sixth major ideological shift of the ever-evolving Coltrane Church since the initial Sound Baptism in 1965 and the church has remained amazingly consistent to the impressions and meanings of that founding moment.

12

The Battle Against Environmental Racism

Damn the Rules, it's the Feeling that Counts.
You play all twelve notes in your solo anyway.
—St. John Will-I-Am Coltrane

October 11, 2007, Archbishop Franzo Wayne King, D.D., now the successor of African Orthodox Archbishop George Duncan Hinkson and presiding Archbishop over a western jurisdiction that includes African Orthodox churches in Chicago, Illinois, and Houston, Texas,[1] sits shoulder to shoulder with Bishop Ernest Jackson of Grace Tabernacle, Minister Christopher Muhammad of the Nation of Islam, Pastor Alex of Sold Out Ministries, Francisco DeCosta and POWER, representatives of GreenAction for Health and Environmental Justice, the Stop Lennar Action Movement (SLAM), San Francisco Supervisor Chris Daly and the Reverend Lelea'e S. Afalava of the First Samoan Full Gospel Pentecostal Church at Bishop Jackson's Grace Tabernacle Church on the hill on Ingalls and Oakdale Streets in San Francisco's Bayview-Hunter's Point (BVHP) neighborhood for a weekly town hall meeting.[2]

A diverse host of activist liberation theologians and community organizers gather every Thursday evening to hear experts talk about the environmental impact of toxic soil bombardment and asbestos friables released in the redevelopment project on the 100-acre Parcel A at the Hunter's Point shipyard. In addition to asbestos exposure under the Lennar Corporation, the Bayview-Hunter's Point neighborhood is home to a Pacific Gas & Electric power plant that represents the city's largest source of air pollution, emitting nitrogen oxides, carbon monoxide, sulfur dioxide, and particulate matter that have contributed to the highest rates of breast

192

cancer in San Francisco.[3] The Nation of Islam. The St. John William Coltrane African Orthodox Church. POWER (People Organized to Win Employment Rights). SLAM (Stop Lennar Action Movement). Members of the San Francisco School Board. Green Party representatives. Grace Tabernacle. The American Samoan Church. The San Francisco Youth Commission. They are building a social justice movement against environmental racism and in 2008 that movement initiated placing ballot measure F[4] on San Francisco's June election ballot.

They hear quantitative evidence of ongoing scientific monitoring data and anecdotes of children and the elderly suffering from nose-bleeds, headaches, and respiratory problems. There is testimony from the elderly. Nurses testify to dramatic new demands for emergency services. Voters from districts as far away as North Beach who remember the overwhelming support San Franciscans cast for Bayview-Hunter's Point residents in the 2001 vote for Proposition P stand and testify to their support for community efforts against Lennar.

According to Jason Browne's March 23, 2011, San Francisco Bay View article "Emails Show Regulators Conspiring with Lennar to Cover Up Shipyard Development Danger," from 2007 to 2011 the Coltrane Church, Nation of Islam, Greenaction for Health and Environmental Justice and their allies in POWER and SLAM engaged Lennar in a series of public hearings and alleged that the Lennar Corporation and officials in the Environmental Protection Agency Region 9 and the San Francisco Department of Health may have engaged in a cover- up of environmental data (http:// sfbayview.com/2011 /03/emails-show-regulators-conspiring-with-lennar-to-coverup-shipyard-development-danger/). Browne writes, "Email correspondence obtained through a public records request now reveals that Mark Ripperda, EPA Region 9 remedial project manager for the Hunters Point Naval Shipyard, and Amy Brownell, environmental engineer at the San Francisco Department of Public Health, used their offices to manipulate environmental data and create false reports in support of Lennar's plan for a major redevelopment project on the shipyard site. Their numerous emails to employees and consultants of the Lennar Corp. show a concerted effort to conceal asbestos exposures in order to avoid the shutdown of redevelopment activities. Additional email correspondence indicates a conspiracy to create a justification for Lennar's redevelopment project to move forward."

In June 2008 Measure F was ultimately defeated by record spending, a dueling ballot measure strategy (Measure G[5] in favor of Lennar's redevelopment plan), misleading campaign advertising linking development to a new San Francisco 49ers stadium, and the manipulation of local African

The church performs at Cité de la Musique in Paris on February 8, 2008.

American churches through the Tabernacle Development Corp. However, the actions of the Coltrane Church and its allies suggested possibilities for subaltern religious communities to initiate counter-hegemonic political action and provide an empirical starting point for building a theory and methodology for the relationship between religion and politics in subaltern communities.

2006–2009: The Battle Against Environmental Racism

On one level the church's involvement in the battle against the Lennar Corporation is historically situated as a backlash against the ineffectiveness of the slow growth progressivism long advocated by San Francisco's African American power bloc since the mid–1960s. And undoubtedly much of this historical disillusionment was revisited by similar contradictions during the mayoral regime of the socially liberal yet staunchly pro-growth former California Assemblyman Willie Brown (1996–2004). On another level, in similar fashion to St. John Coltrane University of Arts and Social Justice proposal, it was an outgrowth of the church's post–1986 mandate to use its legitimation within the African Orthodox Church for a greater role as community activists engaged in community-police relations, urban relocation and removal, and environmental racism and it was also clearly a specific outgrowth of the Caravan for Justice.

Now Archbishop Franzo W. King would align the Coltrane Church with POWER (People Organized to Win Employment Rights), SLAM (Stop Lennar Action Movement), Grace Tabernacle, the Nation of Islam, the Green Party, Chris Daly's lone voice of dissent on the San Francisco Board of Supervisors, and the American Samoan Church against the forces of the multibillion-dollar home builder Lennar, San Francisco Mayor Gavin Newsom, and the Lennar-funded alliance of local African American ministers.

This ideological shift, remains a work in progress, particularly given the electoral defeat of POWER's community-funded measure F in 2009. But the involvement of the Coltrane Church in Measure F and the fight against environmental racism in the Bayview-Hunter's Point is a culminating experience bringing the church further from the margins to the center and affording them an opportunity to draw on their complex history of cultural, religious and political universalism and effectively assist with the mobilization of a broad, diverse political coalition such as POWER.

These contemporary efforts mark the culmination of 50-years of cultural, political, and religious evolution that Archbishop King and Mother Marina, Apostles of Sound, have undertaken in the spirit of John Coltrane to create a spiritual, cultural, and political practice that would meld the progressive impetus of free jazz music, the populism of early black Pentecostal worship, spiritual universalism, Marxist class consciousness, and the radical black nationalist politics of self-help.

Speaking pragmatically of their evolution in preparation for their movement and political campaign against Lennar and their progress from margin to center as a social and political force, Archbishop King states:

> I don't see St. John Coltrane getting comfortable with *A Love Supreme* being a gold record, and thinking that he needed to keep trying to keep duplicating that, but realizing that what he was doing was rooted in love, and even a love supreme. Whatever he did beyond that was an extension of that. When I look at myself and what I'm doing here, I have to make sure that as my saint was always changing and searching and looking and pushing the envelope to the point that John Coltrane wasn't around trying to make friends. It's my job not to see how many friends I can make in this town or how many deals I can cut with people, but to make sure that Coltrane Consciousness is on the cutting edge of the 21st century in terms

of delivering the message of freedom and what that means. All you've got is whether what you're dealing with is in the truth, that you're standing in the truth.

The differential ideological movement of this perpetually evolutionary, transitional church body was building greater momentum toward realpolitik applications of cultural and spiritual activity and related questions regarding the relevance of jazz music as a disruptive cultural form that can initiate social action (Fischlin, Heble, Lipsitz).

Michael Leo Owens has recently begun to explore progressive church-state collaborations in *God and Government in the Ghetto: The Politics of Church-State Collaboration in Black America*. Owens' book fills a void in the scholarship of the black church that has traditionally focused on its limited political role in protest and voter registration.

Owens focuses on church-state collaborations in the 1980s and '90s in the largest and poorest black neighborhoods in New York City: Harlem, Bedford-Stuyvesant, South Jamaica, and Morrisania. He argues that activist clergy utilized a diverse menu of collaborative strategies with secular nongovernmental and governmental groups. Community development corporations (CDCs) are portrayed as the ultimate weapon of activists in the post–civil rights era. *God and Government in the Ghetto* focuses on the collective action of four CDCs—Southeast Queens Clergy for Community Empowerment (SQCCE), Harlem Congregations for Community Improvement (HCCI), Association of Brooklyn Clergy for Community Development (ABCCD), and the Bronx Shepherds Restoration Corporation (BSRC)—and their ability to receive land and money from New York City's Neighborhood Redevelopment Program and the Department of Housing Preservation and Development (HPD) under the auspices of the Ten Year Program to increase the supply of housing for the homeless and poor through the development of 252,000 affordable housing units initially proposed during the Koch administration in 1986 (Owens).

Unlike the protagonists of Owens' text, the Coltrane Church was not involved in collaboration with local governmental authorities but was rather involved in coalitions directly opposed to city policy regarding the Lennar development. Further, the Coltrane Church positioned itself in opposition to a coalition of black churches (The Tabernacle Group[6]) that were operating collaboratively with city government and the private sector. These aspects of their behavior remained consistent with their marginalized past.

In my estimation, the Coltrane Church allied itself with forces directly opposed to black church-state collaborations because in this instance black church-state collaboration represented co-optation and a betrayal of the community, particularly in light of the community's allegations of the health impacts of the Lennar development. The history of slow-growth black progressivism since the mid–1960s also represented a betrayal of community. Certainly collaboration with local government would have been contrary to the history of the Coltrane Church's marginal political involvement before its incorporation within the African Orthodox Church. After 1986, as the Coltrane Church proved during the planning of the Coltrane University, it remained unwilling to compromise its core communal commitment. Although the Coltrane Church was certainly capable of making a dramatic ideological shift, in the case of the Lennar development, an ideological shift toward wholehearted church-state collaboration would have meant a betrayal of perhaps the Coltrane Church's most fundamental value of community.

The Duplicity of Black Middle Class Religion and the Illusive Separation of Religion and Politics

The movement to stop Lennar originated with a conscientious whistle-blower, Chris Carpenter, who was concerned about the health and safety of children attending the Nation of Islam's school located next to Lennar's development. Led initially by the Nation of Islam's Minister Christopher Muhammad, the community began investigating and seeking information about the health of the school children. Archbishop King speaks of the community's initial communications and quest for information from Lennar and the beginning of dialogues with entrenched business and political power rife with duplicity and half-truths:

> It came up that they [Lennar] didn't monitor for the first four months. They said, 'Oh, we had defective monitors.' And then we began to investigate. They can't go defective or undetected for four months. The nature of the instrument is that you have to change the battery every eight hours and then there's something else you have to do every twelve hours. So the longest you could go would be twelve hours to know that these things are not working. So you have this massive grading and no monitors working. So they assure us that there's no problem but because they didn't come and tell and we had to learn it from someone else, I'm not that comfortable with them telling me everything is all right on something that I had to find out on my own. What we asked them to do is stop working temporarily to assess the damage to the health of the children in the school. And then we had the personal physician Dr. Salim Muhammad for Min. Far-

rakhan come out and he did some preliminary testing on the student body and found lead and mercury and things like that in their systems. That was just preliminary and he shared that with the Board of Health.

The complicity and inseparability of organized religion, politics, and money as a cross-cultural constant of human societies has long been obscured from the view of the underclass through the clever play of dominant cultural ideological constructs. But that has never meant that the underclass doesn't know what's going on or what to expect.

The efforts of the Coltrane Church and its allies in the fight against environmental racism were directed against a powerful collusion between African American middle class church leaders, local and state government, and national and local business concerns working against the basic interests of lower middle class to poor African Americans in San Francisco's Bayview-Hunter's Point neighborhood. Writing for the *San Francisco Bay View* on May 6, 2009, Alicia Schwartz indicates that the Lennar Corporation funded the Tabernacle Group "to extract community support for its poisonous development" (http://sfbayview.com/2009/05/bayview-deserves-better/). The Tabernacle Group that at that time consisted of Herman Blackmon, Dr. Aurelious Walker, the Rev. J. Edgar Boyd, Bishop Donald E. Green, the Rev. Calvin Jones and Dr. James McCray, and the Rev. Amos Brown, a former San Francisco Supervisor.[7]

In a May 6, 2009, article in the *San Francisco Bay View* newspaper titled "The Bayview Deserves Better," journalist Alicia Schwartz alleged that the Tabernacle Group worked intimately with Lennar Corporation public relations firm Singer and Associates, wrote and/or signed off on misleading editorials in the *San Francisco Examiner* newspaper, and boldly claimed that Bayview-Hunter's Point residents faced no significant health risks from Lennar's development. Schwartz writes, "The Tabernacle Group claims that there is abundant scientific evidence that community residents are not at risk from Lennar's development, yet they fail to acknowledge that there have been no scientific tests done on residents to assess exposure to chromium, lead and other toxic inorganics. In fact, there is no scientific evidence to back up the San Francisco Health Department's claims that the reckless actions of the Lennar Corp. on the Hunters Point Naval Shipyard have not placed community members at risk for long term health effects brought on by daily exposure to those toxins. While there is no test for exposure to asbestos, there certainly are tests available that can assess short and long term health impacts related to exposure to chromium and lead."[8]

The Tabernacle Group's fierce defense of the Lennar Corporation's development of 10,000 luxury condominiums in the Bayview-Hunter's Point not only marks the dark side of church-state collaboration but is also part of perhaps the oldest racial narrative originating in the history of American enslavement: divide and conquer. Schwartz acknowledges as much when she editorializes, "Now Lennar has stooped even lower, attempting to pit Black people against Black people, Christians against Muslims, resident against resident, all for the promise of a dollar, a seasonal job, some parks on toxic land, and some homes that 80 percent of the community won't be able to afford. It leaves one to wonder—what will they stoop to next, and when are we going to stand up as a community and say, 'Enough is enough!'" (Schwartz).

Archbishop King speaks directly to the collusion of dominant classes within San Francisco's African American communities and Lennar in his remarks about the Tabernacle Group and to Lennar's ability to divide San Francisco's African American religious community as part of a broader history of the betrayal of African American leadership in San Francisco:

> And you've got the Tabernacle Group, who are a group of black ministers. The Tabernacle Group are working with Lennar and Kaiser to do development of affordable housing. In other words, they are supposed to get some of that shipyard. Three of them are working with Lennar. The other two are working with Kaiser, which is going to do something on O'Farrell or Geary.
>
> But back in the day it would be the Waypackers and stuff that would come and get me and say, "Bishop, we need some people to show up." And we'd kind of trust what their thinking was in terms of being guardians. I think some of that trust was mislaid. When I look back I see that these so-called guardians of the Fillmore turned out to be sell-out artists. A lot of them went very cheaply. Even now today they are still hustling from day to day. That's why this city today has just bowed down, because of the so-called leadership that really purchased for the community a death warrant.

Struggles between the community and the Tabernacle Group were further intensified by a significant schism between black Christian leaders and Black Muslim leaders in San Francisco. In effect the struggle over the Bayview-Hunter's Point shipyard development was consistently portrayed in the mainstream San Francisco press as a struggle between the Nation of Islam and black Christian leadership.

Archbishop King was clearly committed to an alternative path that involved his alliance with Minister Christopher Muhammad and the Nation of Islam. This alliance, developed when Archbishop King returned from Chicago in 1989 and began working with Min. Christopher to create a zone of protection around the black community in San Francisco, was now being strengthened by Archbishop King's understanding of the complex manipulation of religious politics by forces outside of the black community.

Speaking to his developing relationship to the Nation of Islam and his love for Minister Farrakhan as well as Min. Christopher, Archbishop King remembers a gathering with Farrakhan and local Chicago ministers in 1995:

> To watch Minister Farrakhan work is a great teaching. And I was thinking about teachers and how close you get to them. For some you're the teacher's pet and for others you sit at the back of the class. Or maybe you had to stand in the corner. But that's still your teacher. I was feeling really blessed and I was looking at him as a teacher. I mean, he teaches you how to be a student. He shows you the hunger that a student needs to have if he's going to grow into the greatness that God created him for. I learned so much from him. And I petitioned him for his help. I told him I needed his help.

Speaking to the Muslim/Christian schism that lay waiting to be exploited in the attempt to undermine the efforts of POWER, Archbishop King comments:

> There's the fear in the community that Farrakhan is interested in stealing all of the members out of the Christian church, and that's so ridiculous, you know what I mean? For a man to even have an ambition like that, he's not even worthy to sit down and talk with.
>
> And to watch the way he dealt with that and to watch and feel the anxiety in the presiding elders that were there.... All you have to do to protect the flock is preach the Gospel. That's all you gotta do.
>
> And what do I care if a no-good Christian up in here is shucking and jiving on his way to hell and Farrakhan grabs him and dusts him off and cleans him up and the next thing I know he's saying, "Allah!" Praise God! That's wonderful.
>
> He's gonna be taking care of his family, his kids, and respecting his mother, his sister, and his auntie. How could you have any fear of that?

The Coltrane Church and its community allies were in the midst of a heightened struggle against corporate development, city government agencies, and the black Brahmin-ism of failed African American leadership in the Bay Area. It has been the singular triumph of the Coltrane Church to recognize the manipulation of politics, religion, and culture by the dominant classes within and without African American communities and to respond to this with their own ideological and practical strategies. They have ultimately rejected the black Christian fear and dismissal of the Nation of Islam and positioned themselves against the black Christian establishment that cooperated with the Lennar Corporation in the struggle over the Bayview-Hunter's Point shipyard development.

Archbishop King speaks further on perceived machinations of state, business, and local African American religious leaders:

> The first time we held a meeting all of the show ponies came out. "Don't stop the work. We need this for development, we need the jobs."And I'm saying, I'm not against development. Just stop this temporarily, stop the work, and assess the damage. All the Tabernacle group have some kind of ties. They'll say, I don't work for Lennar. Yes, but you went to Communities of Opportunities that was coming out of the mayor's office..... You have the Department of Health telling you not to believe your bleeding nose and your increase in asthma.
>
> That neighborhood has been like that for forty or fifty years but there's no long-term health concerns. And I'm saying, wait a minute. The environmental health guys write a letter talking about everything that they found, saying that there is no doubt that the school and the Bayview-Hunter's Point community have been exposed to asbestos-laden dust and other toxins. However, we don't know of any test that's reliable because asbestos has a latency of sometimes as much as up to forty or fifty years. So we look up and we are bombarded with all of these people clamoring for the jobs. And I'm wondering, wait a minute, what do you mean no long-term health concerns? What is long-term? I don't want to be sick for two minutes.
>
> So we started building a coalition.
>
> And it was like opening a can of worms. All kinds of stuff started coming out. They've had all kinds of excesses above what even they say are the acceptable rates of asbestos exposure. Even with the heavy grading over, they were still far exceeding the acceptable rate. Even though the cancer people say there is no safe level.

Discursive distinctions between "religion," "politics," and "money," whether originating from academic disciplinary divisions or other institutions and structures of power, serve only to mask the real lived experience of everyday transgressions between these realms. This masking may be experienced far more acutely in traditionally underprivileged communities in which local leadership conspires to benefit from the perpetual undermining of the community's most basic needs. The contemporary American debate about the role of religion in politics is, in fact, wholly disingenuous and predicated upon a manufactured perception of the invisibility of how long-standing, enduring, and effective the marriage of religion and politics has always been. To unmask the alliance of the African American upper and middle class establishment with state and business interests in specifically African American underprivileged communities is to unmask pernicious structures of power in operation and certainly marks the initial step toward meaningful resistance.

The Coltrane Church allows for present-day analysis of this specific class conspiracy. In light of the historical impact of the black church as the fundamental backbone of anti-slavery and civil rights movements, such collusion reads in one light as the ultimate historical betrayal. It also reflects long-standing field slave-house slave enmities and the history of how every American slave revolt (from Prosser to Vesey to Turner and a host of smaller maroon revolts) was undermined by the slave who thought more of the prospects of wearing the master's coat and eating the master's lean bacon than of ending the system of human bondage into which he had been born.[9]

In the face of this betrayal, the key for marginal and subaltern religious groups like the Coltrane Church is not simply to mimic the cognitive dissonance and gleeful manipulation of dominant religious institutions or duplicitous middle class religious institutions within their own communities, but to acquire a fully functional transitive nature, a transitive consciousness, an ability to strategically manipulate ideology in the moment, and an ability to fully recognize and transgress the illusive discursive separation of religion, politics, and money. Cultural theorist Chela Sandoval suggests, "All social orders hierarchically organized into relations of domination and subordination create particular subject positions within which the subordinated can legitimately function. These subject positions, once self-consciously recognized by their inhabitants, can become transfigured into effective sites of resistance to an oppressive ordering of power relations" (55).

The principal role of functional transitivity in this instance has been that it enables coalition building. The transitions of the Coltrane Church have not only provided exposure and therefore a certain measure of social confidence, but have also enabled a certain cultural multi-lingualism. Archbishop King:

> Coltrane said the whole world was community. And so, we're here with our Muslim brothers and sisters, with the American Samoan church, with other Christian denominations, with atheists and activists, people from outside of this neighborhood who support this cause. Because through Coltrane we can speak this language and understand.

Differential Ideological Movement

San Francisco resident Rebecca Solnit and urban archaeologist Susan Schwartzenberg's *Hollow City: The Seige of San Francisco and the Crisis of American Urbanism* includes a brief chapter on the ceremonial march of the Coltrane Church from their Divisadero location to the St. Paulus

Lutheran Church in 2000. Their narrative effectively locates the Coltrane Church within broader contemporary struggles against urban redevelopment and plainly identifies a transitive and multi-faceted church body that has committed itself to the struggle for the poor.

After following what must have been simply one day of photographing this ceremonial march and notes from one Sunday of a church service preceding their exodus, Solnit and Schwartzenberg instantly and lucidly recognized the social and political dimensions of the mere presence of the Coltrane Church in the Western Addition. "The storefront Church of St. John Coltrane exemplifies culture in every sense: it's religious, artistic, ethnic, political, and social at the same time. It feeds the poor three times a week and serves as one of the last remaining links to the golden age of the Fillmore District before it was gutted by urban renewal. And as an eccentric, individualist cultural hybrid—making free jazz a sacrament—it represents what has always made San Francisco distinctive (23). Solnit and Schwartzenberg "get it" in a fashion reminiscent of Franzo King on July 17, 1967, at Jimbo's Bop City and it is precisely because of the political and social services provided by this small church and its historic link to black ownership and entrepreneurship in San Francisco that it has a counter-hegemonic influence against the trends of gentrification and urban renewal and removal.

Furthermore, Solnit and Schwartzenberg also understand the broader context of an ongoing war against the poor in San Francisco and the steady out-migration of African Americans from the Western Addition in particular. However, Solnit and Schwartzenberg have not been able to identify the principal stakeholders who might benefit from the displacement and exodus of the poor and people of color from San Francisco. Solnit and Schwartzenberg write extensively, "Campaigns to get rid of the poor have a long history in San Francisco. African Americans, working-class seniors, other residential-hotel denizens and the homeless have all had their turn, and other campaigns—against undocumented immigrants and refugees and against Latinos and Asians generally—have attempted to erase or undermine populations on a larger scale. As the Second World War was ending, the city came up with a master plan that featured elements of redevelopment, and by the beginning of 1947 specific proposals were being made to annihilate portions of the Western Addition. Blight was the magical word of the era of urban renewal, a word whose invocation justified the destruction of housing, communities and neighborhoods in many American cities, and San Francisco was no exception. The Western Addition had, not coincidentally, become home to San Francisco's African-

American community, and urban renewal would eventually be nicknamed 'Negro removal'" (43).

Solnit and Schwartzenberg are primarily interested in the demise of San Francisco's artist communities and they do not effectively explore possibilities for subaltern communities to resist redevelopment and removal. However, at the core of the Coltrane Church, on cultural, religious, and ideological terms, is a transitive body that I have argued is well adapted to fighting for its survival in the midst of urban redevelopment and renewal.

The extraordinary transitive nature of the Coltrane Church flirts not only with resistance in discrete social realms, but also with its own set of seemingly contradictory ideologies and practices, including black nationalism and Hindu asceticism and, on some level, jazz and asceticism. Such willful contradictions demand explanation. The persistent transitions of the church demand linkage and confrontation with the broader question of how counter-hegemonic spiritual and cultural ideologies can be manifested or transformed into a politics of resistance just as dominant ideological transgressions have been manifested as public policy.

The Coltrane Church began with a spiritual vision that immediately manifested itself as a cultural movement, then a religious institution, and ultimately a local political force. And all of this without losing the passion for either culture or spirit. This movement is not only related to the classic question of transforming theory into action, but also how social actors and communities can cross and overlap discrete realms of social life, back and forth across religion to culture to politics, for example, and how each of these discrete realms can be transformed or remain intact in the process.

The key is that these realms are not discreet and separable in practice, and social actors approach these transgressions in a far more relativistic fashion that the social sciences appreciate. While social actors daily traverse and integrate cultural, spiritual, and political realms as a process of meeting daily needs, the social scientific translation of such quotidian "cognitive mapping" is lacking in my estimation (Solnit and Schwartzenberg 29). In the end, I am concerned with how such migrations across social spaces enable survival and counter-hegemonic ideologies and practice.

The accumulation of numerous ideological shifts across cultural, religious, and political planes suggests not only a subaltern organization that is fully adept at "differential movement," but also a fully functional transitive organization whose very core principles incorporate evolution and change.

The Coltrane Church is a transitive community held together in large measure by their love and commitment to one another and to John

Coltrane that had been led in effect by the inspiration of John Coltrane to wander across discrete social realms and to evolve in much the same fashion as Coltrane had evolved as both a musician and a mystic. The Coltrane Church is a wholly transitive church body, a transitive group of artists, mystics, seekers, and ultimately also transitive political players whom any long-time observer would be hard-pressed to define within strict ideological terms. The Coltrane Church has manifested several different sets of ideologies and practices over the course of their 50-year history and because of this "differential movement" they have been able to survive even amidst the threat of urban redevelopment that would rather have them depart San Francisco in favor of another upscale, corporate artistic or religious facility. The Coltrane Church is in every respect more of a hermeneutic than an organization, properly speaking, and because of its inherent improvisatory nature and openness to "differential movement," it continues to thrive as a voice for specific subaltern classes.

During the course of its history the community of the Coltrane Church has been building an effective political voice beyond the critique of power from the pulpit. Sandoval identifies an effective mode of resistance that she finds lacking in Fredric Jameson's critique of postmodernism. She answers his longing for a social scientific cognitive mapping of resistance, a theoretical model that at long last catches up with real-time resistance. "I discussed earlier survival skills developed under subordination that revolve around the manipulation of ideology. These skills juggle, transgress, differ, buy and sell ideologies in a system of production and exchange bent on ensuring survival" (Sandoval 30).

These skills necessarily emanate from a differential or oppositional mode of consciousness. In other words, some recognition of dominant cultural abuses of ideology and a willingness to similarly transgress is fundamental. "The differential mode of social movement (that which transforms and allies all other modes of social movement) relies on what I have called a 'cyber' consciousness, a 'differential' consciousness that operates as process and shifting location. Differential consciousness is linked to whatever is not expressible through words. It is accessed through poetic modes of expression: gestures, music, images, sounds, words that plummet or rise through signification to find some void –some no-place- to claim their due" (Sandoval 140).

Implicit in Archbishop King's following remarks is a commentary on the transitive, differential movement of the Coltrane Church:

> What we're about is uplifting people and withstanding the wiles of the devil. And the devil is in the form of corporate developers and agencies

that are really about moving people and transforming communities into a
new kind of image in terms of population. It's going on all across the
country. It's not just in San Francisco.

Here the Archbishop conflates religious and political spheres—a strategy of differential ideology movement not unknown to contemporary
Christian conservatives- and links the enemies of God with the enemies
of the people. In large measure his words hark to black liberation theology
and social justice interpretations of the Gospel of Jesus Christ that mark
Christ as a defender of the poor. Further linking corporate development
with religious evil, and, specifically with the devil, Archbishop King revives
a traditional African American narrative of "trickery." Here he implies the
folkloric trope of Brer Rabbit trickery often used in slave communities as
an origin narrative to explain captivity and bondage and often conflated
with the wiles of the devil. In effect, Archbishop King is speaking of a
community at the crossroads, torn between the promise of jobs and money
for community development and the growing recognition of environmental health issues.

> With Lennar there was a severance package for the community of 30 mil-
> lion. It was supposed to go to the community for education and health.
> That severance package has now fallen to 17 million and it is falling still.
> And it's going to be a situation where the community may not see any
> money at all.

The significance of such differential ideological movement is that it
creates a wealth of alternative strategies and communities that can be
organized for effective action. These two brief statements underscore differential movement between religion and the political expressions of
African American liberation theology and religion and black nationalism.
Such differential movement effectively spans a time frame dating back to
slave-era preaching to 1960s black radicalism, and implies themes from
traditional/folkloric African American narrative commentaries of justice.
Sandoval implies these possibilities in speaking of "charting" social
space. All human experience across social domains is laid out on a grid,
hinting at a relativistic posture and recognition that no one social activity
rests in a dimension above the other and that all social activities are freely
available for counter-hegemonic strategizing. "This differentially moving
force expresses a whole new coordinate in Jameson's knowledge of and
charting of social space. It operates as does a technology—a weapon of
consciousness that functions like a compass: a pivoting center capable of
drawing circles of varying circumference, depending on the setting. Such

a differential force, when understood as technical, political, aesthetic, and ethical practice, allows one to chart out the positions available and the directions to move in a larger social totality" (30).

Of critical importance is the centrality of John Coltrane. Coltrane's music and life operate as the central axis around which strategic ideological moves can be effectuated. Coltrane provides not only an ideological center for movement across cultural, political, and religious planes, but also effectively inhibits church leaders and members from losing core principles in the midst of ideological strategizing. In this fashion, political forays by the Coltrane Church can be interpreted in a less cynical fashion. Archbishop King speaks to the centrality of John Coltrane in the advocacy work of the Coltrane Church:

> You know that quote where Coltrane talks about making things better with music? That's the kind of consciousness that supports our work.

Further, the church's political involvement in the struggle against Lennar is deeply personal. Family therefore also provides a central axis for differential movement. The Bayview-Hunter's Point is not only the home of the first listening clinics and after-hours clubs that preceded the Coltrane Church, but it remains the home of Archbishop King and Mother Marina King and their extended family. Indeed the most significant cultural, religious, and political partnerships of the Coltrane Church are located in the Bayview-Hunter's Point neighborhood.

Archbishop King affirmatively locates this deeply personal connection within his origin narrative of how the church came to be involved in the struggle against Lennar.

> My involvement is Shahada, Tri-Nu, and Little Miles and all of these children who went to Mohammed University. And we did our music program there.
>
> So the way this whole thing came down, we were in a community meeting at the mosque and this brother walks in. We thought he was there for the meeting, but he said, "No, I've been trying to talk you for the past two weeks to ask you if you know about what's going on."
>
> I mean the kids are running up to the gate where there's all the tractors and trucks. And he says, "hey, you guys are not shutting down the school and you're not telling the community anything."
>
> And he starts talking about the construction and the asbestos and the pollution and its possible impact on the children. So he came and he ended up losing his job.
>
> So we left that meeting and we went to the Lennar site on the shipyard and that's how this whole thing started. This guy came on his own. A whistleblower.

Conclusions

The Coltrane Church engaged in political protest and organization in an attempt to stop environmental racism, urban development and removal in San Francisco's Bayview-Hunter's Point. In so doing they positioned themselves in direct opposition to the Tabernacle Group and its church-state collaboration. The fact that the Coltrane Church was able to ally itself with a broad and diverse coalition of interest groups speaks to the ideological movement that the Coltrane Church had undertaken to move from the limitations of narrow black nationalist politics and religious denominationalism towards more inclusive class-based and spiritually universalist approaches. Their alliance with POWER was further indicative of greater moves from margin to center that had begun since their incorporation into the wider African Orthodox Church.

In realpolitik terms, The Coltrane Church and SLAM were able to wrest a measure of community development money from Lennar, what Archbishop King referred to as a "severance package." The money was placed in a trust and designated for the development of Alliance for Californians for Community Empowerment (ACCE), a community rights organization that the Coltrane Church would ally with in a subsequent fight against bank foreclosures.

> SLAM forced Lennar to give money in trust to the San Francisco Foundation for development for ACCE and other groups that determine what is going to happen to that money. That never would have happened without SLAM shaking the tree, there wouldn't be any fruit on the ground.

In the long term, the Coltrane Church and POWER have been unable to stem the tide of African American removal, particularly considering the defeat of 2008 Measure F. Certainly many lessons were learned. However, in the struggle against the environmental racism, the Coltrane Church has proven that it is capable of doing much more than producing a dissonant utopian ideology of resistance. It has demonstrated *the potential* for realizing substantive material gains (political and economic) for the poor and despised of San Francisco.

The limited success that the Coltrane Church and its allies earned in the struggle for Measure F might be measured in terms of the degree of trepidation that their efforts generated from Lennar and the Mayor's office. Certainly the Tabernacle Group's offer to Archbishop King in 2008, to underwrite the church's rent on Fillmore Street in light of the more recent revocation of funds promised to them by New College of California, provides some measure of this fear, as does the advertising effort behind counter–Measure G.

Here Archbishop King speaks of an offer of some $250,000 from the Tabernacle Group to secure funding for the church's lease on Fillmore Street.

> New College, their thing is that they want to drop the lease.... So they came to me with a representative from the Board. He was talking about how they could take care of the lease and do this, that, and another. So I said to him, I said brother, you know what, go back and find out what they want me to do. Do they just want me to step out of the race? Don't start talking to me about how "them people" want to help me. I messed with them. I told them, man, just put some money in a bag. Put forty million dollars in a bag and I can just go to my brother's and tell him I'm going to step back. But me and Minister Christopher already talked. We talked before they even really showed up. We knew what was going to happen and we were just waiting so that when it came I was able to just play it.

The present and ongoing struggle against environmental racism in San Francisco's Bayview-Hunter's Point neighborhood is marked with the kind of progress rarely witnessed in urban redevelopment and civil rights struggles, and perhaps marks an important development in contemporary grass roots politics and relationships between communities and churches. And, arguably, the Coltrane Church's efforts have begun to unmask heretofore obscured alliances and opportunistic and unscrupulous ministers within San Francisco's African American community as well as duplicitous public servants and corporate interests outside of the community.

13

The Ordination of Pastor
Wanika Kristi King-Stephens

There is never any end
There are always new sounds to imagine
New feelings to get at
And always there is a need to keep purifying
these needs and sounds
So that we can really see what we've discovered
in its pure state
So we can see more clearly what we are
In that way, we can give those who listen to the essence
The best of what we are

—St. John Will-I-Am Coltrane

Sunday, September 19, 2010, the Rev. Wanika Kristi King-Stephens was installed as Pastor of the St. John Will-I-Am Coltrane African Orthodox Church. The installation of Pastor King-Stephens fundamentally challenges the gender politics of the black church, furthers the Coltrane Church's legacy of female leadership from Supreme Mother and Alice Coltrane, and marks the fulfillment of the vision of both John Coltrane and the original Apostles of Sound. Her installation necessarily effects a substantive revision of Coltrane Church history and has even greater significance against the historical backdrop of the African Orthodox Church as a whole and the circumstances in which the Coltrane Church became integrated with the African Orthodox Church. It signals a contemporary ideological shift that places the Coltrane Church at the vanguard of progressive social and political action in African American religious movements.

At the age of 65 and after confrontations with prostate cancer and back problems, Archbishop King began to lay the foundation for the next generation of leadership of the Coltrane Church:

> It should be said that we really consider Wanika to be a co-founder of this ministry because she was right there with us when all of this was happening and even as a child she gave me a lot of inspiration for what we were trying to do as a body of believers.

Facing a substantial rent increase for the facility in May 1999, the congregation of the St. John Will-I-Am Coltrane African Orthodox Church sought a new home. After 27 years on 351 Divisadero Street the building was purchased and the rent was raised from $1,100 to $2,250 per month. The church was further instructed by their new landlords to close the food program because of a perceived inadequacy of the kitchen facilities, told to obtain a $1 million insurance policy, and told that there would no longer be a long term lease but merely a month-to-month agreement.

In 2000 the church relocated temporarily to the upper room of the St. Paulus Lutheran Church at 930 Gough Street in San Francisco and continued to draw the same diverse crowds and the occasional renowned spectators. The sojourn of the St. John Coltrane Church to the St. Paulus Lutheran Church on Gough Street lasted for five years until St. Paulus committed to tearing down its structure and building a larger edifice. And in 2006 the St. John Will-I-Am Coltrane African Orthodox Church would find another home in the Western Addition at 1286 Fillmore Street in a post-redevelopment world deliberately feeding off the memory of the Fillmore of the 1940s and '50s as developers sought to create a new and upscale historic jazz district. Here, the New College of California would underwrite the lease for the Coltrane Church for a period of two years and offer educational scholarships for willing members.

This period provided an opportunity for laying the groundwork for a substantive ideological shift, as exile always begets transition. In the years in exile on Gough Street, Archbishop King and Mother Marina King began to reevaluate the direction of the church and broach the possibility of expanding their involvement in local politics and the most relevant and pressing issues of police brutality and environmental racism. These efforts would begin with greater urgency when the Coltrane Church returned to the heart of the Western Addition in 2006.

Pastor Wanika mirrors the spirit and manner of both Archbishop King and Mother Marina. She possesses both the fiery conviction of Archbishop King and the enlightened gentleness of Mother Marina. She has the same lean and angular presence as her father. She is adorned with flowing dreadlocks reminiscent of her father's Bishop Ha'qq phase. She bears an African name from a childhood spent in the midst of the church's black nationalist period. She gracefully dons the mantle of the mystical musician and remains deeply committed to the initial vision of spreading Coltrane Consciousness.

My discussions with the newly ordained Pastor Wanika King-Stephens took place within a moment of great uncertainty for the Coltrane Church, surely the mood of every great transitional moment in the church's history since the initial Sound Baptism in 1965. Our discussions reflected the great expectations and promise of the moment as well as the spirit of faith that Pastor Wanika necessarily relied upon moving forward.

A Vision of Inclusivity for the Future

Peppering our discussions with the same sophisticated integration of the Gospels, the history of jazz music, and the words and wisdom of John Coltrane, Pastor Wanika contextualized her conscious understanding of the church's present evolutionary moment within a rendering of the musical evolution of John Coltrane from the blues to the avant-garde. It is an important statement, because Pastor Wanika here acknowledges the very subtle continuities and adaptations of core discursive practices inherent in every transformational moment:

> John Coltrane's music was always about becoming and coming into being. In other words, he had to go from where he was in the beginning with blues and his days in Philly and in the navy and the Earl Bostic stuff and then Miles and Monk to get to the avant-garde stuff, the Risen Trane stuff. And there's a parallel there with the Coltrane Church in that it is coming into being and trying to get to that point where it becomes a thing of beauty.

Here she demonstrates the very same "multilingual" facility of Archbishop King, speaking with the very same sophisticated integration of Coltrane's wisdom, the history of jazz, and the Gospels of Jesus Christ. The difference, however, lies with Pastor Wanika's decidedly temporal conceptualization of the discourse of Coltrane Consciousness.

Pastor Wanika re-articulates the central discursive practices of Coltrane Consciousness as a blend of "the ancient, the traditional, and the modern":

> I think, like the church, the music is really about to change into something different. That I feel. I feel like there is a need for something contemporary to happen, that there has to be a blending of the contemporary, the ancient, and the classic, and somehow we have to figure out what that sounds like, but we'll know it when we get to it. It's like John Coltrane said, I had a sound that I wanted to hear, I didn't know how I was going to

get to it, I decided to find out. I think that's where we are right now with the music. We're searching and we've just begun a new search or the music.

Archbishop King's interchangeable use of Coltrane and Christ was always centered around a "one mind" concept of spiritual universalism— at least since the influence of Alice Coltrane- that symbolized a horizontal union of world religious beliefs. Pastor Wanika seems to have added a distinct temporal or vertical dimension to the "one mind" concept that may be particularly relevant to her immediate experience and need to locate herself within the history of the Coltrane Church, and the history of women clergy.

Her central vision for the future focuses on providing greater accessibility to the Christian message and securing Coltrane Consciousness (the words, music, and wisdom of John Coltrane) as a gateway to the Gospels. Her message is one of greater inclusivity, mindful of the history of second-class citizenship offered to women, people of color, the poor, and the marginalized. It is a continuation of the message of Archbishop George Alexander McGuire, founding Archbishop of the African Orthodox Church, but, in similar fashion to her re-conceptualization of core Coltrane Consciousness discursive practices, she has clearly augmented Archbishop McGuire's vision with an urgent message of gender inclusivity. What is most encouraging here is her characterization of a kind of "fearlessness" that now guides a more gender-conscious and ever-evolving message of the Coltrane Church:

> It really is a transitional period right now and for me I am still trying to conceptualize myself right now. We at that point like where Miles doesn't have Coltrane in the band anymore and so now, where do we go from here, how do we adapt and go to the next level? For me right now what I am seeing is that there is the need to carry forth the traditional. It is important to keep the vision of our patriarch George Alexander McGuire alive and broaden that circle within the African Orthodox Church by bringing in women and all people and really opening up the table of the Lord to the women. And then at the same time continuing to push forward Archbishop King's vision of spreading Coltrane Consciousness across the globe, which is really how he started. This was his motivation in the beginning. Now there really is this coming together of the two and you have women coming into the picture and I'm not really sure what that looks like when it all comes together.
>
> I do foresee that there will be a greater push with Coltrane Consciousness. I do think that the church has gotten to a point of fearlessness on that level and I think that really is the universal aspect of the church that seems to attract people from all over the world. That seems to be the one thing that we can all come together on are the philosophies behind John

Coltrane's teachings and how they relate to the teachings of Jesus Christ, and even for others, how it relates to other spiritual prophets as well.

I don't think that religiously there's much change because if you are preaching the Gospel of Jesus Christ, you are preaching the Gospel of Jesus Christ and that message remains the same. But when you are talking about John Coltrane and Coltrane Consciousness, what I am seeing is that Coltrane Consciousness is the gateway to the teachings of Jesus Christ and once you start to get familiar with the teachings and the words of John Coltrane, then it opens up that door for people to say, that's what Jesus is saying, and then you begin to see that the message is more universal than you realize, it's not all about dogma and separating people but about unity and bringing people together. And so I think that's the new part of it, I think that's the revolutionary thing that this church has to offer is a new way to look at the teachings of Jesus Christ in a way that accepts all people.

To complete this mission of gender inclusivity, Pastor King-Stephens brings with her a generation of highly educated young women of the church eager to assume leadership and guide the church toward the future:

I've spoken to Makeda and Mildred [Marlee-I-Hand] who have spoken and demonstrated their support. I realize that we have something very valuable with a whole new generation of people and even outside of this family and really tight-knit community there are other people that God is sending to us. I feel like things are starting to generate like God is really putting something into motion and is making it happen. But that seems to be the question in my mind right now, how is it all going to come together?

Pastor Wanika's cultural vision for the Coltrane Church must confront significant challenges, including the possible departure of key members. Every transitional moment in the church's history has been accompanied by an exodus of key members and leaders. At the same time, the church has fortunately experienced an influx of new members and leaders who might assist with the future development of the ministry:

I think there's also going to be a need for significant change with the music as well. Bro. Fred has stepped away to pursue some of his own goals recently. Things have to change, we are going through a metamorphosis right now. But when one thing goes out another thing comes in so I am seeing other talent come in from other areas. We've got poets and we've got tap dancers coming in. It is so spread out right now that it's hard to say this is going to happen or this is what we are shooting for, but Coltrane Consciousness is really coming to the forefront as it relates to the teachings of Jesus Christ. I can say that for sure. There really is a unity of those philosophies that is the spirit of eternal truth. There is definitely a call for something different to happen with the music, for it to evolve.

Pastor Wanika's political vision is compatible with that of Archbishop King and is deeply influenced by the social justice mission of liberation theology:

> In terms of politics, I have been running away from that one, but God is revealing to me—and certainly Archbishop King has been helping me—it's not something I'm going to be able to avoid much longer.
> The church has always been about social justice and standing up and being that voice for those who are the least of the little ones. That's all a part of the work. There's no getting out of that if you are going to have a successful ministry and one that is really dedicated to all of the needs of the people, the spiritual, the political, social needs of the people as well.

Her political vision is necessarily informed by her own experience with the Black Panther Party:

> The Black Panther School was another cultural experience for me certainly. Malcolm X. Bob Marley. John Coltrane. All of these people were icons in my life that I grew up with and they were all people that carried a message, and so this idea of speaking truth to power, speaking truth to help people enhance their lives and enrich their lives as human beings was a concept that I grew up with. And then the music, having Bob Marley as my hero and that the music had a message and that a musician was more than just the player of the instrument or the singer of the song they really are a messenger. For me, whether I am on the bandstand or playing behind Makeda as she's singing "Love Shall Reign" which was inspired by something that Archbishop said in a sermon that was inspired by something that his mother said in a sermon.... I can either do it there or from the pulpit, but it's really all the same thing.

Discursive continuities and adaptations between Archbishop King and Pastor Wanika are significant because they provide a view of the mechanics of differential ideological positioning and how ideologies and practices are necessarily transformed to meet the prerogatives of new leadership and a new era. Pastor Wanika's augmentation of core discursive practices in Coltrane Consciousness is marked by both a need for change and a need for continuity. Her agenda is Archbishop King's agenda, yet with enhanced accessibility and gender consciousness and a distinct temporal dimension. Such subtle augmentations both comfort the faithful with tradition and excite with the adventure of new horizons.

"Rememory"

The discursive alchemy inherent in the narrative testimonies of Pastor Wanika King-Stephens also reminds us that the telling of history is an active and ongoing process fraught with revision and the alterations of "re-memory"[1] or the attempt to understand the role of the past in the present (Morrison). It would be impossible to account for every significant modification of the church's historical narratives. The recent ordination, however, provides an opportunity to witness real-time "rememory," where Pastor King-Stephens has become positioned as co-founder of the church.

> I have heard Archbishop say many times that I am a co-founder. And I just say, Dad, come on, I'm not a founder really. And he's serious about that. When I said that to him, he said, no, you were there. In the beginning I used to think that was a parent trying to make their child feel good and include them, but over the years I've been able to see more clearly what he was saying.
>
> One thought can produce a million vibrations as St. John Coltrane would say and the fact that on that night when they received the news of his death, but the fact that I said, I want to hear some Charlie Parker, that's my man, it did spark in him this concept that John Coltrane lives and that makes a spiritual connection at that point. You can kill Jesus, but you can't kill the truth, and that spirit of truth is eternal.
>
> And the same thing with John Coltrane. He may not be here physically but the truth that came through his horn, the message and the wisdom still lives. And that's really tying into the foundation of the church. And in that sense I feel that I really did contribute in the beginning.

With respect to "rememory," the passing of leadership from father to daughter has also meant not only the transference of the core spiritual message of the Coltrane Church and the metaphorical integration of Christianity, Coltrane, and jazz, but also the transference of many of the important narrative tropes of Archbishop King and Mother Marina's rendering of church history.

Archbishop King's account of the significance of his name and of "naming" in general is reiterated by Pastor King-Stephens in a statement that also echoes Archbishop King's account of how Supreme Mother encourage his preaching and instilled in him a love of Jesus Christ:

> I can remember being a kid in the house before Makeda was born and my mother would have me in the kitchen just reading the Bible to me while she cooked dinner. And I remember very early on in life being impressed by this man Jesus and I really just loved him and thought he was a wonderful human being from what I was able to gather from the Scriptures. And then of course Little Mother who was an evangelist and seriously into Jesus, she taught us how to pray and she said you always end every prayer with in Jesus name. I knew that Jesus was important and someone that I needed to pay attention to.
>
> And then I can mention earlier that with the Black Panther Party and

Pastor Wanika King-Stephens at the sound check before the February 8, 2008, concert at Cité de la Musique in Paris.

having my uncle come home and tell me, you need an African name, we're going to change your name from Kristi to Wanika. That's a black name. And just really understanding the importance of identifying with your culture and your people and the beauty of your people.

Pastor Wanika further reiterates Archbishop King's discovery of music. Pastor Wanika's discovery of the bass through her cousin is a parallel story to Archbishop King's narrative of learning about jazz music from his older brother. In both cases, significant family members introduce Archbishop King and Pastor Wanika to the music and both proceed on a path of self-education, learning the fundamentals of jazz performance through repeated listening and mentorship with the community of musicians that have always surrounded the King family:

> Ron, a cousin of mine who used to be a merchant marine and used to cook on this ship, he would travel all around the world, and one time he came back and he had this beautiful bass in this case and he left it here and he said, "You know, I'm going to leave this here and when I come back, I'm going to play it." And he didn't want anyone to touch it. One day my curiosity got the best of me and I opened the bass case and I looked at it and it was just like one of those "ahh" moments.
>
> I snuck that thing into my room and I started pulling on those strings and it was just love at first site and I couldn't put it down. My Dad came in one time and he said, "A-ha! I see you playing that, I hear you doing stuff on that! You've gotta do it! He was really happy! I thought I was in trouble but he was overjoyed and that was all that I needed. I must have been about 14 or 15 when I did that. And when Ron came back I was playing it and he said, Okay, you can have it. In the beginning I taught myself for a long time.
>
> By the time I had started any formal training I had already written all of the songs on the Mystic Youth[2] album and pulled the other kids together in the church so that we could start making music. I thought then that maybe I should go to school. I then attended City College and managed to get an associate's degree in music. I played with David Hardiman's Jazz Improv at City College. That was a good class.

Pastor Wanika and the Spirit of Little Mother

The key to understanding the church's recent ordination of Pastor Wanika lies in part with Supreme Mother's historical guidance in the spiritual evolution of Archbishop King and Mother Marina that in fact formed the foundation for the church's progressive position on women-centered leadership. Interestingly, Supreme Mother passed in January of 2011, only months before the ordination of Pastor Wanika. Here again the central church narrative of Supreme Mother is opened up in this transitional moment to foreground Pastor Wanika's ascendance and provide clergy with a profound sense of the historical unfolding of this very important transitional moment in church history.

Archbishop King has long testified about the impact of his mother's gendered segregation in the Pentecostal Church and his desire to address this disparity within the leadership of the Coltrane Church.

> I knew still then that the satisfaction of my own life was going to be in carrying the Word. I mean, I love preaching, I love hearing good preaching. When I was a child I used to study the preachers and I'd be excited about, you know the Church of God in Christ preaching, man, those guys are so dramatic, and they tell the story so well, all the intoning and the drama and the preacher running with their handkerchiefs and falling over the pulpit and jumping out and all of this, I used to be fascinated.

> Even until here of late, since I've been in this ministry, since I've been back from Chicago, two or three years ago, I went to get appreciation for her in the church, and she had me to preaching and I talked about her, about her as a powerful preacher, and one of the old preachers, he said, "Did you say she was a preacher?" And I said, "A powerful preacher."

> And I realized after awhile, he said, "Women do not preach in this

Archbishop King and Supreme Mother Dr. Phyllis Proudhomme.

church. I mean they can break the bread of life with us and our hearts can burn within us with fire but we can't let women preach in this church." And this man actually approached her before the services were over with, "Are you a preacher or a missionary?" I mean, and was just jamming her up like that, but she has a husband now, you know, so I kinda let him deal with it because there was a part of me that, you know, really wanted to straighten it out for myself, you know what I'm saying, "Hey man, back up off of this," you know. I was telling them, "Yeah, she's a powerful preacher," I was just pouring it on.

They don't get the acknowledgment, they do the work but they don't get the acknowledgment and they don't become a part of the hierarchy of the church so they're not a part of the decision making body. Which is the same thing that the African Orthodox Church is challenged with where you have women that are doing ninety percent of the work and men are sitting around with their vestments on looking important like they got some divine right born out of gender rather than work.

Throughout the early years of the church, and particularly through its manifestations as the One Mind Temple, Archbishop King and Mother Marina were guided and inspired by the letters of Supreme Mother, known simply as the Epistles of Supreme Mother. Supreme Mother provided confirmation that this fledgling community was acting in accordance with the will of God, in the right spirit and in pursuit of the truth. Following are two representative examples from the Epistles of Supreme Mother.

March 13, 1972

Dear Son, Greetings to you and peace in the name of Jesus the Christ of God. In anticipation of writing you and your flock I have not ceased to pray that you will find the whole truth of the Gospel of Christ and apply it to your daily walk with God. Be ye therefore followers of God as dear children and walk in love as Christ also hath loved us and given himself for us in peace for in the final analysis, peace is all that will count, all else will pass away, but the peace of God will pass from generation to generation. It is like a ray of light, it will go into the smallest opening possible. It is like a vapor, it will seep into the mind if given half a chance. It's like the dawn or the dusk, it surrounds you and closes you in on every side as a protection from the angry world in which you live It is like a lion, it is strong and it will hold you together when others are falling apart. Yet it is like a lamb, it will keep you meek yet not a fool wherein in men will fear treading upon your feelings for they will see in you an image, a glow, and a guide. Son, I say to you, seek peace, seek God, be a good leader. Love to the flock. Mother.

What's most important about the Epistles of Supreme Mother is that they validate then Bishop King as a spiritual leader. Archbishop King remarks:

See, I would get these letters and when we would meet I would read them and she's acknowledging the leadership thing and the flock very early on.

His early congregation developed a strong respect for Dr. Proudhomme and her letters contained powerful teachings that were meditated and commented upon in the course of services. Indeed the title "Bishop" was one first bestowed on Bishop King in these Epistles, and one that provided all the validation then Bishop King required to lead a spiritual community.

March 20, 1972

Dear Son,

Faith is the substance of things hoped for, the evidence of things not seen. Hebrews 11:1. The substance of any edible product is the product itself, notwithstanding that in solid or compact form there is a vast limitation to its use. However, a substance, you might say, the substance, can be used by all and for all barring none. The strong, the weak, the high, the low, the rich, the poor, the intellectual, the illiterate, the old, the young, the sick, and the well can use it. The human body in the very weakest stage can take on a substance, if not by oral intake, it may be given intravenously. Once that substance has been projected into the body then the body begins to gain strength. As a person, though weak in faith he may be or young in his new way of life yet as he takes on faith by degree he will very soon see the evidence. For faith is remembering that you are God's priceless treasure when you feel utterly worthless. Faith is acknowledging God as the giver of abilities when success is mine. Faith is rejecting the feeling of panic when things seem out of control and realizing that God is the God of now. And finally, faith is ceasing to worry, leaving the future to the God that controls the future. Through faith we understand that the Word of God framed worlds so that things which are seen were not made of things which do appear. As I close my letter to you, I say as Jesus said to his disciple, and I quote, "have faith in God."

Greetings to the flock and may they acquire the necessary faith to win the battle.

Love Mother.

Archbishop King frequently speaks of the Holy Ghost Mother in his sermons, and ascribes feminine energy to the Holy Ghost. He speaks of a form of inspiration and comfort that is clearly evidenced in these letters. In faith it is understood that the Holy Ghost was present in the Epistles of Supreme Mother, as a comforter and as a guide toward Christ conscious spiritual expression. The feminine energy that Archbishop ascribes to the Holy Ghost is bound up with that powerful feminine, motherly voice of Supreme Mother in these Epistles, and the way that the Holy Ghost breathes through her words. It would not be an overstatement to proclaim that Supreme Mother was the earliest manifestation of the love and comfort of the Holy Ghost for Archbishop King, and therefore the most important source of Archbishop King's esteem of the elevated position of the Holy Ghost in his spirituality and in Coltrane Consciousness; for the Coltrane Church is above all a Holy Ghost church.

Within the context of the letters of Supreme Mother, there is a powerful feminine dimension to Coltrane Consciousness, without which it cannot fully lay claim to accessing the power of the Holy Spirit. The testimonies of Mother Marina in particular substantiate this claim. From the founding vision of John Coltrane and the Holy Ghost to the development of the Coltrane liturgy, these testimonies bear witness to the spiritual guidance of women. It quickly became apparent throughout the course of my research that at St. John's African Orthodox Church, that which is feminine is not viewed in opposition to the spiritual.

> I want to say something about the women in this church. There is a great amount of feminine power and a feminine aspect that is involved with this ministry. Wisdom, first of all, is feminine. Women have a great role in the church. Often times we, I don't want to say we are the greatest workers, but we are there on all the different fronts. We are the mothers and the nurturers, so if I'm standing in front of the church and I'm singing and holding a child and the Spirit is moving me I am bonding with that child and raising a child in the way that it ought to go. You can't get much closer than that. I'm conscious of that child I am holding and it is learning and I'm trying to encourage the child. It is a part of religious teaching as far as I am concerned. It is a really close type of spiritual teaching that is happening.
>
> One of the other things that I think is important about this church is that this is a progressive church and the Holy Ghost doesn't stop at gender. So women, if they are apt to teach, preach, head different committees, coordinate committees, they should be allowed to do so. I don't think our church is really so different from all of the other churches. Women are your main workers in the church a lot of times. If it's preparing the food, raising the funds, doing the programs, we're out there meeting the people and telling them about our work, promulgating the word and the teachings, raising the children, and I think it's befitting ... and also Jesus loved the women. That's one of the things I really love about Jesus, he loved the women and he had them close to him. They were very close to him and he used them in a special way and a way that the men weren't able to be used.
>
> We also understand the Holy Ghost as mother and feminine aspect. The feminine aspect is also the active force. The doers. Women are doers. One of the early visions of the church was that we were to come together in our infancy and it wasn't planned that we would stay together under one

roof. It was planned that we would grow in our leadership roles and establish other churches. In that respect some of the women would become spiritual leaders of their own churches, and bishops in their own right.

In large measure, the ordination of Pastor Wanika marks continuity with the spiritual guidance of Supreme Mother. Supreme Mother's "Epistles" certainly set the stage for woman-centered leadership and a reverence for the spiritual interpretations of church women. Further, Archbishop King's recognition of his mother's true status and title within the black church becomes in effect fully realized through the official ordination of Wanika King-Stephens as pastor.

Black Womanist Theology

The broader historical context of American religious institutions— against which the Coltrane Church now seeks to draw sharp contrast— have been marked with ongoing resistance to the ordination of women. Indeed it should come as no surprise that the largest institutions in North America that continue to deny equal rights to women are conservative Christian denominations: Roman Catholicism, Eastern Orthodox and many other denominations within Protestantism, like the Church of Jesus Christ of Latter-day Saints and the Southern Baptist Convention.

In spite of the fundamentally different historical trajectory of black womanism and the persistent racialization and segregation of religion in America, the "black church" in many respects reflects rather than rejects these broader American religious histories of gender discrimination. However, African American denominations can broadly speaking be categorized as either progressive or conservative on the issue of the ordination of women largely in terms of the histories of social class embedded within the ecumenical histories of each denomination. In other words, the historical record reveals that the older, more established African American churches that tend to have greater upper and upper-middle class stability are, generally speaking, far more progressive on the issue of the ordination of women than those denominations whose members have only begun to find advancement towards the middle and upper-middle class in recent decades. Certainly these histories of class advancement are also linked to the broader histories of post-slavery African American rural-urban migrations.

The most authoritative text on the history of the ordination of black women preachers is Bettye Collier-Thomas' *Daughters of Thunder: Black Women Preachers and Their Sermons, 1850–1979*. Collier-Thomas does

Pastor Wanika King-Stephens conducts the wedding ceremony of Deacon Max Hoff and Hallie Green, 2010.

not present a class-based argument generalizing ordination patterns across African American Christian denominations. She does, however, provide a lucid history of ordination and its consequences across a broad range of denominations over a period of one hundred and twenty-nine years.

The first African American denomination to officially ordain women to the ministry was the African Methodist Episcopal Zion Church. "The AME Zion Church was the leader in the African American movement to ordain and grant laity rights to women. Black women were first ordained by the AME Zion Church, which was one of the few denominations to grant women of any race ordination rights in the nineteenth century" (26). Julia A. Foote was ordained as a deacon in 1894 in Poughkeepsie, New York, and Mary J. Small was ordained deacon in 1895 at the Philadelphia/Baltimore conference. Both women were subsequently ordained "elder" by 1900.

Collier-Thomas distinguishes the impact of legitimacy earned by Foote and Small as well as the differential impact of ordination and elder status, suggesting that black male clergy in the AME Zion Church were most threatened by the Mary J. Small ordination's as deacon and later as elder because of Small's relative youth. "The Small ordination threatened the male clergy in ways that the Foote ordination did not. Julia Foote was seventy-one years old at the time of her ordination. Having preached for over fifty years by 1894, she was well known among white and black Methodists and revered by many for her intellect and the power of her preaching. Foote's ordination was more a form of recognition than empowerment, because her career was in its twilight. It was not expected that she would be appointed to pastor a church" (23). And on the matter of Small's ordination as elder, Collier-Thomas writes: "Small's ordination as an elder cut the ground out from under the black male clergy's feet. In the view of many males, a woman elder was functioning out of her sphere. Unlike an un-ordained preacher or an ordained deacon, an elder possesses power and authority over other ordained clergy" (24).

The AME Zion's ordination of women happened 50 years before any other similar action took place in any other black Methodist denominations. The ordination of women in the AME Church began in 1948—in spite of attempts to achieve gender equality dating back to 1868—and the CME Church did not allow the full ordination of women until 1954. The progressive attitudes of the AME Zion, AME and CME churches may indeed have something to do with their status as black America's first churches or with their historical origins in slave rebellion (e.g., Denmark Vesey in Charleston, South Carolina, in 1822) or radical anti-slavery and anti-lynching black social movements.

There is little documentation of the history of black women preachers in the Baptist church. As the Baptist faith grew during the First Great Awakening in the mid–18th century there was some freedom for women to establish themselves as church leaders. Early Separatist churches in the South ordained women as deaconesses and allowed women to preach.[3] In 1800, when regular and separatist Baptists merged, the freedom that women had experienced became far more restricted and eventually leadership became almost exclusively male (Collier-Thomas 24). The National Baptist Convention that split with Southern Baptists in 1895 in light of racism, and the Progressive National Baptist Convention that began in 1961 have not had specific policies against the ordination of women and the Baptist principle of congregational autonomy has allowed many to ordain women.

In the largest African American Pentecostal group, the Church of God in Christ, there is generally a firm policy against the full ordination of women as elder, bishop, or pastor. COGIC churches generally allow some women to preach but only as evangelists or missionaries performing a teaching function where there is no requirement for ordination. Official sanctions against the ordination of women in many African American denominations have led to the spread of many independent Holiness or Pentecostal churches that typically begin in private homes, apartments, or storefronts (Wilmore 185). Examples of women clergy who have come from this Independent Holiness movement include Elder Lucy Smith, founder of All Nations Pentecostal Church in Chicago in the 1930s; and Bishop Ida Robinson, founder of Mount Sinai Holy Church of Philadelphia in 1924. Bishop Robinson's church practiced "faith healing, foot washing, and extensive female participation" (185). There are further contemporary examples of the ordination of women in independent Holiness churches including the Rev. Barbara King of Hillside International Truth Center in Atlanta and the Rev. Johnnie Colemon of Christ Universal Temple in Chicago, both of whom have congregations that total in the thousands.

Interestingly the early history of the African Orthodox Church and of the Garvey movement places the Black Madonna in an elevated position, and it might well be argued that the relative gender progressivity of the African Orthodox Church played a contributing role in the possibility of the ordination of Pastor King-Stephens. In his article "Garvey and Black Liberation Theology," the Reverend Ernle P. Gordon discusses the practical and theological impact of the UNIA's use and propagation of the image of the Black Madonna. the Rev. Gordon writes, "The concept of the Black Madonna is traced to hieroglyphics on stone found in Egypt (Upper Nile) in 6000—5900 BC. This research was done by George C.M. James and Yosef Ben-Jochannan and documented in 1982. An interesting situation developed at the 4th International Conference of the Negro Peoples in 1924 when UNIA members marched with a large portrait of the Black Madonna and child. This was very significant, because it was making a theological point: not only that man should demonstrate the feminine nature of God, but also that the black woman can rise to great heights and is also equally human. In other words, this movement began to assert the primacy of women in black religion" (Lewis and Bryan 138–139).

Coltrane Consciousness Is Womanist Consciousness

In her essay "The Church of Aretha," included in Gloria Wade-Gayles' anthology, Margo V. Perkins makes an important analogy between the spirituality and sainthood of John Coltrane and that of Aretha Franklin. "When I listen to Aretha Franklin sing, I understand why there came to be, for instance, a church of Coltrane. Lovers of John Coltrane's music honor not just his brilliant saxophone playing, but the spiritual power of his melodies to transform both space and consciousness. Aretha (her first name, alone, being sufficient to evoke a mood), like Coltrane, is one of those rare artists whose unique voice conjures the breadth and depth of African American experience" (Wade-Gayles 128).

As Wade-Gayles has suggested, the power of women at the Coltrane Church is most immediately manifest in key clergy and leadership roles maintained by women, the presence of women as musicians, the exaltation of motherhood, and the opportunity for women to preach the word of God and thereby provide their own critical voices and interpretations. Although the role of women in maintaining and furthering a Christian ministry is not uncommon in African American church communities, the St. John Will-I-Am Coltrane African Orthodox Church differs substantially from other religious institutions—and indeed even from the practices of other African Orthodox Churches—in its open recognition and celebration of the power of women as preachers and interpreters of the word of God.

What establishes and maintains the power of women at St. John's African Orthodox Church is the identifiable feminine aspect of John Coltrane's music, the notion that the Holy Ghost is a woman and the Mother figure of the Holy Trinity, the understanding that the ancient wisdom of music was attributable to women, and the appreciation of the role of women in the development of blues and jazz music.

　　Among the most revolutionary facets of the interpretation of the Holy Ghost at St. John's African Orthodox Church is the perception of the Holy Ghost as a woman, as Mother in the Trinity. I became familiar with this church concept first through the Sunday School teachings of the Rev. Sis. Deborah. The Rev. Sis. Deborah often stressed that the hand of the Holy Ghost is like the hand of a mother guiding worship and spiritual dedication. Archbishop King has often commented during sermons that the Coltrane Church is a Holy Ghost church. The notion of the Holy Ghost as Mother combined with the understanding of a Holy Ghost Church finds powerful and concrete expression in the leadership roles that women assume at the Coltrane Church.

　　When discussing the role of women in the founding, ministry, and furthering of Coltrane Consciousness, the Coltrane Church celebrates the feminine side of John Coltrane: the blessing of the soprano horn, the influence of women on John Coltrane's spiritual and musical development, and Coltrane's communication with a feminine image of the Holy Ghost Mother. Coltrane Consciousness is a celebration of male and female aspects of the sound and life of John Coltrane. Through the use of the tenor and soprano saxophones, and specifically by including the soprano horn as a spiritually elevated sound, John Coltrane unified the gender dichotomy that so often divides conventional worship practice and placed both male and female voices on an equal footing in the devotion and praise of God. In fact, it is widely understood among believers that Coltrane's attempts to bridge the gender dichotomy are related to his understanding of the one-ness of all God's creation. Indeed Coltrane's emphasis on one-ness in his testimonies, quotes, and music church practice is a celebration of this unification, departing from traditional conceptions of women's roles.

　　Certain facts of Coltrane's own biography are told and re-told in formal and casual settings and serve to underscore the spiritual power of women in the church. It is widely believed, both among the community of the faithful at the St. John Will-I-Am Coltrane African Orthodox Church as well as among many of Coltrane's biographers, that John Coltrane was greatly encouraged in his adult spiritual life by his first wife, Naima, after whom one of his favorite compositions was named, and who was a devout Muslim.

　　Coltrane's inclusion of the women in the performance of his music is also widely discussed. Although the only woman to perform in Coltrane's band was his second wife, Alice Coltrane, Alice had an incredible impact on the early spiritual development of the St. John Coltrane Church as well as on the avant-garde and overtly spiritual recordings of the post—*A Love*

Supreme John Coltrane. Archbishop King frequently cites the fact that John Coltrane ended his addiction to heroin by first stating his intentions to his wife, Naima, and then by retreating to the seclusion of his mother's home for prayer and fasting. He uses this piece of biographical data throughout his sermons to support the importance of the spiritual leadership of women, and it frequently surfaces in casual conversation. What is important here is that Coltrane elevates his mother to the status of mother-protector, a real-world image of the Holy Ghost mother-protector, and signifies to the followers of Coltrane Consciousness that our mothers are indeed our first examples of the manifestation of the Holy Ghost in our lives.

The fact that Coltrane sought to develop a sound that mimicked a woman's singing voice, and at the same time to develop through music a means of communication with God, is evidence of Coltrane's understanding of some essential feminine aspect of his praise and devotion. C.O. Simpkins alludes to Coltrane's interest in mimicking male and female voices: "At the Woodbind club John met Odean Pope, a 16-year-old tenor saxophonist who was seeking a musical direction. Odean soon learned that John would rarely initiate a conversation, but when asked questions, a fountain of words would flow. John spoke to him of his involvement with changes, and methods of constructing a solo. He told Odean that two of his favorite songs were 'Come Rain or Come Shine' and 'Lush Life.' He explained to Odean that he liked to sing through his instrument and that it was valuable to listen to good singers like Billy Eckstine or Sarah Vaughn" (Simpkins 49).

The notion that music and wisdom were originally attributable to women also maintains a strong sense of the power of women at the St. John Will-I-Am Coltrane African Orthodox Church. During his sermon of December 4, 1994, Archbishop King commented:

> You know I've been seeking out and searching out some motivation of our music, and I thought it was interesting that in the music of African classical music there's almost a man's thing, you know that? Mostly men playing the music, but the Scriptures tell me and my research that the wisdom was originally attributed to the women. I don't know what happened, at some point in time they tried to exclude you, Wanika, and make it sound like you were on new ground. But it sounds to me like you were claiming ground that was yours from ancient times. Amen. Praise God! Keeping alive the tradition, that is a tradition of women. That's what's so sweet about John Coltrane, he reached and got down and said, "Come on, we're taking you back to the place from which you come." Amen. Because women are a powerful entity in the making of music in the house of God.

In addition to the sermonic references of Archbishop King, there are a number of critical scriptural sources which emphasize the power of women and which are frequently cited in formal and informal contexts to provide some understanding of the range and depth of women's roles and discursive practices involving gender at the Coltrane Church. These scriptures are cited in sermons, testimonies, Sunday school, Devotion service, Wednesday night testimony service, and in everyday conversation by male and female clergy members. In the midst of one of our many interview sessions, Archbishop King carefully outlined the most critical of these Scriptures.

1 Samuel 2:1 indicates that women will be included among those who raise their instruments in praise of the Lord. Hannah in 1 Samuel 2:1 is depicted as exalting and praising the Lord with her horn: "And Hannah prayed, and said, My heart rejoiceth in the Lord; mine horn is exalted in the Lord; my mouth is enlarged over mine enemies; because I rejoiceth in thy salvation" (1 Samuel 2:1).

This Scripture is made manifest in the involvement of women in the liturgical sound praise. While none of the women who serve in the clergy and leadership at St. John's are horn players, 1 Samuel 2:1 validates the power of the song of women in general and is interpreted to elevate the voices of the Sisters of Compassion, the song of Mother Marina, as well as the instrumental playing of Ohnedaruth bassist Pastor Wanika Kristi King-Stephens.

The Sunday School lesson for Easter, 1995, delivered by Reverend Sister Mary Deborah, dealt with the role of women in the Resurrection of Christ and the manner in which Christ first revealed himself to women. Women came to the tomb to find the dead body and cleanse it with herbs but instead found the heavy stone rolled away. While the women were confused upon seeing the stone rolled away and an angel of the Lord that appeared to them, they soon recovered, strong in their faith, and went forth to disseminate the good news of the resurrection of Christ.

In the New Testament Scriptures detailing the Resurrection, women are given the central role in the defining moment of Christianity, the Resurrection of Christ. That the angel of the Lord appeared first to the women who were thereby required to accept on faith the resurrection of Christ, presents women as the strongest in faith. That the women were then asked to disseminate the good news of Christ's resurrection surely imparts on women a critical teaching role. In fact this Scripture opened up a lively discussion of women's power in the Sunday school. Reverend Trotter was given deference to speak at length about how women really are the teachers, and how the church is considered to be the bride of Christ. However it was Reverend Sister Mary Deborah's comment that the Holy Ghost was the female aspect of the Holy Trinity, acknowledged as the Mother figure, which most forcefully brought out the importance of women.

Several church ministers have also discussed how the Scripture reveals that the men to whom the women later spoke at first refused to believe them. In one particular Sunday school session in the fall of 1997, Reverend Arthur Trotter offered a view that the men refused at first to believe what the women were telling them because of jealousy, and Reverend Sister Mary Deborah and I introduced into the discussion the fact that in these times a woman's testimony was not valid according to the law.

Reverend Sister Mary Deborah commented, "Truly the presence of the angel of the Lord empowered the women to speak, where previously their testimony was considered invalid, through the power of the Lord, their words are given force."

Even in the midst of that particular Sunday school lesson, the New Testament notion of women as speakers and teachers powerfully substantiated the Rev. Sis. Mary Deborah's leadership and voice.

The significance of that Sunday school discussion and that particular ethnographic moment was that it initiated more dialogue among church members about women's spiritual power. The leadership of the Coltrane Church views itself in the same light as the early Christians, as members of an avant-garde spiritual movement, as spiritual trailblazers. It was clear that a progressive position with respect to gender equality was considered by many in the church to be a fundamental part of their self-understanding as a vanguard movement.

Conclusions

Coltrane Consciousness is black womanist theological consciousness. The origin narrative of the Coltrane Church, the 1965 Sound Baptism, provides Mother Marina King with an independent and definitively black womanist ownership of the ministry. The evolutionary development of the Coltrane Church reflects the profound influence of Dr. Phyllis Proudhomme, not to mention the leadership of Alice Coltrane. The discursive practices of the Coltrane Church include key scriptural references and black womanist theological archetypes that all reflect an awareness of the connection between gender equality and progressive politics. Finally, the ordination of Pastor Wanika King-Stephens and the legacy of her leadership are the most important markers of gender equality in the Coltrane Church.

14

The Apostles of
Sound Occupy SF

*History will have to record that the greatest tragedy of
this period of social transition was not the strident clamor
of bad people, but the appalling silence of the good people.*

—The Rev. Dr. Martin Luther King, Jr.

As activist movements loosely grouped under the title of Occupy SF
began to address the inequity of corporate bailouts in the wake of the
2008 mortgage crisis, the Coltrane Church would continue to broaden its
political activities even further. Archbishop King and Mother Marina
joined the Alliance for Californians for Community Empowerment (ACCE)
and allied the church with the 99% Power Movement and began protesting
predatory lending practices that profited from community losses, including foreclosures, predatory lending, tax dodging, and private prison investment (McKitrick).

The Coltrane Church's involvement with Occupy SF, ACCE and 99%
Power—99% Power included a coalition of workers, retirees, families fighting foreclosure, students, immigrants, environmentalists, and such notable
activist groups as the Rainforest Action Network—was the latest stage of
an ongoing evolution since their ecumenical legitimation in 1982 as
African Orthodox and found the church building on many of the community alliances that it had developed during its struggles against police
brutality and environmental racism. Further, their involvement with 99%
Power emerged in a new era of womanist leadership under the pastorship
of the Rev. Wanika King-Stephens.

What had changed during the course of the church's evolving political

Archbishop King and Mother Marina protesting bank foreclosures in downtown San Francisco, 2009.

engagement, from the African American Community Police Relations Board and Caravan for Justice and SLAM to the present struggle, was that the Coltrane Church was now involved in a national movement that foregrounded much more aggressive and confrontational nonviolent direct action strategies than they had ever before utilized, marking their latest ideological shift.

99% Power

The 99% Power movement in San Francisco was largely inspired by Occupy Wall Street and related Occupy SF and Occupy Oakland movements. Cathy McKitrick, writing for *The Salt Lake Tribune* notes, that the leadership of 99% Power "credited the Occupy Wall Street protest movement for having 'opened up a real space to talk about inequality and corporate power in this country.' 'The coalition is taking what we consider the next step,' Tarbotton said. 'We're channeling that energy into focused pressure on the worst corporate offenders in the country.' Other corporations that can expect similar action at their upcoming shareholder sessions include Bank of America, General Electric, Verizon Wireless, Walmart and Sallie Mae, a publicly traded student loan association" (McKitrick).

Although 99% Power credited Occupy Wall Street for its inspiration, the Coltrane Church's involvement in local housing issues was consistent with a broader history of black church involvement in this area including the community's long struggle with San Francisco Redevelopment. Occupy SF was in fact only engaging in the kind of consciousness raising that the Coltrane Church had been involved in since the late 1960s. In fact, the Occupy SF manifesto, "Why We Are Here," expressed many of the political interests of the Coltrane Church, most specifically the first listed grievance: "They have taken our houses through an illegal foreclosure process, despite not having the original mortgage" (Occupy SF).

For the Coltrane Church, the Occupy SF-inspired 99% Power movement represented a moment to gain new allies in their ongoing struggle against the corruption of mortgage bankers and foreclosures. It also marked an important strategic development as the Coltrane Church now began to engage in more aggressive non-violent direct action, ultimately fighting power at its source through protests and bank shareholder meeting, and even engaging purchasers of foreclosed properties outside of their homes and businesses.

Towards and More Aggressive Nonviolent Direct Action

The strategies of the Coltrane Church and 99% Power Movement involved direct nonviolent confrontation with the decision-makers of the major banks and mortgage lenders engaged in predatory practices that had long undermined the economic aspirations of middle-class and poor citizens in San Francisco's predominantly African American Bayview-Hunter's Point and Fillmore/Western Addition neighborhoods. There was additionally an attempt to occupy and live in abandoned buildings and foreclosed homes, and occupy city lots and use them to farm.

In the spring of 2012, 99% Power began disrupting a series of corporate shareholder meetings for the largest American banks, including Wells Fargo and Chase Bank, and protesting outside of the private homes and other businesses of persons who had purchased recently foreclosed properties. Archbishop King:

> The tactics were to go to John Stump's $5 million condominium on Russian Hill and be out there with a whole bunch of people and talk crazy and

go to the jobs of some of the board members and act up. They took Josephine's house and we had a demonstration in front of her house but then we went down to the company that bought it down on Ocean Avenue with about 50 or 60 people and demonstrated and then we went down to the restaurant that they owned on Portola and had signs, "Don't Eat Here, The Food Tastes Like Foreclosure." They gave that building up and the sister is in it right now. Just small victories but they were more than anything anybody was getting.

There was a union brother, Dexter, and he lost his house and we occupied that house and set up offices inside of it and had barbecues, and set up bands on the sidewalk and they gave it back to him. He's still in there.

There was also an important traditional lobbying component to the Coltrane Church's strategies of nonviolent direct action. Here, Archbishop King specifically addresses the church's lobbying efforts in Sacramento to create stronger state legislation protecting people from "dual tracking" wherein a mortgage lender simultaneously offers the consumer opportunities for loan modification at the same time that it initiates foreclosure proceedings.

And there were some legal things. We went up to Sacramento and made sure that law was passed on dual tracking. Dual tracking is like when the bank calls you and says they see you're in trouble and they offer to put you on a plan and send you some paperwork because they say they don't want you to lose the house. And then when you get all excited and you start getting all the paperwork another guy from the bank says, we have to move on this. So while you're working on the paperwork, the trust people have moved on eviction. They've moved on foreclosure while you're filling out the paperwork. That was the most disheartening thing for people. You give them a sense that they are winning and then you foreclose on them. Corporate people understand the fickle mind of the people and they have these fear tactics and who is not one paycheck away from being homeless.

So they have you in this fear and ignorance thing. When I got into this thing I didn't know how this worked with banks selling your loans to other banks. Dual tracking and uncertified transference of property ... the average person knows nothing about that. This is what a lot of black folks and people of color got caught up in. And that's the way they were rolling with me.

Some of us went up to Sacramento and lobbied for that law with phone calls and so on and that law is the biggest victory that we got. And they had to assign a particular person to deal with you in trying to mend your mortgage agreement. We also got the auctioneers off the steps of City Hall so they have to do it on the sidewalk.

And we are still fighting against the foreclosures.

An Alliance with Occupy SF

A collection of Occupy SF documents—including letters, meeting notes, programs, flyers, etc.—currently housed at the San Francisco Public Library's Historical Room suggest that core members of the purposely ad hoc Occupy SF movement very much desired that the movement should be culturally inclusive. Echoing the prerogatives of the Weather Underground movement of the 1960s, Occupy SF clearly intended to build substantive alliances across ethnic groups and, in effect, to "join" activists of color in a broad-based class struggle against predatory lending and the ravages of monopoly capitalism.

To this end, the "leaders" of Occupy SF listened to the concerns of people of color, acknowledged the recent history of grassroots movements like the Caravan for Justice, and enlarged their agenda to include the community's fight against police brutality and corporate redevelopment. It was here that European American protestors began to understand the relationship between predatory policing and predatory lending that had been articulated in the alliance between Min. Christopher and Archbishop King as they sought to serve as "watchmen" for the community.

Properly speaking, Occupy SF joined the struggle that Archbishop King and the Coltrane Church had long been engaged in with the Caravan for Justice, ACCE, and SLAM. And this alliance of leadership and members of the Coltrane Church with the Occupy SF movement legitimated Occupy's attempts at building a multi-racial movement. Archishop King:

> People from the Occupy movement joined us. They had a religious group that was standing up against foreclosures. It was a big coalition of Jewish, Lutheran, and other Christian leaders. I met with them and brought them to Hunter's Point and Double Rock Baptist Church so that they could talk to some of the people about what was happening. It was hard to get the black preachers involved. When I talked about meeting Christopher, this is when Amos Brown brought it to everyone's attention the loss of black people in the city. He was then talking about how he didn't have to put out extra chairs for Easter. I didn't get that concerned about that because my congregation isn't necessarily black but I could sense that this is going to be a problem. So I was willing to get into that fight.

With respect to the integration of issues of police brutality, the Occupy SF Manifesto "Why We Are Here" resonated Coltrane Church concerns about the policing of Bay Area communities: "They have used the military and police to prevent freedom of the press" (Occupy SF). The City College of San Francisco International Socialist Club staged an Occupy rally December 6, 2011, at the CCSF Creative Arts Bldg. headlined by Denika Chatman, mother of Kenneth Harding, a 19-year-old African American man shot in the back by the San Francisco Police Department for evading a $2 MUNI bus toll, and Rob Slaughter, a St. Mary's College student brutally beaten by police at the first Occupy Cal rally. Flyers for the CCSF rally proclaimed "In the U.S. the 1 percent uses racism against blacks, immigrants and other ethnic minorities to divide and conquer the 99 percent. If the Occupy struggle is to succeed, it needs to represent and involve all of the 99 percent—and that means putting issues affecting people of color at the center of our movement. Some of the most pressing issues facing communities of color are police brutality, the war on drugs, the foreclosure crisis and the mass departation of immigrants. Join us in a discussion about racism in America today, and the potential to build a mult-racial struggle" (CCSF International Socialist Club).

Further, the SF Occupy Action Calendar for Friday October 28, 2011, through Monday October 30, 2011, that began with a protest of Federal Reserve policies at 101 Market Street and a Halloween Critical Mass bike ride beginning at Justin Herman plaza, included teach-ins on gender issues, Anti-Oppression, Homes Not Jails and Working Groups/Committees on Gender and Racism. There were events held at the Mission Cultural Center hosted by the city's Latino artists, and coalitions built with the Bay Area Latin American Solidarity Coalition. Multi-ethnic iconography was plentiful in the flyers and posters of the movement.

The handwritten notes of Occupy SF protester Derek Whaler dated January 26, 2012, indicate significant communication with the Occupy Oakland movement, itself a movement characterized by greater leadership of activists of color, and communication with the organizers of the National Tour with John Carlos and Dave Zirin in late December 2011, an Occupy "Visionary Group" that was focused on issues of economic justice. On December 3, 2011, Occupy SF joined with tenant and homeowner groups in the Bayview, Castro, Mission and Tenderlon neighborhoods for a mass march against sub-prime lending, bank bailouts, homelessness, and the Ellis Act. The flyer for this event featured the iconography of an African American woman shouting into a megaphone labeled "Occupy" against a backdrop of Victorian houses. They flyer was also rendered in Spanish. On December 21, 2011, Occupy SF participated in an Interfaith memorial for the Homeless Dead in San Francisco.

Thus a significant working relationship between the predominantly European American led protest movement of Occupy SF and the Coltrane Church and its broad coalition of people of color activists was achieved. Historically, it might properly be considered an expansion of the mission of the Weather Underground in the 1960s to renounce racial privilege and join the global decolonization struggle of people of color that would have national implications for Occupy movements across the country and for deconstructing whiteness.

A Deeply Personal Struggle

The foreclosure movement was also a deeply personal movement for the Coltrane Church, just as personal as the fight against the Lennar Corporation had been. In the *Salt Lake Tribune*, Cathy McKitrick made Archbishop King's personal narrative of an exploitative negative amortization loan a central feature of her story.

Although the "Coltrane Church's" political engagement with the foreclosure crisis was initially motivated by self-interest, Archbishop King and Mother Marina quickly understood that the banks were coming after black churches and, by extension, African American cultural institutions. The

Pastor Wanika King-Stephens and Archbishop King fight against foreclosures, 2011.

foreclosure movement thus became, at least for Coltrane Church activists, part of the broader struggle to preserve African American cultural institutions and the African American cultural heritage of San Francisco.

> The banks have closed down churches in this town. The foreclosure movement went to being concerned about how we need to save cultural institutions.
>
> I tried to organize NAACP and all these other folks but there wasn't many really trying to hear it. The foreclosure movement was after the community and police relations board, after SLAM and Lennar.
>
> So now I'm kinda independent out there and Min. Christopher is not with me in the flesh but he's with me in spirit. So when I go down to the HUD approved counselor about my own personal thing, that's when I hear from Ed Donaldson who is running for supervisor of the 10th District that there are some progressives working with foreclosure and after checking them out I meet with them and I join with them on this principle: my community is disappearing. If I save my house I'm thrilled because I have a domestic responsibility. But I'm not getting in this fight to save my house, I'm getting in the fight to save the community.
>
> So when I come out in the foreclosure movement people are losing their houses and not saying anything because black people are proud people. If I owe you a dime I'm not going to bring you a nickel I've got to bring you that dime or else I am going to cow out. When I came out it was like, take off your garbs of shame. Be the proud black people you are and put your war clothes on and let's fight against these banksters.
>
> I'd rather borrow money from Al Capone than to borrow it from the bank. Al Capone will break your legs. You can have them re-set. The banks will break your inheritance for your children, your retirement.
>
> And then somebody told me that "mortgage" is a French term for "death contract."
>
> So we have entered into a death contract. But we didn't realize that they were leading us into a grave situation to bury our children's inheritance, our retirement, to bury our dignity. So that's how I got into the movement.

The Battle for Marcus Books

Resonating its awareness of the significant threat to African American cultural institutions, the foreclosure movement engaged in a highly publicized struggle in 2013 and 2014 to save an important African American cultural site from foreclosure. Marcus Books at 1712 Fillmore Street, the nation's oldest existing African American bookstore and the former location of Jimbo's Bop City where Archbishop King experienced his second Sound Baptism upon learning of John Coltrane's untimely passing in 1967, missed a couple of rent payments in 2013 and mortgage holder PLM Lender foreclosed on the building housing the bookstore, according to Rebecca Bowe reporting on May 8, 2014, for the *San Francisco Bay Guardian*. The foreclosed property was sold to the Sweis family who owned the Royal Taxi company in San Francisco in a bankruptcy "auction" for $1.6 million. The Johnson family—Greg, Tamiko, and Karen Johnson— who owned Marcus Books offered $1.8 million, at which point the Sweis family raised their price to $3.2 million. In the wake of public protests against the Sweis investment group, the asking price was lowered to $2.6 million and the Johnson family launched a community fund-raising effort to retain the property (Bowe).

Archbishop King and his family, and by extension the Coltrane Church, had an established relationship with the Johnson family and Marcus Books. Archbishop King considered Marcus Books founder Julian Richardson a mentor and elder in the community from whom he sought advice and counsel.

> My first contact with Marcus Books was with Julian Richardson, the founder, who was a Garveyite and when I first started the church the typesetter was working out of his place on McAllister and Van Ness. So I would get the privilege of asking him questions and he was quick to start teaching on stuff and he was very encouraging. I always felt I needed the encouragement of the elders in the community because what I was doing was so out and radical and not a part of established religion. I'm indebted to him and I see him as a part of the royal family.

Conscious of the Johnson family's role as one of the "first families" or "royal families" in the Fillmore, Archbishop King joined a broad coalition as part of his larger efforts with Occupy SF and the foreclosure movement to save Marcus Books. According to Bowe, the coalition to save Marcus Books included "the local chapter of the NAACP; ACCE; Japantown activists; Westside Community Services; Julian Davis, our fearless legal counsel; Carlos Levexier's "Keep it Lit" campaign committee; local literary community including writers and other bookstores; people from all over the world: friends, family, customers, churches and unions took a stand against the bulldozing of community."

Archbishop King:

> That family is royalty in this town and they have been treated horribly. When I hear about Marcus being in trouble, I wonder what are we going to do about that.

In spite of donations and pledges from individuals, unions, churches, the Community Land Trust of San Francisco and a $1.6 million loan from Westside Community Services, the Sweises filed for eviction.

Further, the community's activism and impressive fund-raising support motivated the San Francisco Board of Supervisors to support initiatives to preserve Marcus Books as a historic landmark. Archbishop King remarks on the ability of the community to pressure the Board of Supervisors and the cultural importance of Marcus Books against the backdrop of the Jazz Heritage Center and Yoshi's:

> Mirkarimi made a statement about three cultural institutions when he was supervisor in the Fillmore. I tried to capitalize on that to say to the Jazz Heritage Center that has closed, in terms of us being able to survive down here as cultural institutions we can't compete with feeding troughs and gin joints. We need to come together but they have us so divided, everybody is trying to fend for self that they don't get to selflessness and boom, both of them are gone, the Jazz Heritage Center and Yoshi's is bankrupt and they're on their way out.

But on May 6, 2014, Marcus Books was officially evicted from 1712 Fillmore. Interestingly, Archbishop King cites the emergence of the very same coalition of community accomplices in the defeat of Marcus Books that had undermined the African American Community Police Relations Board and that had so vigorously defended the Lennar Corporation in the Coltrane Church's earlier battles with corporate and governmental power.

> Marcus Books thing would have been on silence. Grace Martinez is the local head of ACCE who really organized the whole save Marcus Books thing and made sure that the meetings were happening and introduced them to the tactics that we were using to put pressure on the banks to talk to us. The city retirement board, we went down there to their board meeting because Brenda Wright is on the retirement board and also a representative for Wells Fargo. And the retirement board had this policy that they would not put their money in anything that was discriminatory. So we put pressure on that and went down there.
>
> And then the opposition took out a full-page ad in the *Chronicle* saying what a nice person she was. So we have had that kind of opposition. There has always been an element of so-called leadership in this community that would stand up and speak for the master.

Conclusions

In spite of the bitter failure to save Marcus Books, the foreclosure movement that continues in the present day had real, material successes. In the first place, the Coltrane Church, ACCE, and Occupy SF were able to persuade the legislature and city to pass legislation outlawing dual tracking, a central practice of predatory lending. Archbishop King:

That foreclosure movement was responsible for getting that law passed
that outlawed dual tracking. And we saved some peoples' houses. We
made banks sit down and negotiate new contracts with people.

There were real people in the community whose homes had been
saved by the efforts of the foreclosure movement:

> The group that I was working with was ACCE. Alliance for Community
> Empowerment. We saved in the first couple of months a number of houses
> including a 75-year-old sister, Josephine, running a daycare center. She left
> to go do something and came back with the children and they had changed
> the locks. We made the bank rescind the foreclosure and give that sister
> her house back. And then Vivian Richardson, we got her house back. We
> won some houses back. We made the banks sit down and negotiate.

Furthermore, the foreclosure movement yielded an important ideological transition toward more aggressive and confrontational nonviolent
direct action tactics, as well as furthering the church's ongoing ethnic coalition building and the dismantling of white privilege in leftist, community-
based social and political movements as Occupy SF engaged in meaningful
dialogue with the Coltrane Church, ACCE, and a host of other people of
color activists.

15

Answering the Prophetic Call

In that great getting up morning,
Fare you well! Fare you well!
In that great getting up morning,
Fare you well! Fare you well!

The Lord spoke to Gabriel
Go behind the altar
Take down the silver trumpet
Blow your trumpet Gabriel

Lord how loud shall I blow it
Blow it right calm and easy
Do not alarm my people
Tell 'em to come to judgment

"*In That Great Getting-Up Morning*"—*traditional*
Negro spiritual (Southern 1983, p. 174)

Analyses of the narratives of the Coltrane Church reveal that over the course of a 50-year history, founders and members have dynamically evolved different ideological and realpolitik positions in response to changing times. This dynamic, evolutionary process has been integral to the sustainability and continued relevance of the Coltrane Church. Rather than abandon previous ideological and realpolitik positions upon each evolutionary shift, every contemporary manifestation of the church utilizes counter-hegemonic methodologies from its history in complex and nuanced manipulations of past and present.

The narratives of Archbishop King and Mother Marina King begin with the communicative and community building potential of jazz music and produce possibilities for a sovereign counter-hegemonic politics of representation through music. The narratives of the Coltrane Church tell stories of how the Coltrane Church community imaginatively represented the jazz music of John Coltrane to create and re-create a de-colonized and democratic ideological terrain for the social and cultural practices of a sovereign counter public.

I have sub-titled this book *Apostles of Sound, Agents of Social Justice* in order to explicitly draw attention to the agency exhibited by this remarkable group of people who operated as free men and women in the face of racial prejudice and represented the music and the words of wisdom of St. John Coltrane and constructed revolutionary spiritual, ethical, political, and dietary practices. The foregoing discussions of communication and representation occur against the backdrop of power and racial inequality in America. Communication, whether linguistic or musical, must always be linked with power. In *The Coltrane Church*, everything from the critical reception of Coltrane's music to contemporary dismissals of the Coltrane Church in jazz scholarship illustrate representational tensions and the ideological practices of American racism.

The stories of the Coltrane Church involve the same response to the call of the drums in the era of slavery for the hush harbor gathering of community and the planning of insurrections and ultimately the building of a new America. The core members of the St. John Will-I-Am Coltrane African Orthodox Church in San Francisco bear a unique resemblance to the prophets and agents of insurrection in ante-bellum America: David Walker, Nat Turner, Frederick Douglass, Henry Highland Garnet, Denmark Vesey, Sojourner Truth and Gabriel Prosser. Narratives of the Coltrane Church mark an important continuation of the insurgent political spirit of the ring-shout of the ante-bellum period (Stuckey), the history of radical black liberation theology (Cone) and the roots of black womanist theology.

The founders and members of the Coltrane Church are the Apostles of Sound, followers after a latter day gospel "written" in the musical discourse of flatted fifths and swinging triplets by jazz giant Saint John Will-I-Am Coltrane. In their love of John Coltrane, this community pursued him through Hindu chanting, Sufi mysticism, radical black politics, and Orthodox Christian practice. This is a church community that has seen myriad transitions, from the belief in Coltrane as Christ to Coltrane as Blue Krishna to Coltrane as the Holy Ghost. It is the post–civil rights love child of the music and thought of John Coltrane, free jazz improvisation and the new black music, black Pentecostalism, Garveyism and the African Orthodox Church, Alice Coltrane's Hindu teachings, the writings of Sufi mystic and musician Hazrat Inayat Khan, and the political philosophy of Huey Newton and the Black Panther Party. Like the early history of the apostles of Jesus Christ, the Coltrane Church is similarly marked by stories of transition and constant searching. There's a tremendous openness in these stories to a myriad of devotional styles. At the core of these movements and transitions is an abiding love of the Master teachers, Jesus Christ and John Coltrane. Perhaps the true energy of Christianity or any other mode of spiritual devotion is best exemplified here in the spirit of change and openness of hearts to receive the message of Christ.

I have used the word "Apostles" in the subtitle to equate the Coltrane Church with the experience of early Christians in the New Testament Book of Acts, a people who leaned on the words of Christ and went forth trying to do even greater works than he, healing the sick and raising the dead. The Coltrane Church indeed represents John Coltrane as a latter day apostle with a Gospel for the new millennium composed in the language of jazz music. As a "Gospel" of music, the Gospel according to John Coltrane, and indeed the language of jazz—with its blue notes, flatted fifths, suspended fourths, 13ths, 11ths, sharp and flat ninths, diminished sounds, tri-tone substitutions, and syncopations—certainly deconstructs the tyranny of the safe and saccharine tones of popular music, major scale harmony, and indeed of western tonality and rhythm itself. And as a spiritual, social,

The church performs at Cité de la Musique in Paris, 2008.

political, and cultural "Gospel," the Gospel according to St. John Will-I-Am Coltrane deconstructs racist constructions about the divinity and spirituality of African people, legitimates non–Western spirituality, and embraces a utopian paradigm of brotherhood and peace.

The evolution of the Coltrane Church through ideologies of black nationalism, class consciousness, spiritual universalism, environmental activism, and womanism—coupled with enduring beliefs in the miracle healing power of jazz music—is the key to the sustainability of this ministry as a spiritual, cultural, and political force. These ideological transformations mark the Coltrane Church as dynamic and indeed pragmatic in its responses to ever-changing contexts. They also mark the Coltrane Church as a community that aspires to remain vanguard figures in the ongoing social, cultural, spiritual, political struggles of all oppressed peoples through constant self-examination and self-conscious transition.

While Coltrane Consciousness explicitly foregrounds cultural and ideological formations, real material re-locations and empowerment have never lacked relevance for the community of the Coltrane Church. I trust that this book has not only illustrated the effective application of Chela Sandoval's notion of differential ideological movement but how this movement has worked collaboratively to produce limited and yet developing material change in the lives of its adherents and its community, particularly in the fight against corporate redevelopment, police brutality, foreclosure, and environmental racism. Without espousing a ministry of prosperity, Coltrane Consciousness, allied with a good old time religion of Holy Ghost—centered ecstatic worship, has been effectively employed to cure illness, halt impending death, end drug addiction, secure housing, provide a livelihood, and feed the people. The experience of Coltrane Consciousness isn't merely about elevating one of America's greatest musicians to the level of sainthood. Coltrane Consciousness is about elevating every one of its adherents beyond social injustice and toward a visionary conception of freedom.

Avant-garde jazz composer Albert Ayler once remarked, "John [Coltrane] was like a visitor to this planet. He came in peace and he left in peace; but during his time here, he kept trying to reach new levels of awareness, of peace, of spirituality. That's why I regard the music he played as spiritual music–John's way of getting closer and closer to the Creator" (Wilmer 31). Ayler was not alone in his elevation of John Coltrane, nor has the reverence for the music and wisdom of John Coltrane ceased since his ascension July 17, 1967. In an essay included in the Rhino/Atlantic Jazz Gallery two–CD anthology *The Last Giant*, Amiri Baraka places Coltrane at the epicenter of ongoing African American struggles for freedom: "But Trane still sounds inside us as the freedom we seek, the total expression of the Human-headed Soul, the teaching that the flaming paradise of his music is in us to create the world we live in."

The genius of Franzo Wayne King and Marina King was that by 1967 they recognized that John Coltrane was so much more than the sum of his musical contributions. They recognized that he was a cultural, spiritual, political, and ideological force who transcended his role as an African American musician of the bop, cool, and free jazz eras of the 1950s through late 1960s and emerged as a universal icon of the human struggle for freedom. Because of the Coltrane Church, John Coltrane remains an important symbol for universal desires for freedom.

Coltrane Consciousness answers the prophetic call issued by composer and scholar William C. Banfield in his eclectic ruminations on black music, *Black Notes: Essays of a Musician Writing in a Post-Album Age.* Banfield issues the call: "There is a growing urgency in our society to hear, heal, and revisit the idea of meaningful exchanges between people. Our society has become a common playground for violence, selfishness, social ambivalence, complacency, mean-spiritedness, and political and spiritual emptiness. There is definitely a cry, a need for prophetic voices, impulses and movements. These needs have driven us to rely on waves of bad substitute teachers who take the role and the money and write 'mess' on the chalkboard. It is important to identify places in our culture that have meaning, and also to unearth compelling figures, expressions and movements which slow the downward spin and provide more moments of 'truth platforms'" (Banfield 19).

Archbishop King directly echoes Banfield's demands on the music, elevating Coltrane's music and person as opportunities for spiritual transformation.

> You have to understand that for us, John Coltrane was God, was the anointed one, the spirit of God, was Blue Krishna. I mean, Coltrane had written songs telling us about "Evolution" and "Transition" and "Meditation 4 a.m." and these were all helping us to evolve into higher spiritual beings and so we knew that John Coltrane had the power to assist us in our remaking.

Core ideologies and beliefs of the St. John Will-I-Am Coltrane African Orthodox Church centrally deconstruct visually and linguistically-biased prerogatives of traditional Euro-American Judeo-Christian worship in favor of aural engagements with the divine. Simply stated, God is Sound. Not text. Not image. Reminiscent of the extensive teaching of Sufi mystic

Hazrat Inayat Khan, Coltrane Consciousness interprets sound as a universal conduit to divinity where the true essence of the divine is revealed, transcending artificial constructs of race, class, gender, sexual identity and indeed even time itself. Sound is immanent Truth. But, perhaps even more significantly, practices embedded in and guided by Sound lead to the kind of social utopia around which the cultural politics of the Coltrane Church began to take shape.

In the wake of a nihilistic cultural space articulated by Banfield, the Coltrane Church offers a return to the use of music and aesthetics for articulating oppositional identity and giving rise to subaltern counter-publics. In my humble estimation, the Coltrane Church offers that prophetic voice demanded by Banfield in what he terms a "post-album age" where most American music has generally come to represent materialist excess rather than subaltern politics, spirituality, or culture.

Chapter Notes

Preface

1. From liner notes of *Kulu Se Mama* (Impulse! AS-9106), 1966.

2. "The Coltrane Church" is not the name that the St. John Will-I-Am Coltrane African Orthodox Church gives itself. It is, however, the colloquial name by which the church has come to be known in local media.

3. John Coltrane preferred to call "jazz" music "American classical music."

4. There was literally an "Upper Room" in the 351 Divisadero Street location, but at the church's present location on 1286 Fillmore Street the "Upper Room" has been substituted by a "back room" where musicians gather and tune up before the commencement of the worship services. The term "Upper Room" refers to the Cenacle or site of the Last Supper and the place where the Apostles stayed in Jerusalem from Acts 1:13. The "Cenacle" or "Upper Room" is also considered by some to be the site of the first "official" Christian Church.

5. Rev. Mark Dukes, the official iconographer of St. John's, has termed his icons "neo-Byzantine." The term signifies his attempt to extend that style of iconographic representation.

6. "Will-I-Am" refers to God's words to Moses uttered from the burning bush. In Exodus 3: 14, it is written, "And God said unto Moses, I AM THAT I AM: and he said, Thus shalt thou say unto the children of Israel, I AM hath sent me unto you."

7. The Coltrane Liturgy is the unique product of the St. John Will-I-Am Coltrane African Orthodox Church. The music of John Coltrane is integrated within the order of service for the African Orthodox liturgy.Worship services are organized in order from the opening to "A Love Supreme: Acknowledgment" and the singing of Psalm 23, "Lonnie's Lament" and "Tunji."

8. According to *The John Coltrane Reference*, Coltrane appeared at the Jazz Workshop in San Francisco, California, from September 14 to 26, 1965, a Tuesday through Sunday with Monday off (Porter, DeVito, Wild, Fujioka, Schmaler, 2013).

9. In my view there is no greater evidence of this tendency toward dismissal than in a brief aside in Eric Nisenson's *Ascension: John Coltrane and His Spiritual Quest* (1995).

Chapter 1

1. Haqq is the Arabic word for "truth." Under this general concept, Archbishop King created a theology of "Haqq-ism" emphasizing the pursuit of Truth.

2. A document produced by the San Francisco Redevelopment Agency dated July 21, 1964, titled Appendix C to the Report on the Redevelopment Plan for the Western Addition Project Area A-2, states, "Negro leadership has also been consulted and kept informed of planning for Area 2. Agency staff has had continuing contact with a number of community groups and organizations whose primary interest is that of minority group consideration.

Included among them are the Afro-American Association, Council for Civic Unity, National Association for the Advancement of Colored People, and Bay Area Urban League. Extensive discussions have been held with individual Negro ministers as well as with their coordinating groups known as the Baptist Ministerial Alliance and the Inter-denominational Ministerial Alliance."

3. Appendix C to the Report on the Redevelopment Plan for the Western Addition further notes, "Another avenue through which Negro leadership in the community has been consulted is the Western Addition District Council and its subcommittee on redevelopment. The Council acts as the coordinating body for public and private agencies and citizen groups with an active interest in the Western Addition. The organization has included in its membership a number of minority group representatives. The following excerpt from the Council's subcommittee on redevelopment report concerning the Relocation Plan for Western Addition Area 2 is indicative of the attitude of organizations in that area: "The Committee recommends a District Council expression of confidence in the Redevelopment Agency's approach to the planning of the Area 2 Project and specific endorsement of the following aspects of the plan: 1. The provision for early contact with residents to inform them about the redevelopment program; and 2. The provision for attention to social problems and needs of residents, either resulting from, or brought to light by, the redevelopment process."

4. WACO included the Bay Area Urban League, the Black Anti-Draft Union, the Blackman's Freestore, the Fillmore Neighborhood Peace and Freedom Club, the Buchanan YMCA, Holy Cross Roman Catholic Church, and the Holy of Holiness Baptist Church, among diverse others.

5. *San Francisco Chronicle*, November 1, 1967, p.4

6. Former ILWU representative Wilbur Hamilton served as head of the San Francisco Redevelopment Agency from 1977 to 1987, a tenure second only to Justin Hermann, under the administrations of George Moscone and Dianne Feinstein. He was hired as Area 2 project manager

in 1967 in the wake of WACO's successful to halt redevelopment until the agency could submit a federally certified plan for the relocation of Western Addition residents, a move which effectively slowed the progress of redevelopment in the Western Addition.

7. http://www.salon.com/2012/05/01/jim_jones_sinister_grip_on_san_francisco/.

8. In late July 2003 Archbishop King journeyed to Ghana and Liberia with Al Sharpton and Dr. Cornel West. Conservative writer and television commentator Tucker Carlson chronicled the trip in an article for *Esquire* magazine. Carlson writes, "Fourteen of us gathered across from the gate one afternoon in late July and held hands. On my left was Sanford Rubenstein, Abner Louima's lawyer in the NYPD brutality case. On my right was His Eminence Franzo W. King, D.D., Archbishop and lead sax player of the St. John Coltrane African Orthodox Church in San Francisco. Across the circle was former D. C. mayor Marion Barry's wife, Cora Masters Barry, and three guys from the Nation of Islam, two of them named James Muhammad." (www.esquire.com/features/ESQ1103-NOV_LIBERIA_rev).

9. African American religious blogger Michael Corcoran, in an essay titled "Hungry for More God: The Rots of the Black Pentecostal Movement," writes, "Tagged 'the American Jerusalem' for the thousands of seekers who descended on the City of Angels from 1906–1909, the Azusa Street Revival is acknowledged as the birthplace of the Pentecostal movement, whose doctrine of speaking in tongues as the only true evidence of being baptized in the Holy Spirit is practiced today by an estimated 500 million churchgoers worldwide." (www.michaelcorcoran.net).

10. The Church of God in Christ's officicial website speaks of the inspiration that Bishop Charles Mason recevied from his attendance at William Seymour's Asuza Street Revival in Los Angeles: "The turning point in Elder Mason's life came in March, 1907, when he journeyed to Los Angeles, California, to attend a great Pentecostal revival with Elder D.J. Young and Elder J.A. Jeter. Elder W.J. Seymour was preaching concerning Luke 24:49, 'And behold I send the promise of my Father upon you; but tarry ye in the city of

Jerusalem until ye be endued with power from on high." Elder Mason became convinced that it was essential for him to have the outpouring of the Holy Ghost" (www.cogic.org/our-foundation/the-founder-church-history/).

11. Ohnedaruth is a Sanskrit word meaning "compassion."

12. Writing for *NPR Music*, John Burnett notes, "Of all the virtuosic Hot Five recordings, it is 'West End Blues' that collectors, critics and scholars hail as a mile marker in the evolution of jazz. On a personal level, Armstrong emerges for the first time as a mature musician" (http://www.npr.org/2000/08/06/1080400/west-end-blues).

Chapter 2

1. *Bitches Brew*, a double album released on Columbia Records in April 1970, was Miles Davis' first gold record and garnered a Grammy Award for Best Large Jazz Ensemble Album in 1971.

2. Archbishop King and Mother Marina have not been able to recall the specific date of John Coltrane's 1966 performance. However, according to *The John Coltrane Reference*, Coltrane appeared at the Jazz Workshop in San Francisco between January 25 and February 6, 1966, on a Tuesday through Sunday with Monday off (Porter, DeVito, Wild, Fujioka, Schmaler, 2013).

3. The reference is to a letter John Coltrane wrote to *Down Beat* critic Don DeMichael June 2, 1962.

4. According to Peter Lavezzoli, John Coltrane studied the Bible, the Qur'an, the Kabbalah, astrology, Hinduism, Jiddu Krishnamurti, African history, Plato, Aristotle, and Zen Buddhism. Among the many books in his collection were *The Gospel of Sri Ramakrishna*, the Bhagavad Gita, and Paramahansa Yogananda's *Autobiography of a Yogi*. Lavezzoli, *The Dawn of Indian Music in the West* (New York: Continuum, 2006), pp. 272–286).

5. The classic quartet refers to John Coltrane on saxophone, Jimmy Garrison on bass, McCoy Tyner on piano, and Elvin Jones on drums. This unit was responsible for some of the more popular Coltrane recordings, including *My Favorite Things* and *A Love Supreme*.

6. For example, music publisher Hal Leonard's transcriptions suggest other diminished sounds, including G7flat5, G flat 7, A flat 7, A flat min7 flat 5, B flat minor 7 flat 5, G7 flat 5 flat 9, and E flat minor sharp 5/D flat in addition to the written F diminished chord in "Day."

7. Every diminished scale has an intervallic pattern of alternating half and whole steps. Diminished scales may begin with either a half or whole step, thus creating distinct patterns and different scales. The F diminished half-whole scale from which the melody for "Day" is created is spelled out as F, F sharp/G flat, G sharp/A flat, A, B, C, D, D sharp/E flat.

8. John Coltrane's first wife, Naima, was a Muslim. The relationship between Coltrane's prayer schedule and the Islamic prayer schedule is probably no coincidence.

Chapter 3

1. Known affectionately as "Bishop Norman 'New Testament' Williams," Norman Williams would later become an integral part of this burgeoning church community.

2. The death of St. John Will-I-Am Coltrane is commonly referred to by church members as his "Ascension" into heaven.

3. While John Coltrane died from liver ailments that may have stemmed from substance abuse, Archbishop King's reference to John Coltrane being killed specifically indicates his belief that the proliferation of drugs in African American communities is tantamount to murder and genocide.

4. According to Carol P. Chamberland's 1998 documentary, *The Legend of Bop City*, Jimbo's Bop City was a safe location for intercultural couples to meet and interact within the context of the "informal" racial segregation of San Francisco between the end of World War II and the civil rights era of the 1960s.

Chapter 4

1. Albert S. Broussard, *Black San Francisco: The Struggle for Racial Equality in the West, 1900–1954* (Lawrence: University of Kansas Press, 1994), p.73

2. Ohnedaruth is the Hindu name given to John Coltrane by his widow Alice Coltrane. Sri means wealth or prosperity. Rama is one of the highest names of the Lord. Rama translates into English as: Ram. RA also is Universe, MA is world. Ohnedaruth means compassion.

3. The "jazz left" is a term used by Herman Gray in *Cultural Moves* to describe community-centered jazz practice and is distinguished from corporate and state-controlled cultural institutions, e.g., the Lincoln Center.

4. Acid jazz is a fusion of jazz, funk and hip-hop beats. It presumably originated in Britain during the 1980s by musicians influenced by the jazz-funk of Jimmy Smith, Grant Green, etc. Acid jazz made its mark on the San Francisco jazz scene in the 1990s.

5. Yoshi's Oakland moved from Claremont to Jack London Square in 1997 during the revitalization of the Port of Oakland, with the assistance of funding from the Oakland Development Agency. The new facility included a 330-seat, 17,000-spare-foot concert hall with an attached 220-seat Japanese restaurant. In 10 years (2007) Yoshi's would engage in a similar relationship with the San Francisco Redevelopment Agency to establish another state of the art facility in San Francisco's redeveloped Western Addition/Fillmore neighborhood.

6. The final price tag for Yoshi's was $10 million (Jesse Hamlin, *San Francisco Chronicle*, September 19, 2004).

7. The online version of the Western Edition newspaper provides a thorough resume for Michael Johnson. "Johnson, president and founder of EM Johnson Interest, Inc. has over 20 years of experience in urban real estate development around the country. A native of Philadelphia, Johnson studied architecture at the University of Maryland and then went on to Georgia Tech, where he got a Masters Degree in Real Estate Development. ... He did not enter the San Francisco market until 1998, when he decided to bid on the St. Regis project on Third and Mission Streets, a mixed use, housing, hotel and open space, which would eventually become the Museum of African Diaspora." (http://www.thewesternedition.com/?c=117&a=1110).

8. The centerpiece of the fine dining partnerships with the San Francisco Jazz Heritage Center is chef David Lawrence's 1300 on Fillmore, featuring a sophisticated Southern cuisine born of his Jamaican and English roots (www.1300fillmore.com).

9. The current board is comprised of a retired university advancement officer at San Francisco State University, who served on boards of directors in Silicon Valley including Villa Montalvo Arts Center in Saratoga and Cultural Initiatives Silicon Valley; a founder and president of Apperture Media Group, which assists clients in creating and maintaining corporate vision and strategy, in conducting business and product development including market research and analysis, and with managing high-level project engagements; a chief financial officer affiliated with San Francisco Botanical Garden Society, with over 20 years experience in various CFO positions in private and non-profit entities specializing in turnaround and re-engineering; a development consultant with Center for Investigative Reporting with 22 years in development leadership positions at Stanford University; an Oakland-based graphic designer and graduate coordinator of design and industry at San Francisco State University; and a committee member, Alameda County Public Art Advisory Committee. The Fillmore Heritage Center, of which the Jazz Heritage Center is a critical cultural centerpiece, is led by Atlanta-based minority owned EM Johnson Interest, Inc., a real estate development firm founded by developer Michael Johnson (www.jazzheritagecenter.org).

10. A term coined by Stanford anthropologist Renato Rosaldo in *Culture and Truth: The Remaking of Social Analysis* (1993)

11. www.sfgate.com/cgibin/article.cgi?f=/c/a/2007/06/02/MNG6QQ69RE31.DTL.

12. Rubien mistakenly refers to John Coltrane's second son as "Ravi Shankar." Although Coltrane's second son is named in honor of the great sitar player, his name is Ravi Coltrane.

13. Among the more important precursors to the AACM, George Lewis evaluates Will Marion Cook and James Reese

Europe's Clef Club; Gigi Gryce and Benny Golson's Melotone Music and Totem Music; Charles Mingus and Max Roach's Newport Rebels festival in 1960 as well as their publishing firm, Debut Records; Horace Tapscott's Union of God's Musicians and Artists Ascending (UGMAA) in Los Angeles; and Bill Dixon and Cecil Taylor's New York-based Jazz Composer's Guild.

14. Rasselas opened in 1986 at California and Divisadero streets and has since opened a second location on 1534 Fillmore Street and continues to feature such local talent as Ledisi, John Handy, and Kim Nalley, and serves Ethiopian food.

15. Sheba's was opened in 2006 by Ethiopian immigrants and features such local artists as the Robert Stewart Experience. The club also serves an Ethiiopian cuisine.

16. www.jackboulware.com/writing/church-of-john-coltrane.

17. In recent years Yoshi's has moved well outside of the boundaries of jazz music and featured such artists as Mos Def.

18. Ohnedaruth, the "Coltrane Church" band, remains largely unrecorded, with the exception of a compact disc of its liturgy produced by a small New York label in the late 1990s. When Yoshi's was a smaller, more community-centered organization on Oakland's Claremont Avenue, the "Coltrane Church" was an annual guest for its John Coltrane Birthday celebration. Since their move to Jack London Square in Oakland and the birth of their second location in the heart of the Fillmore Center, Ohnedaruth has received sporadic invitations. The San Francisco Jazz Festival finds little interest in the musicians of Ohnedaruth, and the church has arguably received greater interest from state-sponsored festivals abroad, including the Premier Festival de Gospel de Provence in France in which they performed in 1996 and 1998.

19. http://sfist.com/2014/06/04/yoshis_sf_sold_will_get_new_name_ne.php.

Chapter 5

1. A community that began with a vision in 1965 and a subsequent listening clinic evolved first into the Yardbird Club and then the more spiritually oriented Yardbird Temple. It then went through a number of other manifestations as the Yardbird Revolutionary Vanguard Church of the Hour, the One Mind Temple Evolutionary Church, and the One Mind Temple Evolutionary Transitional Body of Christ. By 1969, the community was known as the Yardbird Vanguard Revolutionary Church of the Hour and it is in this period that they met Dr. Huey P. Newton.

2. Black Liberation Theology is a term drawn from James Cone's groundbreaking interpretation of African American religious history, *A Black Theology of Liberation*. Drawing heavily from the earlier writing of theologian Howard Thurman, Cone provides a definition in the opening sentences: "a rational study of the being of God in the world in light of the existential situation of an oppressed community, relating the forces of liberation to the essence of the gospel, which is Jesus Christ. This means that its sole reason for existence is to put into ordered speech the meaning of God's activity in the world, so that the community of the oppressed will recognize that its inner thrust for liberation is not only consistent with the gospel but is the gospel of Jesus Christ" (1). Cone defines Christian theology as inherently liberational, proclaiming, "There can be no Christian theology that is not identified unreservedly with those who are humiliated and abused" (1). I have adhered very strictly to Cone's definition and have tried throughout to demonstrate the consistency between Cone's interpretation of the Christian Gospels and Coltrane Consciousness.

3. Then Archbishop King received a copy of Khan's *Mysticism of Sound and Music* from friend and fellow musician Michael White. King remembers, "a gentleman named Michael White who's a violinist saw me reading all of these books and he gave me a book called *Mysticism and Sound* by Hazrat Inayat Khan, who was a musician himself and had gotten to the point where he said that he had played for all the maharajahs in India, you know, the kings and all that, and he had been given jewels and awards for his music ... and he said one day he left all of his precious awards and things on a plane, and I

think how he said it that that was a signal to him that God wanted him to stop tuning instruments—because he played a stringed instrument- and begin to tune souls, and he stopped playing music and started dealing with the orchestration of life and tuning of souls."

4. As the Coltrane Church enters its current transition in the ascension of Wanika King to pastor, the church has reconsidered its position on membership and is certainly poised for a substantive effort at growing its ranks.

5. Supreme Mother Phyllis Proudhomme's parents were privileged to have Church of God in Christ founder Bishop C.H. Mason as a frequent dinner guest. Supreme Mother's uncle was Rev. Hercules Benbow, who pioneered black Pentecostalism in Sacramento, California, in the 1960s.

6. The hippie movement is worth mentioning in this context because of its representation as an outgrowth of the 1950s Beat Generation that specifically endorsed Eastern religious practices.

7. Interestingly, Wuthnow has also written about the relationship between artistic creativity and spirituality in *Creative Spirituality: The Way of the Artist* (Berkeley: University of California Press, 2003).

8. Notable scholars and works in this movement include Charles T. Gloch and Robert N.Bellah, eds., *The New Religious Consciousness* (Berkeley: University of California Press, 1976), Robert Wuthnow, *The Consciousness Reformation* (Berkeley: University of California Press, 1976); and Stephen Tipton, *Getting Saved from the Sixties: Moral Meaning in Conversion and Cultural Studies* (Berkeley: University of California Press, 1982).

9. www.pbs.org/wnet/religionand ethics/week534/rwuthnow.html.

10. The reference is from Matthew 12:8.

11. Ira Levin founded the "time traveling vaudevillian slamswing band" Comfy Chair in the late 1990s and by the early 2000s was no longer a regular presence at the Coltrane Church.

Chapter 7

1. Given the degree of national, ethnic and class markers that accompany most forms of popular, folk, and classical music, it seems fair to make this judgment. Here I am referring to everything from Thomas Mann's work on Wagner and German nationalism to Amiri Baraka/LeRoi Jones' writings on African American music to Paul Gilroy's work on contemporary black music in America and England. In spite of the apparent universalism of sound and the hybrid origins of most musical traditions, there are numerous historical incidents of the use of sound in constructing ethnic identity, philosophies, and political agendas. Paul Gilroy, in particular, adroitly treats issues of music and ethnic essentialism in *The Black Atlantic: Modernity and Double Consciousness.* Indeed Gilroy understands the range of dialogue on black music to fall between the notion of "music as the primary means to explore critically and reproduce politically the necessary ethnic essence of blackness and those who would dispute the existence of any such unifying, organic phenomenon" (100).

2. Among the suggestions translations for this chant once expressed to me by the late Fr. Roberto DeHaven was that "Om" signifies God or the realms of the gods; "Ma" designates purification from jealousy; "Ni" signifies purification from human passion and desire; "Pad" purifies ignorance and prejudice; "Me" purifies greed; and "Hum" purifies hatred and violence.

3. Alice Coltrane died of respiratory failure January 12, 2007, at the age of 69 and was buried alongside her late husband, John Coltrane, at Pinelawn Memorial Park in Farmingdale, Suffolk County, New York.

Chapter 9

1. Specifically these categories are drawn from Jacques Derrida's critique of speech and writing acts in *Margins of Philosophy* and *Dissemination.* Here, Derrida's categories serve to ground and structure far more esoteric discussions of the mystical power of sound drawn largely from Eastern and Christian mystical traditions. I would argue, however, that Derrida's work as a whole, and his deconstructionist agenda of liberating us from metaphysical origins, does strive for some sort of spiritual urgency.

2. There are certainly exceptions to this statement that deserve mention. Joscelyn Godwin's *Harmonies of Heaven and Earth: Mysticism in Music from Antiquity to the Avant-Garde* (1995) deals not only with mystical musical traditions in Sufism and other eastern religions, but provides a concise history and explanation of everything from the Planetary Scales of Greek antiquity to the Tone-Zodiacs of Rudolph Steiner of the early twentieth century. Godwin's work sheds little light on mysticism and jazz. I am far more interested in Godwin's appreciation of the spiritual power of music and of her comparison of musical performance with spiritual worship. Further, Godwin discusses musicians as mystical alchemists. Her book seeks to uncover the basic formulae of these alchemists. Godwin writes, "This secret function of musical creation and performance 'made of that stage on which a soul was thus called into being one of the noblest altars on which a supernatural ceremony could be performed.' There are only a few real artists, composers, or poets, meaning those abundantly endowed with both the memory of the realm of Ideas and the skill to embody that memory. Theirs is the privilege to conceive the progeny of the Gods, called by the alchemists the Philosophic Egg. At the appointed time these divine children are brought forth for all to behold, incarnated in bodies of paint, of marble, of vibrating air. For a time these substances undergo a veritable transmutation, becoming transparent to realities of a higher order. Paint may last a few centuries, marble and words a few millennia. But musical entities are more reluctant: no sooner are they born, with the indispensable help of the performer as midwife (or, to continue the alchemical analogy, as *soror mystica*), than they vanish. Again and again they have to be conjured back to earth on the altar of stage, studio, or living room. No art so closely parallels those religious rites, such as the Mass, which demand constant re-enactment" (74).

3. Further, it may serve to indicate that Khan's position is something of an elaboration of Derrida's statement that "the voice is the being that is proximate to itself in the form of universality, as consciousness [con-science]; the voice is consciousness" (Peggy Kamuf, ed., *A Derrida Reader* [New York: Columbia University Press, 1991, 23]).

4. Indeed for Khan language not only develops after music in his conception of the history of the universe, but also is further conceived as a "simplification of music." Khan comments, "Language may be called the simplification of music; music is hidden within it as the soul is hidden in the body. At each step towards simplification the language has lost some of its music" (159).

5. Jacques Derrida also addresses the performative aspects of speech. Again, the categories provided by Derrida only set the stage for discovering the important Eastern mystical, biblical, and Coltrane-inspired precepts for the performative power of sound. For Derrida, performative speech is uttered to call something into being, literally to perform an action, such as calling a meeting to adjourn with the pronouncement of words, or calling a courtroom to order. In his critique of J.L. Austin, Derrida defines performative speech as "the utterance which allows us to do something by means of speech itself" (Kamuf, ed. *A Derrida Reader*, 97).

Chapter 10

1. Many of these are captured by Ansar El Muhamad's 2013 documentary *Crimes of the Police*.

2. The San Francisco 8 consisted of eight former members of the Black Panther Party for Self Defense arrested in 2007 for their alleged involvement in the 1971 murder of Police Sgt. John V. Young at the San Francisco Police Department's station in the Ingleside neighborhood. The San Francisco 8 were Herman Bell, Jalil Muntaqim, Richard Brown, Richard O'Neal, Ray Boudreaux, Francisco Torres, Harold Taylor, and Hank Jones. The courts set an extraordinarily high bail of 3 to 5 million dollars for each defendant. Within a year, conspiracy charges were dropped against five of the defendants and Richard O'Neal was completely removed from the case, which changed the name of the case to the San Francisco 7. By mid–2009, Herman Bell pleaded guilty to a charge of voluntary manslaughter and charges against Brown, Jones, and Boudreaux were

dropped. Taylor and Muntaquim pleaded no contest to conspiracy to commit voluntary manslaughter.

3. http://truth-out.org/archive/compo nent/k2/item/83641:california-caravans-for-justice.

4. This is a reference to Jerry Brown's first term as governor of California, 1975–1983. The Arnold Schwarzenegger administration was 2003 to 2010, and Jerry Brown's second iteration as governor began in 2010.

Chapter 11

1. http://campbellarchitects.blogspot. com/2009/07/development-proposals. html.

Chapter 12

1. Archbishop King would preside over St. Augustine's African Orthodox Cathedral on 5831 Indiana Ave. in Chicago and the St. Simon of Cyrene African Orthodox Church at 3430 Prospect Street in Houston, Texas.

2. These meetings actually began at the Nation of Islam Mosque on 3rd Street in the San Francisco neighborhood of Bayview-Hunter's Point and were later relocated to Grace Tabernacle.

3. www.greenaction.org/hunterspoint/factsheet.shtml.

4. San Francisco Hunter's Point Redevelopment Measure F appeared on the June 3, 2008, ballot, where it was soundly defeated. It required the development plan for the Bayview-Hunter's Point area to include a "significant amount of affordable housing." (http://ballotpedia.org/wiki/index.php/San_Francisco_Hunter%27s_Point_Redevelopment_Measure_F_(June_2008).

5. San Francisco Bayview Jobs and Housing Measure G appeared on the June 3, 2008, ballot, where it passed by an almost two-thirds majority. Measure G allows the Lennar Corporation to develop an 800-acre parcel in Bay View-Hunter's Point with shops and high-rise office and residential space, and clean up toxins from the Naval Shipyards (http://ballotpedia. org/wiki/index.php/San_Francisco_Bayview_Jobs_and_Housing_Measure_G_(June_2008).

6. The Tabernacle Group is a non-profit community development program and describes its origins and activities on its website: "The *Tabernacle Community Development Corporation* (TCDC) has been working for years to enhance the health, stability and diversity of the San Francisco's neighborhoods. The Tabernacle Community Development Corporation (TCDC) is a non profit affordable housing development company founded by 5 of San Francisco's most prominent African American ministers who serve on the Board of Directors. Incorporated in 2001 and located in Bayview Hunters Point, the TCDC's primary goal is to provide access to safe, clean and reasonably priced housing-rentals and homes to buy for working families. As a faith based organization, the TCDC's divine goal is to close at least 3 projects per year for the next few years and to increase participation of local ministers in the Tabernacle Community Development Corporation. Its long term goals include providing consultations and workshops assisting other ministers—locally, statewide, and nationally—with their real estate development agendas and affordable housing goals" (http://www.tcdc-sf.org).

7. http://sfbayview.com/2009/05/bay view-deserves-better/.

8. http://sfbayview.com/2009/bay view-deserves-better/.

9. Archbishop King consistently refers to these historical and modern day figures as "slave chasers."

Chapter 13

1. "Rememory" is a concept derived from Toni Morrison's novel *Beloved* (1987). Within the novel the term refers to the act of remembering memories and is raised in the context of the central character Sethe, who understands that the past is alive in the present.

2. Mystic Youth was a musical group formed by the children of the Coltrane Church between the departure of Alice Coltrane and the church's 1982 incorporation into the African Orthodox Church. In this brief period the church embraced some elements of Rastafarianism, including the appreciation of the spirituality of Bob Marley. The band included Pastor

Wanika and Rev. Franzo King, Jr. Pastor Wanika recounts: "Mystic Youth was the group we formed. Bishop had a group of brethren that he was yoked with and they were called the Mystics and they would study philosophy and talk about different things. And so they had their little group and we decided we would be the Junior Mystics. Later this became Mystic Youth."

3. www.baptisthistory.org/contissues/huffman.htm.

Bibliography

Allen, Ray. *Singing in the Spirit: African American Sacred Quartets in New York City.* Philadelphia: University of Pennsylvania Press, 1991.

Analahati, Rev. Sis. Nancy Jean, ed. *John Coltrane Speaks.* San Francisco: Sunship, 1981.

Banfield, William C. *Black Notes: Essays of a Musician Writing in a Post-Album Age.* Lanham, MD: Scarecrow, 2004.

Behar, Ruth. *The Vulnerable Observer: Anthropology That Breaks Your Heart.* Boston: Beacon, 1996.

Berliner, Paul. *Thinking in Jazz: The Infinite Art of Improvisation.* Chicago: University of Chicago Press, 1993.

Blackwell, James E., and Morris Janowitz, eds. *Black Sociologists: Historical and Contemporary Perspectives.* Chicago: University of Chicago Press, 1975.

Blassingame, John W. *The Slave Community: Plantation Life in the AnteBellum South.* New York: Oxford University Press, 1990.

Broussard, Albert S. *Black San Francisco: The Struggle for Racial Equality in the West, 1900–1954.* Lawrence: University Press of Kansas, 1993.

Bowe, Rebecca. "Marcus Books of San Francisco Evicted." San Francisco Bay Guardian Online, www.sfbg.com/politics/2014/05/08/marcus-books-san-francisco-evicted, May 8, 2014.

Brown, Leonard L., ed. *John Coltrane and Black America's Quest for Freedom: Spirituality and the Music.* New York: Oxford University Press, 2010.

Carter, Crystal. *San Francisco Bayview,* May 28, 2009.

Coan, Carl. John Coltrane Solos (transcriptions). Milwaukee, WI: Hal Leonard, 1995.

Cole, Bill. *John Coltrane.* New York: Da Capo, 1993.

Collier-Thomas, Bettye. *Daughters of Thunder: Black Women Preachers and Their Sermons, 1850–1979.* San Francisco: Josssey-Bass, 1998.

Cone, James H. *A Black Theology of Liberation.* Maryknoll, NY: Orbis, 1986, 1990.

Curtis, Edward E., IV, and Danielle Brune Sigler, eds. *The New Black Gods: Arthur Huff Fauset and the Study of African American Religions.* Bloomington: Indiana University Press, 2009.

De Coster, Philippe Laurent. *African Orthodox Church: A General History.* http://www.scribd.com/doc/2199133/African-Orthodox, 2008.

DeLeon, Richard Edward. *Left Coast City: Progressive Politics in San Francisco, 1975–1991.* Lawrence: University Press of Kansas, 1992.

Derrida, Jacques, and Gianni Vattimo, eds. *Religion: Cultural Memory in the Present.* Stanford, CA: Stanford University Press, 1996.

Drake, St. Clair. *The Redemption of Africa and Black Religion.* New York: Third World Press, 1990.

DuBois, W.E.B. *The Philadelphia Negro: A Social Study.* Philadelphia: University of Pennsylvania Press, 1903, 1995.

_____. *The Souls of Black Folk*. New York: Dover, 1904, 1994.

Ellison, Ralph. *Invisible Man*. New York: Vintage, 1990.

Fanon, Frantz. *Black Skin, White Masks*. New York: Grove, 1967.

Fauset, Arthur Huff. *Black Gods of the Metropolis: Negro Religious Cults in the Urban North*. Philadelphia: University of Pennsylvania Press, 1971.

Fiorenza, Elisabeth Schussler. *In Memory of Her: A Feminist Theological Reconstruction of Christian Origins*. New York: Crossroad, 1983.

Fischlin, Daniel, Ajay Heble, and George Lipsitz. *The Fierce Urgency of Now: Improvisation, Rights, and the Ethics of Cocreation*. Durham, NC: Duke University Press, 2013.

Foster, Frances Smith. *A Brighter Coming Day: A Frances Ellen Watkins Harper Reader*. New York: Feminist Press at City University of New York, 1990.

Foucault, Michel. *Politics, Philosophy, Culture: Interviews and Other Writings*. New York: Routledge, 1990.

Frazier, E. Franklin. *The Negro Church in America (1963)* and Lincoln, C. Eric. *The Black Church Since Frazier*. New York: Schocken, 1974.

Gargani, Aldo. "Religious Experience as Event and Interpretation." *In Religion: Cultural Memory in the Present*, eds. Jacques Derrida and Gianni Vattimo, Stanford, CA: Stanford University Press, 1996.

Gilroy, Paul. *Against Race: Imagining Political Culture Beyond the Color Line*. Cambridge, MA: Belknap Press, 2001.

_____. *The Black Atlantic: Modernity and Double Consciousness*. Cambridge, MA: Harvard University Press, 1993.

_____. *Small Acts: Thoughts on the Politics of Black Cultures*. New York: Serpent's Tail, 1993.

Gioia, Ted. *West Coast Jazz: Modern Jazz in California, 1945–1960*. Berkeley: University of California Press, 1992.

Gitler, Ira. *Swing to Bop: An Oral History of the Transition in Jazz in the 1940s*. New York: Oxford University Press, 1987.

Godwin, Joscelyn. *Harmonies of Heaven and Earth: Mysticism in Music from Antiquity to the Avant-Garde*. Rochester, VT: Inner Traditions, 1987, 1995.

Gray, Herman. *Cultural Moves: African Americans and the Politics of Representation*. Chicago: University of Chicago Press, 2005.

Hall, Stuart. *Representation: Cultural Representations and Signifying Practices*. Thousand Oaks, CA: Sage and Open University, 1997.

Hamlin, Jesse. "Jazzy S.F. Fusion Catches On." *San Francisco Chronicle*, July 30, 1995.

_____. *San Francisco Chronicle*, 1998.

_____. *San Francisco Chronicle*, 2004.

_____. *San Francisco Chronicle*, May 6, 2010.

Harmanci, Reyhan. "Occupy San Francisco Is Nothing Like the Old Days." *New York Times*, October 14, 2011.

Heble, Ajay. *Landing on the Wrong Note: Jazz, Dissonance, and Critical Practice*. New York: Routledge, 2000.

Hoyle, Lydia Huffman. "Baptist Women in Ministry." www.baptisthistory.org/con tissues/huffman.htm.

Jackson, Michael. *Paths Toward a Clearing: Radical Empiricism and Ethnographic Inquiry*. Bloomington: Indiana University Press, 1989.

James, William. *The Varieties of Religious Experience*. New York: Modern, 1999.

Jones, LeRoi [Amiri Baraka]. *Blues People: The Negro Experience in White America and the Music that Developed from It*. New York: William Morrow, 1963.

_____. *Selected Plays and Prose of Amiri Baraka/LeRoi Jones*. New York: William Morrow, 1979.

Jost, Ekkehard. *Free Jazz*. New York: Da Capo, 1994.

JT the Bigga Figga. "On the Frontline for the Community." *Mandatory Business* 9 (2009).

Kamuf, Peggy, ed. *A Derrida Reader: Between the Blinds*. New York: Columbia University Press, 1991.

Khan, Hazrat Inayat. *The Mysticism of Sound and Music*. Boston: Shambhala, 1996.

King, John. *San Francisco Chronicle*, February 16, 2013.

King, Rev. Bishop Franzo Wayne, D.D., and Rev. Sis. Nancy Jean Analahati. *Coltrane Consciousness*. San Francisco: Sunship, 1981.

Kofsky, Frank. *John Coltrane and the Jazz Revolution of the 1960s: Black Nation-

alism and the Revolution in Music. New York: Pathfinder, 1998.

Krebs, Albin, and Robert McG. Thomas Jr. "Coltrane's Widow Sues San Francisco Church." *New York Times*, late edition (East Coast), October 24, 1981, 2.26

Lavezzoli, Peter. *The Dawn of Indian Music in the West.* New York: Continuum, 2006.

Lavie, Smadar, Kirin Narayan, and Renato Rosaldo, eds. *Creativity/Anthropology.* Ithaca: Cornell University Press, 1993.

Levine, Lawrence. *Black Culture and Black Consciousness: Afro-American Folk Thought from Slavery to Freedom.* New York: Oxford University Press, 1977.

Levine, Mark. *The Jazz Theory Book.* Petaluma, CA: Sher Music, 1995.

Litweiler, John. *The Freedom Principle: Jazz after 1958.* Dorset, UK: Blanford House, 1984.

McKitrick, Cathy. "Progressive Groups Plan Wells Fargo Protest." *Salt Lake Tribune*, April 25, 2012.

Mamiya, Lawrence, and C. Eric Lincoln, eds. *The Black Church in the African-American Experience.* Durham, NC: Duke University Press, 1990.

Miller, James. *The Passion of Michel Foucault.* New York: Simon and Schuster, 1993.

Monson, Ingrid. *Saying Something: Jazz Improvisation and Interaction.* Chicago: University of Chicago Press, 1996.

Moore, Rebecca. *Understanding Jonestown and Peoples Temple.* Westport, CT: Praeger, 2009.

Morrison, Toni. *Beloved.* New York: Random House, 1987.

Muhammad, Keith. "(i am) Oscar Grant." *Mandatory Business* 9 (2009).

Murray, Albert. *The Blue Devils of Nada: A Contemporary American Approach to Aesthetic Statement.* New York: Vintage, 1996.

Nisenson, Eric. *Ascension: John Coltrane and his Quest.* New York: St. Martin's, 1993.

_____. Blue: *The Murder of Jazz.* Press New York: St. Martin's, 1997.

Novak, Philip. *The World's Wisdom: Sacred Texts of the World's Religions.* San Francisco: HarperCollins, 1995.

Owens, Michael Leo. *God and Government in the Ghetto: The Politics of Church-State Collaboration in Black America.* Chicago: University of Chicago Press, 2007.

Paden, William E. *Interpreting the Sacred: Ways of Viewing Religion.* Boston: Beacon, 1992.

Pepin, Elizabeth, and Lewis Watts. *Harlem of the West: The San Francisco Fillmore Jazz Era.* San Francisco: Chronicle, 2006.

Pinn, Anthony B. *Varieties of African American Religious Experience.* Minneapolis: Fortress, 1998.

Porter, Lewis. John Coltrane: *His Life and Music.* Ann Arbor: University of Michigan Press, 1998.

Porter, Lewis, Chris DeVito, David Wild, Yasuhiro Fujioka, and Wolf Schmaler. *The John Coltrane Reference.* New York: Routledge, 2013. Kindle.

Radano, Ronald M. *New Musical Figurations: Anthony Braxton's Cultural Critique.* Chicago: University of Chicago Press, 1993.

Rivelli, Pauline, and Robert Levin. *Giants of Black Music.* Boston: Da Capo, 1980.

Rosaldo, Renato. *Culture and Truth: The Remaking of Social Analysis.* Boston: Beacon, 1993.

Rubien, David. "Coltrane: Final Edition." *San Francisco Chronicle*, March 6, 2005, 44.

Sandoval, Chela. *Methodology of the Oppressed.* Minneapolis: University of Minnesota Press, 2000.

Scheinin, Robert. *San Jose Mercury News*, March 16, 2003.

Schultz, G.W. "A Half Century of Lies." *San Francisco Bay Guardian*, March 21–26, 2007.

Sernett, Milton C., ed. *African American Religious History: A Documentary Witness.* Durham, NC: Duke University Press, 1999.

Shadwick, Keith. *The Illustrated Story of Jazz.* New York: Crescent Books, 1991.

Shange, Ntozake. *Nappy Edges.* New York: St. Martin's, 1972.

Simmonds, Yussuf. "The Murder of Oscar Grant." *The Sentinel*, July 1, 2010.

Simpkins, C.O. Coltrane: *A Biography.* Baltimore: Black Classic, 1975.

Smith, Theophus H. *Conjuring Culture: Biblical Formations of Black America.* New York: Oxford University Press, 1994.

Solnit, Rebecca, and Susan Schwartzenberg. *Hollow City: Gentrification and* the Eviction of Urban Culture. New York: Verso, 2001.

Southern, Eileen. The Music of Black Americans: A History, 2d ed. New York: W.W. Norton, 1983.

Spencer, Jon Michael, ed. "Sacred Music of the Secular City: From Blues to Rap." Black Sacred Music: A Journal of Theomusicology 6 no. 1 (Spring 1992), special issue.

Stoddard, Tom. Jazz on the Barbary Coast. Berkeley, CA: Heyday, 1982, 1988.

Stoller, Paul. Embodying Colonial Memories: Spirit Possession, Power and the Huaka in West Africa. New York: Routledge, 1995.

Sullivan, James. "A Show of Faith for Church of Coltrane: Benefit Show Honors Patron Saint's Spirit." San Francisco Chronicle, March 17, 2000.

Swift, Donald. Religion and the American Experience: A Social and Cultural History, 1765–1997. New York: M.E. Sharpe, 1998.

Talbot, David. "Jim Jones' Sinister Grip on San Francisco: How the Peoples Temple Cult Leader Ensnared Harvey Milk and Other Progressive Icons" Salon.com, May 1, 2012, www.salon.com/2012/05/01/jim_jones_sinister_grip_on_san_francisco/.

Taussig, Michael. Mimesis and Alterity: A Particular History of the Senses. New York: Routledge, 1992.

Thomas, J.C. Chasin' the Trane: The Music and Mystique of John Coltrane. New York: Da Capo, 1975.

Thurman, Howard. Jesus and the Disinherited. Boston: Beacon, 1976.

Turner, Victor. The Anthropology of Performance. New York: PAJ, 1987.

Ugwu, Catherine, ed. Let's Get It On: The Politics of Black Performance. Seattle: Bay, 1995.

Wade-Gayles, Gloria, ed. My Soul Is a Witness: African American Women's Spirituality. Boston: Beacon, 1995.

Weinstein, Norman C. A Night in Tunisia: Imaginings of Africa in Jazz. New York: Limelight, 1994.

Williams, Delores S. Sisters in the Wilderness: The Challenge of Womanist GodTalk. Maryknoll, NY: Orbis, 1996.

Williams, Melvin. Community in a Black Pentecostal Church. Pittsburgh: University of Pittsburgh Press, 1974.

Wilmer, Valerie. As Serious as Your Life: The Story of the New Jazz. Westport, CT: Lawrence Hill, 1980.

Wilmore, Gayraud S. Black Religion and Black Radicalism: An Interpretation of the Religious History of African Americans. Maryknoll, NY: Orbis, 1998.

Wilson, Bryan, and Jamie Cresswell, eds. New Religious Movements: Challenge and Response. New York: Routledge, 1999.

Wuthnow, Robert. Experimentation in American Religion: The New Mysticisms and Their Implications for the Churches. Berkeley: University of California Press, 1978.

Index